BOUNTY CHORDS

PHILIP HAYWARD

To Rebecca
whose ana'ana smile lured me to the South Pacific in the first place and to
Rosa and Amelia for their love and laughter (and hours shared at Emily Bay).

BOUNTY CHORDS

Music, Dance and Cultural Heritage on Norfolk and Pitcairn Islands

PHILIP HAYWARD

John Libbey

LONDON • PARIS • ROME • SYDNEY

Cataloguing in Publication Data

Bounty Chords: Music, Dance and Cultural Heritage on Norfolk and Pitcairn Islands

    1.Norfolk and Pitcairn Islands – music and dance culture
    2.Pacific Studies

Hayward, Philip 1956-

ISBN: 0 86196 678 3 (Paperback)

Design and Setting: John Libbey Publishing
Front Cover Photo: Norfolk Island delegation attending the 8th Festival of Pacific Arts in Noumea (photograph: Don Christian-Reynolds)

Published by
John Libbey Publishing, Box 276, Eastleigh SO50 5YS, UK
e-mail: libbeyj@asianet.co.th; web site: www.johnlibbey.com

Orders: **Book Representation & Distribution Ltd**. info@bookreps.com

Distributed in North America by **Indiana University Press**, 601 North Morton St, Bloomington, IN 47404, USA. www.iupress.indiana.edu

Distributed in Australasia by **Elsevier Australia**, 30–52 Smidmore Street, Marrickville NSW 2204, Australia. www.elsevier.com.au

Distributed in Japan by **United Publishers Services Ltd**,
1-32-5 Higashi-shinagawa, Shinagawa-ku, Tokyo 140-0002, Japan. info@ups.co.jp

Printed in Malaysia by Vivar Printing Sdn. Bhd., 48000 Rawang,Selangor

Contents

Acknowledgements

In addition to the various musicians and dancers on Norfolk and Pitcairn Islands who contributed to my research (and who are quoted in these pages) I would also like to thank Les Brown, Alice Buffett, David Buffett, Eddie Driver, Joyce Dyer, David 'Bubby' Evans, Merval Hoare, Rick Kleiner, Marie Lewis, Tim Lloyd, Tom Lloyd, Patricia Magri, Margaret Meadows, Raymond Nobbs, Eve Semple and Bob Tofts for their help and encouragement.

Many thanks to the staff and institutions of the administration, public library and Bounty Folk Museum on Norfolk Island; the Kinder Library in Auckland; the Alexander Turnbull Library in Wellington; and the Mitchell and Macquarie University libraries in Sydney for providing research assistance for this project. Don and Maree Christian-Reynolds also provided invaluable help (and frequent accommodation) during my various visits to Norfolk.

Thanks also to my colleagues in the Department of Contemporary Music Studies at Macquarie University, Sydney – Denis Crowdy, Mark Evans, Dave Hackett and Robin Ryan – who assisted my research in various ways and made useful comments on final drafts of the book. Jonas Baes, Irene Byron, James Revell Carr III, Leigh Carriage, Rebecca Coyle, Jon Fitzgerald, Junko Konishi, Danny Long, Jerome Madulid, Don Niles, Helen Reeves Lawrence, Neil Rosenberg and John Whiteoak also provided valuable information and advice at various stages.

As always, my family has fully supported my research on this project and they deserve thanks for coping with my frequent absences. Their participation in local social and cultural life during our residence on Norfolk Island in April-June 1999 was a major factor in cementing my resolve to research and document the history related in this volume.

Publication of this book was assisted through a grant from the Australian Academy of Humanities.

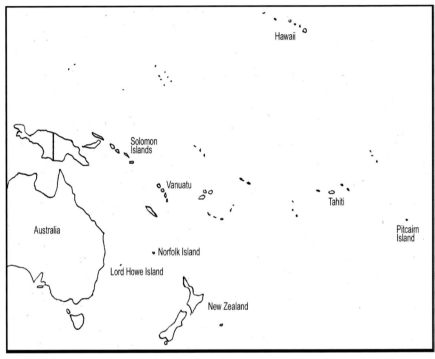

Map of the southwestern and central Pacific showing the positions of Norfolk and Pitcairn islands

INTRODUCTION

Pitcairn Island is located at latitude 25-04 south, longitude 130-05 east, at the south-eastern edge of Polynesia. While there is archeological evidence of earlier settlement on the island, Pitcairn was uninhabited at the time of European arrival in the Pacific. The present-day community was founded in 1789 when a group of mutineers from HMAS *Bounty* and their Tahitian companions arrived and stayed in an attempt to conceal themselves from anticipated pursuit by the British Navy. In 1856 the entire community was relocated to Norfolk Island, latitude 29-02 south, longitude 167-57 east (1440 kilometres east of the Australian city of Brisbane and 1120 kilometres north west of the New Zealand city of Auckland).

Like Pitcairn, Norfolk had evidence of Polynesian settlement in the pre-colonial era. Similarly, Norfolk Island was also unpopulated at the time of the Pitcairners' arrival, following the closure of its British colonial penal facility in the previous year. In 1858 sixteen Pitcairners left Norfolk to return to Pitcairn and in 1863 a second party of twenty-six returned home to assist in the re-establishment of the community. Since this period, the islands have been linked by their common ancestry and heritage and through various contacts and movements between them.

I. Culture, identity and heritage

This book charts the development of the music and dance cultures of the two islands and the manner in which these relate to and express broader issues of cultural identity. In the pages that follow I have attempted to document and account for processes of cultural selection, adoption, innovation and what might be termed *traditionalisation* (the inscription of cultural forms as heritage items). In particular, I offer analyses of the manner in which the cultures of Norfolk and Pitcairn Island have been created and re-created through processes of adoption and synthesis.

My research for this volume – and the analyses of the cultural practices, material and perceptions I present – were substantially informed by consideration of a set of assertions published to accompany UNESCO's 'Year of Cultural Heritage' (YCH) in 2002 (archived online at http://portal.unesco.org[1]). While there was little in the UNESCO statements that was

1

conceptually new[2], their collation and presentation as an agenda provided a grid against which I could map and orientate the areas I address. The Afterword to this volume reflects on aspects of the YCH assertions drawing on the specific analyses I advance.

While heritage and tradition are often invoked as something fixed and essential, they are – conversely – fluid and contentious, subject to various changes and interpretations, disputes and affirmations. Always in flux, heritage and tradition show different faces to those looking from different positions. One of the most significant aspects of the YCH statements is that their sense of 'cultural heritage' is one that acknowledges a whole range of contemporary, vernacular and/or popular practices (rather than just ancient relics, officially recognised 'folk' practices[3] or well-established 'high' cultural forms). My approach in this volume concurs with this.

As importantly, the YCH statements assert the notion that cultural heritage encompasses and interacts with a natural heritage, one *of* environment and *between* species. This is, of course, a notion that has been examined by a variety of western anthropologists, with particular regard to non-western (pre-development) cultures (Feld's work with the Kaluli people of Papua New Guinea being one striking example[4]). The UNESCO assertions move this concept to a more prominent position in the 'mix'. If we use the framework of ecology, UNESCO's assertions encourage us to attribute a 'deep-ecology'[5] to aspects of culture and heritage. Consequently, the YCH statements refer to (their concept of) cultural heritage as:

> *a more global and holistic approach that alone can testify to the universal nature of the human spirit in all its creations.*
> (http://portal.unesco.org[6])

As the documentation states:

> *Today, the notion of heritage is an open one which can develop new objects and put forward new meanings as it reflects living culture rather than an ossified image of the past. We have become aware over the last thirty years that nature and culture cannot be separated in our approach to heritage if we are to render a true account of the diversity of cultural manifestations and particularly those in which a close link is expressed between human beings and their natural environment.* (ibid)

As subsequent chapters attest, a "close link... between human beings and their natural environment" is an important aspect of the two island cultures considered in this volume, an aspect celebrated and expressed in song and dance, in language and in a variety of other aspects of local culture. Section IV of this Introduction describes how localised language use is an important aspect of Norfolk and Pitcairn Island cultural heritage and one that has a complex interaction with song traditions and contemporary innovation. As in any culture, individual practices – such as song and dance – are interlinked with others and together provide the broad field of cultural heritage.

The YCH statements propose a set of components of cultural heritage[7] that matches their expanded, inclusive vision. The framework incorporates elements often identified as folkloric:

2

- Music and Song
- The Performing Arts
- Oral Traditions
- Languages
- Literature
- Festive Events
- Rites and Beliefs
- The Movable Cultural Heritage
- Handicrafts
- Traditional Medicine
- Culinary Traditions
- Traditional Sports and Games

along with broader environmental aspects:

- Cultural Heritage Sites
- Natural Sacred Sites
- Cultural Landscapes
- Historic Cities
- The Underwater Cultural Heritage

and with practices that are, themselves, representations of cultural heritage:

- The Documentary, Media and Digital Heritage
- Museums

While such a list – and schematisation – is open to debate and further refinement[8], it provides a useful, multiply-facetted characterisation of cultural heritage. Obviously, as researcher primarily concerned with music and dance, the topmost categories have been prominent in my study. But, in a process that was initiated in 1998 and informed by the complementary emphasis of the UNESCO YCH agenda in 2002, all of the identified elements of the body of cultural heritage have contributed to my understanding and discussion of the phenomena I analyse. Indeed – at least from the viewpoint of its writer – the research and writing of this volume has provided further confirmation that the most productive study of culture should seek to *implicate* specific genres (such as music and dance) in an interactive, shifting continuum of heritage. While any study of specific forms must, necessarily, *extricate* these from a wider field (in order to focus on them), it is important to acknowledge and analyse the skeins of meanings and associations that bind them to broader sweeps of heritage.

3

II. Island Cultures

Islands are marked by a duality. On the one hand they are insular, sea-bound and cordoned off from other communities. On the other, they are (multi-directionally) connected through sea-lanes (and, more latterly, air routes). Different islands occupy different places within this polarity at different historical moments. The isolation and insularity of one period can be replaced by the connectivity and interaction of another, dependent on both local-internal and regional-global factors. Any discussion and analysis of island cultures needs to proceed with an awareness of these dualities and their influence on local cultures. As Doreen Massey argued, with regard to a very different location (an arterial road in London[9]):

> *What gives a place its specificity is not some long internalized history but the fact that it is constructed out of a particular constellation of relations, articulated together at a particular locus... The uniqueness of a place or a locality... is constructed out of particular interactions and mutual articulations of social relations, social processes, experiences and understandings.* (1993: 68)

Massey's emphasis is that while locations may have particular identities, these are formed within a wider context, determined by social, political, economic, cultural and environmental factors. While she was not writing with islands in mind, her characterisation is singularly apposite for the subject of this book. The history of the Norfolk and Pitcairn communities, with their roots in the *Bounty* voyage and the encounter of the ship's crew with Tahitian culture, is a vivid example of the influence of a wider matrix on specific localities. The history of the islands offered here is, consequently, contextualised within international frameworks and with consideration of international media forms and influences. Within these pages heritage is considered not simply as some micro-local practice but rather as something affected by broad planetary factors.

Flipping back to the other pole of islandness, the bounded nature of small island cultures such as Norfolk and Pitcairn gives them a distinct character. The frequency of individual, familial and social interaction in everyday life produces a society that is not so much *imagined* (as in Benedict Anderson's famous characterisation of the nation-state [1983]) as *actual* – in that individuals and families *are* known to eachother, often intimately. Within this intensely socialised environment, specific aspects of repertoire (such as songs and dances) are regarded as socially located, in the sense that they are tied into a social network and a network of claims and assumptions of origin, ownership and/or right to perform. In this regard, Massey's characterisation of place specificity as "constructed out of particular interactions and mutual articulations of social relations, social processes, experiences and understandings" is equally applicable to the creation and continuance of cultural heritage.

While the Pitcairn Island community, re-established in 1858, has remained a relatively homogenous one, Norfolk Island has experienced a series of developments that have diversified its population (and also seen the presence of temporary communities – in the form of the Melanesian Mission [between 1866 and 1924] and the New Zealand military garrison [from 1942–48]). The arrival of a number of Australian, New Zealand (and other) settlers on Norfolk from the 1850s on – and the employment of many more on fixed-term working visas – has created a cultural plurality for the island that has been apparent in various facets of its music and dance culture. While the cultural heritage of the Pitcairn-descended population of Norfolk Island is central to this book, I have also endeavoured to represent the variety of inputs into Norfolk Island culture provided by those who have resided on it.

III. Research and Readership

Aside from my professional status as an academic specialising in the postcolonial music history of the south western Pacific, my credentials for writing this book comprise eight years of research into the music culture of the two islands (including three months residence on Norfolk Island with my family in 1999) and a continuing involvement in recording and song-writing projects with Norfolk and Pitcairn Island performers. While I had anticipated being able to undertake research on Pitcairn in 2002–2004, the social tension and upheaval arising from the sexual abuse cases on the island and subsequent disputes between the islanders and British authorities (discussed in Chapter 12), made such a visit unviable[10]. My primary research into Pitcairn culture derives from interviews I conducted with Pitcairn singer-guitarist Trent Christian (who has resided on Norfolk Island since the mid-1990s), interviews and subsequent correspondence with Pitcairn singer-guitarist and composer Meralda Warren (who was on extended vacation on Norfolk Island while I was living there in 1999), conversations with other Pitcairners I encountered during visits to Norfolk Island, e-mail communications with Pitcairners and research inquiries pursued on my behalf by Warren on Pitcairn Island following her return. Draft copies of Chapter 12 of this volume were sent to Pitcairn Island and were revised and amended following advice received.

I have several audiences in mind for this book. The first comprises the communities who are the topic of my study. In deference to them, I have attempted to keep extended theoretical reflections to a minimum in the individual chapters that form the core of this volume. These kinds of discussions, which might be more of interest to fellow academics and researchers, have been introduced above and are otherwise corralled into the Afterword. I am also hopeful that the general reader interested in *Bounty* history and the experiences of the islands' populations will find material to engage them.

My research has uncovered a considerable number of individuals who participated in the social history of music making on Norfolk and Pitcairn islands. In the chapters that follow I have discussed the careers and achieve-ments of the most prominent performers and those who made significant contributions to the specific practices I explore in detail. Since I have not endeavoured to write an encyclopedic catalogue of social performers, there are – inevitably – individuals whose names are omitted from discussion. My apologies to any islanders for whom such omissions cause offence.

All the material in the chapters that follow has been written with extensive reference to published sources and research gained from conversations, interviews and correspondence with Norfolk and Pitcairn islanders. I have made every effort to limit errors of fact and untenable interpretation and I have passed draft chapters to various members of the island communities for comment and correction. Despite these best intentions there will inevitably be material open to dispute, contested information and questions of interpretation – such occurrences are all but inevitable in collating a study of over two hundred years of cultural history amongst two island cultures. I will be pleased to receive suggestions, corrections, caveats and/or alternative interpretations and to address these in future revisions of this volume.

This book is organised in a manner that blends chronology and topics. The music histories of Norfolk and Pitcairn are separated into thematic sections that overlap while moving to a contemporary focus that provides the springboard for my final set of critical reflections. I have refrained from attempting to re-tell the narrative of the *Bounty* mutiny and settlement of the islands in any great detail, relying on other works (such as Nicholson, 1965 and Hoare, 1978) to provide this. I have however provided a summary chronology after this Introduction in order to allow the reader to orientate my discussion of music and dance against the broader history.

IV. Notes on Norfolk Island and Pitcairn language and spellings used in this volume

Several chapters of this book include reference to words, terms or concepts expressed within local speech on Norfolk and Pitcairn Island. Linguistically, there several ways of understanding the nature of Norfolk and Pitcairn vernacular speech. One is to view them from the standpoint of language structure, along a continuum of English variation, whereby underlying English language grammar structures are found along with non-standard terms. In the case of Norfolk and Pitcairn languages, the variant terms are mainly derived from 18th Century dialects of English and 18th Century Tahitian. Another is to view Norfolk and Pitcairn in terms of language genesis, as a *creole*, combining elements of two or more languages. From the standpoint of language function, Laycock (1989) has also provided a third characterisation of Pitcairn language as a *cant*, an artificially constructed language form used to exclude outsiders.

In deference to common usage in Norfolk and Pitcairn Island cultures I have avoided such terminologies and simply refer to the two forms as 'languages'. This accords with local advocacy of these forms as distinct and important aspects of cultural heritage. In the case of Norfolk Island, Alice Buffett's pronunciation guide and dictionary (1988 and 1999) and Beryl Nobbs Palmer's earlier volume (1986) have been significant as local political assertions of distinct linguistic identity.

Despite Buffett's work on Norfolk language, a number of problems present themselves to an author trying to survey and analyse uses of Norfolk and Pitcairn language in songs (and related written and oral material). With particular regard to Norfolk Island, one major difficulty is that, despite Buffett's research and presentation of a standard grammar and dictionary of terms, Norfolk language – both historically and presently – shows a high degree of internal variation. Linked to this is a continuing practice of expression in an intermediary zone along a continuum between the poles of most distinctive Norfolk language usage[11] and Standard English (SE). Many of the songs discussed in this volume – including several of those written by the same songwriter – occupy various positions on this spectrum. The two main issues arising from this are those of literary re-presentation (on the printed page) and translation. There are also unfolding complexities within these. With regard to the written versions of song lyrics I include in this volume the situation is, in some ways, easiest when I have transcribed song lyrics (with the assistance of Buffett [1999] and Palmer [1986] and the help of various local language speakers). In these cases I have chosen to use an approach that combines the spelling of distinct Norfolk Island terms provided by Buffett and the orthodox spelling of elements of the SE language usage I have identified in song texts. One result of this is that my written versions combine two separate systems – SE and Buffett's phonetic spellings. Awkward as this is, it serves to identify distinct Norfolk Island terms and usages in print. However, difficulties occur with regard to sung and/or spoken terms which are ambiguous as to which linguistic pole they belong – ie how should they be spelt, in SE, or phonetically as Norfolk/Pitcairn words? Despite my best attempts at scientific discrimination I have often had to rely on personal interpretative assessments for such cases.

An associated issue to those discussed above is how to render words and usages that are clearly not part of SE usage but are also not specified in Buffett's or Palmer's work. In these cases I have sought advice from native Norfolk speakers but, since this advice has frequently been uncertain and/or contradicted by the opinions of other language speakers, I have often made my own judgments as to spelling and usage. My own uncertainty here, as an outsider, is also one shared by Norfolk Islanders concerned with public communication and education. One of the most significant insights into issues of Norfolk Island usage to arise during my research was provided by Ivens 'Toon' Buffett during the course of an (unpublished) interview with my colleague Rebecca Coyle in 1999 about the minimal use of Norfolk Island language in local radio broadcasting. Reflecting on responses to a single radio show that he presented in Norfolk language in the 1980s, Buffett asserted that:

> *Every single person who is a Norfolk Islander has got their own version of the Norfolk language.*

He identified this as a major impediment to language broadcasting since:

> *Some people said it is good, some people said that you are pronouncing it the wrong way, you're using the words in the wrong spot, you don't know what it means ... One of the real difficulties you have using the Norfolk language ... is that a single word or a phrase can have up to six different meanings just purely on the tone of the voice that you use.*

Any use of written forms of Norfolk language is thereby problematic. In order to give the book a standard rendition of various song texts I have, necessarily, had to standard*ise* spellings. One particular issue has arisen from situations when songwriters have supplied me with their own written versions of song lyrics. While these represent the songwriters' own written representations of their sung words, since it is the *sung* word texts that I am referring to, I have, in some instances, produced my own written versions of their sung texts. While few of the songwriters concerned have been particularly happy with this, my clear statement of this practice here should serve to emphasise that my written transcriptions are *my* renditions. In defence of this position, it is significant to note that various versions of 1980s' and 1990s' song lyrics that have appeared in written and/or printed form differ in spelling, largely, it seems, due to both shifting fashions in how particular words should be spelt and, more latterly, through some attempt to standardise spellings using Buffett (1999) as a reference source. Perhaps the most tangled situation I have become embroiled in is that with regard to written versions of the texts of songs by George 'Toofie' Christian. As author of the CD booklet notes accompanying his debut CD *Pilli Lornga N.I.* (2001) I collaborated in producing written versions of his song lyrics. The versions that appeared represented a compromise between his desire to use SE spellings (using Palmer's dictionary as a spelling source) and my wish to use a number of the Buffett spellings for standard Norfolk terms. This, and his use of words and phrases that were not found in either source, caused the process to be a highly protracted one[12].

Translations have also been problematic. Many of the problems that have arisen are inherent to the general practice of translation. First amongst these has been the issue of what position to take between the poles of literal and interpretative translation. I have tried to take a middle ground and have provided any additional information or qualification via endnotes. Related to this have been disputes over specific meanings. These have been caused by either ambiguities arising from the potential multiple meanings identified by 'Toon' Buffett above and/or different understandings and usages amongst different generations, families etc. When the songwriter has been alive and willing to advise me, I have followed their understandings in these cases. In other instances I have had to make informed assessments.

Traversing the whole field of issues that I have discussed above is the question of the extent to which the use of language in songs – with particular modifications of grammar and the additional signifying elements of melody and sung intonation – constitutes a distinct linguistic (sub-)zone that has a relative autonomy from that of spoken language. My approach here has been to regard Norfolk language song as an element of Norfolk Island heritage that has been developing in patterns of inter-relation with Norfolk speech, dance and other cultural forms. Since the focus of this book is not primarily a linguistic one I will leave analysis of such 'sub-zonal' issues to other, more specialist writers.

Discussion of Pitcairn language songs in this volume have been less complicated due to both the smaller body of Pitcairn language songs that have been written (to date) and common use of either Standard English or a Pitcairn inflected English by Pitcairn songwriters. Issues of Pitcairn language development have therefore been somewhat tangential to the focus of this book (aside from references to Norfolk Island language's roots in that form)[13]. Such discussion of Pitcairn language variationism as I offer is limited to my observations on Meralda Warren's songs and poetry in Chapter 12.

V. Note on Abbreviations and Quotation Sources

Throughout this book there are various references to and quotations from short, unattributed lineage items published in Norfolk Island, Pitcairn Island and Sydney newspapers and magazines. These articles are referred to by date and page alone and are not individually listed in the Bibliography. The principal publications (and the abbreviated form in which they are referenced) are as follows:

NI:	The Norfolk Islander
NINE:	Norfolk Island News Edition
NIP:	The Norfolk Island Pioneer
NIT:	Norfolk Island Times
NIWT:	Norfolk Island Weekly Times
PIM:	Pacific Islands Monthly
PM:	The Pitcairn Miscellany

Two other publications are referred to on various occasions, the Norfolk Island magazine *Dem Tull* and the WW2 New Zealand forces' Norfolk Island publication *Duffy's Gen*.

Throughout this volume the terms 'Norfolk Island' and 'Norfolk' are used interchangeably to refer to the island (reflecting local language usage). There are no references to the British county of Norfolk anywhere in the volume, so confusion should not arise.

The abbreviation 'SE' is used on occasion to refer to Standard English language usages – as opposed to Norfolk and/or Pitcairn languages (as discussed above).

Notes

1. At time of writing (early 2005), these were located at: http://portal.unesco.org/culture/en/ev.php-URL_ID=1335&URL_DO=DO_TOPIC&URL_SECTION=201.html

2. Hobsbawm and Ranger's 1983 anthology having provided a significant early orientation for such debates.

3. I have avoided using – or invoking – the term and concept of 'folk' and 'folk culture' in this study. For a thorough excavation of the concept of 'the folk' and of how folk culture is constructed via processes of cultural selection, see McKay (1994).

4. See particularly Feld (1991) and his CD recordings *Voices of the Rainforest* (1991) and *Rainforest Soundwalks* (2001).

5. An eco-centric perspective on human existence in global/local environments.

6. See endnote 1 (above).

7. NB the order of items listed is modified from that of the original.

8. One element, for instance, that is particularly apparent at various points of the analyses I offer is the manner in which the natural world and 'cultural landscapes' have an intermediary zone with music and song in the form of the audioscape of the environments concerned. Other specialist studies might, presumably, point to visual

(and other sensory) -scapes as other broader continuums. While the YCH schema does not refer to these intermediary zones, its framework allows for their insertion.

9. Kilburn High Road in north London.

10. In the sense that I received no encouragement nor indication that such a visit would be welcome at this time – a response that was in marked contrast to the willingness of Pitcairners to assist and encourage my general research for the book.

11. I use the phrase 'most distinctive' carefully here, since it is still open to debate whether there is a (single) 'pure' Norfolk vernacular that exists in a binary opposition to English or whether there is an interconnected set of Norfolk language usages within which a group of most distinctly different aspects can be identified.

12. Given that I am attempting to follow a standard approach throughout this book I have provided modified versions of the lyrical transcriptions appearing in the original CD booklet in the chapters in which I discuss his work.

13. This absence of discussion in no way attempts to diminish the importance of the Pitcairners' vernacular to their sense of identity and their identity politics. It is, rather, that with regard to songwriting, linguistic variation issues have not played as prominent role in Pitcairn as they have on Norfolk Island.

SUMMARY CHRONOLOGY
of the *Bounty* mutiny and the establishment and history of the Pitcairn and Norfolk Island communities

1774	Captain Cook's expedition discovers and names Norfolk Island and claims it for Britain.
1787	The *Bounty* departs from England on voyage to Tahiti under the command of Captain William Bligh.
1788	First penal colony established on Norfolk Island; The *Bounty* arrives in Tahiti.
1789	Mutiny on the *Bounty*, led by Fletcher Christian. Bligh and others set adrift. Mutineers sail to Tubuai, then Tahiti, then to Tubuai again, where they try and establish a settlement before abandoning the attempt and returning to Tahiti. At Tahiti some crewmembers leave the ship and some Tahitians join and the *Bounty* departs in search of refuge.
1790	The *Bounty* arrives at Pitcairn Island, a settlement is established and the *Bounty* is scuttled.
1793	Violent disputes between Pitcairn settlers result in a number of men being murdered, including Fletcher Christian.
1808	US sealing ship *Topaz* chances upon Pitcairn Island and discovers mutineers, resulting in regular visits by British and US ships in subsequent years.
1814	Norfolk's penal colony removed from the island, convicts transported to Van Diemen's Land (present-day Tasmania).
1823	British sailors John Buffett and John Evans join the Pitcairn community.

1825	Second penal colony established on Norfolk Island.
1828	George Hunn Nobbs joins the Pitcairn community.
1829	Death of John Adams, the last surviving *Bounty* mutineer on Pitcairn.
1831	Unsuccessful attempt to relocate Pitcairners to Tahiti.
1832	English eccentric Joshua Hill joins Pitcairn community.
1837	Hill departs Pitcairn.
1838	Pitcairn becomes a British colony.
1855	Second penal colony on Norfolk Island disbanded and convicts removed to Australia.
1856	Pitcairners re-located en masse to Norfolk Island.
1859	Small party of Pitcairners returns to Pitcairn.
1863	Second party of Pitcairners returns to Pitcairn.
1866	Melanesian Mission established on Norfolk Island.
1886	First Seventh Day Adventist missionary arrives at Pitcairn Island.
1890	The population of Pitcairn converts en masse to Seventh Day Adventism.
1913	Norfolk Island constituted as a territory of the Commonwealth of Australia.
1942	Military airfield built on Norfolk Island and New Zealand garrison stationed there until 1948.
1967	Historical pageant staged on Norfolk Island.
1975-76	Australian Government Royal Commission into the status of Norfolk Island (Nimmo Report).
1977	The Committee for Democratic Self Government for Norfolk Island established (later renamed The Society of Pitcairn Descendants).
1979	Norfolk Island Legislative Assembly established.
1980	Governor General of Australia assents to Norfolk Island being granted its own flag.
1984	A Norfolk Island delegation attends the Pacific Arts Festival in Tahiti (for the first time).
1993	United Nations Year of Indigenous Peoples. Following the Society of Pitcairn Descendants' assertion of the Pitcairn-descended population of Norfolk Island as the Island's indigenous occupants, a Norfolk Island representative is invited to attend a meeting of the International Working Group on Indigenous Peoples in Geneva.
1994	Inaugural annual Country Music Festival held on Norfolk Island.
2002-5	Social and political crisis on Pitcairn Island triggered by sexual abuse charges laid against a number of Pitcairn men and prosecuted by British authorities.

Chapter One

ACTS IN THE *THEATRUM MUNDI*
The *Bounty*, Tahiti and the Mutiny

The years between 1767 (when Samuel Wallis 'discovered' Tahiti) and 1797 (when the first sustained missionary efforts of the London Missionary Society began in Tahiti) were a short and intensive period in which the Pacific was theatrum mundi *[the theatre of the world]. It was a period when the nations of Europe and the Americas saw themselves acting out their scientific, humanistic selves ... self-righteously conscious of their obligations to observe, describe and publish ... It was a time of intensive theatre of the civilised to the native, but of even more intensive theatre of the civilised to one another.* (Dening, 1992: 372-373)

Introduction

It has been estimated that there have been somewhere between 2500-3000 books and articles, and several more films and plays produced relating to the mutiny aboard the British naval vessel *Bounty* in 1789[1]. Given the highly limited nature of period sources on the incident itself, such a number principally attests to the enduring fascination of the drama of the *Bounty* saga, and the willingness of generations of writers to speculate upon, interpret and revise earlier accounts. Inevitably, given this characterisation, there is a massive overlap, and (effective) redundancy to much of the material. There has also been a recurrent tendency upon the part of successive writers to focus upon the two principal protagonists, the deposed captain, William Bligh, and leader of the mutineers, Fletcher Christian. While an emphasis on these historical players is perhaps understandable, given their centrality to the narrative, the focus has tended to marginalise and/or exclude other significant aspects of the circumstances and history of the *Bounty*'s voyage and the mutineers' later settlement on Pitcairn Island.

The principal facts of the voyage and mutiny are relatively straightforward. The *Bounty* set sail from England on December 23rd 1787, bound for Tahiti, under the captainship of William Bligh. The express purpose of the voyage was to gather breadfruit plants in order for them to be transported to the West Indies (as a crop intended to feed plantation slaves)[2]. The ship arrived in Tahiti in on October 26th 1788 and remained there for five months, due to various delays. During its stay, its crew received considerable hospitality from their Tahitian hosts and mingled, socialised and formed various sexual and/or emotional relationships with local women. The *Bounty* departed on its return journey on April 4th 1789. On April 28th friction between Bligh and his second-in-command, Fletcher Christian, led Christian to stage a mutiny, in the course of which Bligh and several others were cast adrift in a rowing boat. Christian and his party of mutineers then returned to Tahiti and attempted to find an uninhabited island upon which they could secrete themselves so as to avoid detection and capture by the British naval expedition that they (rightly) assumed would be dispatched to locate and apprehend them. After an unsuccessful attempt to settle on the island of Tubuai, they eventually located the uninhabited (and mis-charted) Pitcairn Island upon which they settled, together with a number of Polynesian women and men in 1790.

The following sections of this chapter describe and reflect upon the role that music and dance played in the narrative sketched above.

I. From Spithead to Tahiti

One of the most vivid and detailed discussions of daily life aboard the *Bounty* (and life onshore at Tahiti immediately prior to the mutiny), is provided by Greg Dening's study *Mr Bligh's Bad Language: Passion, Power and Theatre on the Bounty* (1992). Dening details a variety of contextual elements (such as the design of the ship, punishment procedures and conventions in the British navy, and of Tahitian social organisation and customs at the time of the *Bounty*'s visit) yet for all that, his book's account is an oddly silent one. The music that accompanied the voyage from England, provided by the ship's fiddler Michael Byrne, and the music that accompanied the *Bounty* crew's stay on Tahiti, is barely mentioned. This is, in no small part, due to the paucity of written references on the topic. Indeed, Byrne remains a shadowy figure who has not been subject to the same attention as other figures in the drama of mutiny. One of the few exceptions is Charles Chauvel's 1933 film *In the Wake of the Bounty*[3]. This opens with the narrative device of Byrne, in his later years, sitting in a tavern reminiscing about his days in Bligh's service and introducing the narrative that follows.

Little is known about Byrne apart from that he was born in Ireland in the early 1760s, raised in Kilkenny (in the southeast) and that he suffered from substantial visual impairment. While the violin is now regarded as a core element of traditional Irish music, it was a relatively recent innovation in Byrne's time, being introduced to Ireland in the early 1700s (following its invention in Italy in the mid-1600s). It soon became popular and by the mid-late 1700s had become established as widespread vernacular instrument. It is likely that Byrne's visual impairment was a spur to his acquiring instrumental proficiency since musical performance was a standard means for visually impaired children and adults to earn an income at this time. Fiddle players began to appear onboard British Navy ships around 1750. Prior to this, instruments such as the harp, fife and drums had been used to accompany singing and dancing and to provide a general distraction for crews during long voyages, and the fiddle was deployed to similar ends. Byrne found his way to England by the 1780s and was a late addition to the *Bounty's* party, enlisted by Bligh specifically to provide musical accompaniment and stimulation to the *Bounty's* crew.

Despite the myth of Bligh's vicious tyranny as a captain, promulgated by many versions of the *Bounty* story, and most obviously manifested by stories of repeated floggings and other cruelties, the historical record shows that (whatever his intemperate language) Bligh was in fact far less inclined to flog his sailors than many other contemporaries (Nicolson, 1997: 5-13) and was also ahead of the times in being actively concerned with the health and fitness of his crew. One of the ways in which this manifested itself was through music and dance. Byrne was employed to provide musical accompaniment to daily, three-hour long dance workouts on deck. In the course of these sessions each sailor would dance for a twenty minute period, either jogging on the spot or performing the dance known as the hornpipe[4]. While the scheduling and compulsory nature of these daily sessions were somewhat unusual, dancing was a common form of exercise on board British naval vessels until the late 1800s.

While the British writer Alexander McKee fancifully recounts that Byrne struck up a "traditional air" entitled *Drops of brandy* upon the *Bounty's* departure from Spithead quay (1989: 13)[5], there are no surviving references to the specific material performed by Byrne. However it would seem likely that his repertoire would have drawn on the reels that were common in both public music performance and specific naval contexts in the late 1700s, possibly with additional material learnt during his youth in Kilkenny. Such a repertoire would have been eminently suited to the sailors' performances of common dances such as the hornpipe. While there are no specific references in *Bounty* documentation – due to the commonplace nature of the activity – it also seems reasonable to assume that members of the crew would have performed various sea shanties, popular songs and/or material from their areas of origin as a personal and/or social activity intended to alleviate the boredom of a long sea voyage. Assuming this to be the case, the backgrounds of the crew suggest a wide potential repertoire of material. In a crew of forty five, along with the ship's Cornish captain, eight members were Scottish, one Irish, two were from the Isle of Man, two from the Orkney and Shetland islands and one from Guernsey. In the late 1700s, these regions of the (then somewhat tenuously) United Kingdom had distinct languages (or dialects) and local music and folkloric cultures. Added to this, the remaining English portion of the crew, which was regionally diverse in its make-up, was also complemented by two United States sailors, a West

Indian and a German (giving an even greater range of linguistic diversity and available song repertoire).

One of the few references to song performance on the *Bounty* comes from Bligh's own pen. Defending himself from James Morrison's criticism of the quality of food and the fairness of its allocation on board the *Bounty*, and the (alleged) discontent this caused; Bligh argued that the opposite was true and that the crew were so pleased with their treatment "that songs were made on him extolling his kindness" (1794: 45). Were this remark to be taken at face value, as a celebration of Bligh's shipboard cuisine, it would sit somewhat oddly with the weight of evidence concerning his management of provisions. Assuming that such material was performed, Gavin Kennedy has argued that it is more likely that:

> there may have been a touch of irony in the songs composed by Byrne[6] ... and sung by the men and that, fortunately for all involved, Bligh missed out on the joke. (1989: 219)

In either case, the origination and performance of topical songs on board accords with the intense and introverted nature of shipboard life and the frequent discussion of this by crewmembers in various contexts, one of which is discussed by Dening in terms of "yarning". Describing this verbal practice as one of the various maritime "rituals of sociability", he emphasises this was "very political" in that it "educated participants in the language and signs of institutions" (1992: 73). He also emphasises that through its practice sailors "raised grumbling to an art form" (ibid). In one of his few discussions of dance and music on board, Dening produces a notable characterisation of what might be termed the crew's micro-politics of resistance on board the *Bounty*:

> The ways human beings exercise power over one another in an institution such as a ship... are subtle and complex. Hegemony is made of trivia ...
> One defence against the power of exaggerated rage [such as that practiced by Bligh] is to watch its boiling theatre with mockery. (ibid)

Referring to Bligh's regime of compulsory daily exercise for the crew, Dening comments that the crew responded by using the very 'space' designed and enforced by their captain to reply to him:

> Bligh did not win his duel with his crew over dancing, because, as Michael Byrne fiddled, they mocked their captain in the ditties they sang and the steps they danced. (ibid)

The voyage from England to Tahiti was, therefore, one in which music played a substantial part. Byrne's fiddle playing, in particular, was both a source of friction, accompanying compulsory dancing, and an assuager of the same, allowing the crew a cultural reply to its imposition. Singing also enlivened the spirits of those on board and vented feelings of anger and resentment (and, no doubt, also served as relaxation and entertainment).

II. The Tahitian Interlude

In between the journey to Polynesia and the fateful mutiny was a period we might refer to as the 'Tahitian interlude' – a pause in the drama when all, including Bligh, relaxed on Tahiti. The reasons for the extended stay on the island remain unclear but appear to have involved issues to do with seasonal factors relevant to the successful collection of breadfruit plants and/or the choice of a favourable time of year to embark upon the lengthy return journey. Whatever the reason, the extended stay contributed significantly to the subsequent development of the narrative of the *Bounty*. During their stay the crew had little more to do than relax and wait the seasons out. One central aspect of their recreation was that the particular social morés and culture of welcoming guests on Tahiti at that time meant that the crew were well fed and entertained by their hosts and provided with sexual companionship by Tahitian women – on an apparently voluntary and enthusiastic basis. Along with sexual pleasures, the sailors, and their Tahitian hosts, also indulged in repeated feasting and musical and dance performances, practices which the sailors also indulged in with enthusiasm.

Aside from all but the broadest similarities, these activities were a far remove from the kind of cultural events the (soon-to-be) leader of the mutineers, Fletcher Christian, had grown up with. One such event, held at Christian's school, St Bees in Whitehaven, Cumbria, when Christian was fourteen, was described in a local newspaper in the following terms:

> *Last week the young gentlemen students at St Bees gave a very elegant ball to the ladies of Egremont and other neighbouring places. Upwards of thirty couples danced country dances, and the whole was conducted with the greatest propriety.* (quoted in Christian, G, 1999: 32–33)

By contrast, energetic sexual indulgence, together with abandoned feasting and drinking *were* a common feature of British (and other western) sailors' lives while in port, with wives or girlfriends (if available) or (more usually) prostitutes being visited ashore or transported on board during ships' visits. One vivid contemporary representation of such activities is provided by a period illustration archived at the National Maritime Museum of London (reproduced in Christian, G, 1999: np). This depicts a boat being rowed out to a ship in port carrying a group of drunken prostitutes, barrels of gin and brandy and a leering fiddler bowing a tune. While Byrne and his fiddle were present on Tahiti with the crew of the *Bounty*, the principal difference between the scenarios was not simply that the *Bounty* crew's hedonistic pursuits took place on shore; but rather that these occurred as an interactive social activity rather than as, in the case of consort with prostitutes and purchase of food and alcohol in port, a commercial one designed to exploit and satiate the needs of visiting sailors. It is likely that the pursuits were all the more appreciated by the crew for that very reason.

So, having danced their way across the Atlantic, Indian and Pacific oceans to the tune of Byrne's hornpipes and reels, singing various songs, satirical and otherwise, members of the *Bounty*'s crew arrived on Tahiti. The fact of there being no mention in any account of the Tahitian interlude that members of the *Bounty* crew danced or sang for and/or in the company of their Tahitian hosts means that any consideration of this is conjectural. However, several elements suggest that such performances were likely. To begin with, singing and dancing were a central aspect of sailors' conviviality and were also an available reciprocal option at any social event at which they were entertained. As Joseph Banks's journal attests, such interactions had taken place during Cook's initial visit to Tahiti in 1769:

> [A group of Tahitians] *seeing us entertaind with their musick, askd us to sing them an English song, which we most readily agreed to and receivd much applause, so much so that one of the musicians became desirous of going to England to learn to sing.*
> (Beaglehole [ed] 1962: 290)

In the light of this there may even have been an expectation that the *Bounty* crew would perform during their stay.

Along with any performances of their own material, members of the crew were given the opportunity to adapt their steps and rhythms to the percussion and vocal chant-based music of late 18th Century Tahiti[7], and indeed, danced and watched dance regularly for the next five months. If we pause to consider the events which occurred over the period, we can perceive a quite extraordinary process of acculturation through performance (both dance/musical and sexual), after which a substantial proportion of the crew were evidently never the same again. This was confirmed by the manner in which one crewmember, George Stewart, celebrated Bligh's departure from the *Bounty*. As Bligh later recalled, Stewart came on deck and "danced in the Otahetian manner" as the castaways drifted off (cited in Christian, G, 1999: 185).

As Oliver has identified:

> *Tahitians danced on many occasions, from carefree informal gatherings of a handfull of neighbors, to solemn assemblies of thousands. Dancing took place at welcomings and departings; at births and deaths; before, during, and after battles; as preludes, interludes and postludes to contests, theatricals and religious ceremonies. They danced for sheer pleasure or to vent rage, to express happiness or grief, to invite or defy, to entertain or terrify, to worship the spirits or humble their opponents.*
> (1988: 105-106)

Bligh's observations about Stewart's dancing reflect the manner in which Bligh had become well acquainted with Tahitian customs during his stay and his accounts of the island include several descriptions of dancing and music. Some of these were modest, low-key affairs. On October 31st 1788, for example, Bligh attended an entertainment organised for him by a chief named Tinah that he described as "a concert of one drum and three flutes, with singing by four men" (1792: 75). The description of the size of ensembles and the instruments used accords with those noted by earlier observers. Visiting the islands some twelve years prior to the arrival of the *Bounty*, as a member of the crew of Captain Cook's *Resolution*, John Webber sketched a scene he entitled 'Dance in Otaheite' (reproduced in Clarke, 1986: 34) which showed three slender women dancing, two demonstrating hula-style hand gestures, with a third dancing more languorously. Their accompaniment, shown on the left hand side of the image, comprises a flautist (playing in frontal recorder/oboe style) and two squatting drummers beating a rhythm with their hands on vertical conical drums (of approximately two foot in height).

Other performances appear to have been less restrained in their movements, costume and physical explicitness, particularly those enacted by members of the *arioi* sect of celebrant-entertainers[8]. One performance Bligh witnessed on November 8th 1788 appears to have been so 'colourful' that Bligh demurred from describing it in any detail, simply commenting that:

> *a dancing heiva began, which was performed by two girls and four men: this lasted half an hour, and consisted of wanton gestures and motions, such as have been described in the account of former voyages.*
> (1792: 88)

To add to Bligh's discomfort, the wrestling match that was scheduled as the second entertainment rapidly developed into a "scene of riot and confusion" (ibid) as a group of *arioi* took advantage of the melee to seize and forcibly disrobe various women.

Despite his earlier demurral, Bligh appears to have become less shy by February 1789, since he both readily accepted an invitation from a group passing en route to Tettaha on Wednesday 11th and gave a more explicit description of the performance:

> *They had the civility to send me word, that, if I chose, they would stay to perform a short heiva before me: and I immediately attended. It began by a dance of two young girls, to the music of drums and flutes, which lasted no long time; at the conclusion, they suddenly dropped all their dress, which was left as a present for me, and went off without me seeing them any more. After this, the men danced: their performance was more indecent than any I had before seen, but was not the less applauded on that account by the natives, who seemed much delighted.* (ibid: 127)

This description accords with that offered by a crewmember on the *Resolution* in 1776, midshipman George Gilbert, who had previously reported that Tahitian "songs and dances, which are very frequent, appear exceeding lascivious in the eye of a European ... the custom of the country ... seemingly permits them to pursue the natural impulse of their passions" (quoted in Clarke, 1986: 35).

III. The Mutiny and its Aftermath

The mutiny took place on 28th April 1789. Despite his protestations, the mutineers prevented Byrne from joining Bligh and the other crewmembers cast adrift in a crowded boat. As Byrne testified at his court-martial:

> *I do not know whether I may be able to ascertain the exact Words that were spoken on the Occasion; but some said, "We must not part with our Fiddler," and Charles Churchill threatened to send me to the Shades, If I attempted to quit the Cutter, into which I had gone, for the Purpose of attending Lieut. Bligh.* (Rutter [ed] 1931: 161)

Commenting on the moment of the mutiny, Dening has identified that:

> *What stuck in the memory of those who tried to describe Christian on the morning of the mutiny was the sort of Tahitian-English pidgin he was using. 'Mammoo' (mamu), 'Silence', they remember him shouting. While it is difficult to point to anything stronger than hints in James Morrison's and Peter Heywood's accounts of the mutiny, there is a*

19

suggestion that the crew of the Bounty *had been marked by something more than tattoos at Tahiti. They had begun to intersperse Tahitian words in their speech with one another... On the* Bounty, *their pidgin would* [have] *... underscore[d] a relationship changed by their Tahitian experience. It bred familiarity. It lessened distinction between them and increased distance between their present and their former selves.* (1992: 57-58)

After the mutiny the mutineers sailed to the island of Tubuai, which Christian had identified as a possible hiding and settling place. Here, for the first time, the hedonistic rapture of the mutineers' Polynesian experience began to unravel. On arriving at Tubuai, the crew was first assailed by the noise of blown conch shells from the land, which unsettled them with its ambiguity. Fifty canoes put off from shore and surrounded the ship, one canoe conveying young women garlanded with flowers and pearl shells. Morrison later recalled that those onboard "stood up and beat time to a song which was given by one of them which appeared to be a person of some consequence" (1789: np[9]). Members of this party came on board but the crew soon realised that it was a trap and had to fend off armed men attempting to board the boat, as the conch shells again sounded out.

After returning to Tahiti to re-provision and to add Tahitian women and men to their party, the *Bounty* returned to Tubuai, moored off a different part of the coast and established an encampment at a place later known as Fort George. Keen to establish good relations, Christian and two other crewmembers who had sufficient Tahitian to communicate arranged a meeting with Tahoohoo'hoo'atumma, the chief whose area the encampment was in. In the contact that followed, traditional Tahitian dance played a significant role in establishing mutual respect (emphasising the manner in which the *Bounty* crew led by Christian were engaging with traditional Tahitian morés). Morrison recorded that at the first meeting:

At the request of the Old Man [Tahoohoo'hoo'atumma] *the young women* [who accompanied him] *performed a dance beating time and singing and went through the performance with much regularity after which the Taheite Women* [from the Bounty party] *entertained them with a dance in turn, when they took their leave Mr Christian invited them to see a Heiva Next day, which they readily accepted and before they arrived in the Morning two of the Weomen were Neatly dressed, & two Men in Pairs of the Mourning dress of Taheite and when the Company were arrived they were entertained with a Heiva after the manner of the Society Isles at which they seemed highly pleased, they were quite taken with the dress of the Weomen"* (ibid).

Despite these elegant festivities, the *Bounty* mutineers' attempt to settle on Tubuai proved unsuccessful and they returned briefly to Tahiti in September 1789, with the addition of three Tubuaian men. At this point, several members of the crew decided against accompanying Christian in his quest for a safe hiding place and opted to remain on Tahiti. One of these was Byrne[10]. The fiddler awaited the arrival of the British navy, which duly occurred when the *Pandora* moored offshore in 1791. He was duly arrested and transported to England, where he was tried for mutiny but eventually acquitted. After persuading a number of Polynesian women to board, the *Bounty* set sail, with nine mutineers, six Polynesian men (three Tahitians, two Tubuaians and a Raiatean), twelve Tahitian women and a baby, starting on the looping voyage that was to bring them to remote, mis-charted Pitcairn Island on January 12th 1790.

IV. Cultural Commemorations

The *Bounty* crew's visit to Tahiti and the subsequent mutiny were events of such scale, for both Tahitians and the British Empire, that they were reported and commemorated in a range of media. For Tahitians, the inter-action of the *Bounty* crew with locals (and the novel material goods the ship possessed) were the most significant elements and these were duly inscribed in local folklore in the forms of tales, verse, song, dance and mime.

While no trace of the songs and dances the *Bounty's* crew may have performed on Tahiti appear to have persisted to present, Australian film maker Charles Chauvel, who visited Tahiti in 1932, noted that another aspect of their stay had been inscribed in local folklore:

> The men of the Bounty, who seemed to have suffered an epidemic of sprains and rheumatic pains during their stay upon Tahiti, are still massaged in pantomime during the course of an old interpretive dance which, when it is performed to-day, is not understood by its performers. (Chauvel, 1933: 33)

Chauvel's passage is ambiguous in that it appears to suggest that the dance referred to was still performed in the 1930s and was one of the few early "interpretive dances still existant" (ibid). However, this might have been simple surmise on his part, since he makes no reference to having seen the massage dance or having heard contemporary reference to it. Chauvel's insight into the origin of the dance appears to have originated from William Ellis's book *Polynesian Researches* (1830/revised 1832), which includes material based on his residence in Tahiti in between 1816 and 1822 – a period within generational memory of the *Bounty's* visit.

Chauvel also offers another example of folkloric memory, drawn from Ellis, who related that he witnessed a dispute between two Tahitians about what happened to an anchor buoy belonging to the *Bounty*, and that:

> after disputing it for some time without convincing his opponent, the individual who had stated the fact referred to the following lines in one of their ballads relating to that event.
>
> "O mea eiá e Tareu eiá
>
> Eiá te poito a Bligh."
>
> Such a one a thief, and Tareu, a thief,
>
> Theived (or stole) the buoy of Bligh.
>
> The song was one well known to most, and the existence of this fact, the remembrance of which the ballad was designed to preserve, was conclusive, and appeared to satisfy the parties by whom it had been questioned. (Ellis, 1832: 286-287)

Research for this book has not located the full text of the ballad referred to by Ellis. From the description, it seems likely that it was an example of a *ute*, a topical (and often satirical) form of Tahitian song. While the buoy song appears to have persisted several decades after the *Bounty's* visit, there is no evidence that it continues in local oral transmission.

In Europe, representations of the event were also quick to follow.

In May 1790, shortly after the mutineers landed on Pitcairn, the mutineers became the subject of dramatic presentations in London and Paris in the form of *The Pirates! or The Calamities of Captain Bligh*, a play staged at the Royalty Theatre in London. The drama featured an "Otahetian Dance" performed by members of the cast, dressed in some semblance of Tahitian appearance, in role as the Tahitians who welcomed the *Bounty* crew on their initial visit[11]. A fully musical version of the story was also staged in Paris shortly afterwards[12].

While the musical and theatrical commemorations of the *Bounty's* mutiny and the efforts of the British navy to locate and seize the mutineers comprised the British responses to the mutiny; further dramatic developments in the narrative were unfolding on Pitcairn itself, creating another layer in a rapidly mythologised narrative which was only to become apparent when a New England sealing ship named the *Topaz* chanced across the island in 1808.

Notes

1. Speaking at the Norfolk Island Museum in April 1999, British Pitcairn history enthusiast Maurice Allward estimated that around 3000 articles, books, films and television documentaries had been made about the mutiny and its aftermath.
2. An enterprise promoted by Sir Joseph Banks, scientific adviser to King George III and president of the Royal Society, who had previously visited Tahiti on Captain Cook's first voyage to the Pacific.
3. Which was bought up and withdrawn from circulation by MGM prior to the release of their major budget production *Mutiny on The Bounty* in 1935.
4. See discussion of the hornpipe in Chapter 2.
5. McKee includes the following description:

   As the men walked the capstain bars round, and the dripping anchor ropes came inboard, the half-blind Irish fiddler, Michael Byrne struck up the traditional air, "Drops of Brandy", and the men hummed the words to themselves:

   And Johnny shall have a new bonnet,
   And Johnny shall go to the fair,
   And Johnny shall have a blue ribbon,
   To tie up his bonny brown hair.
   And why should I not love Johnny
   And why should not Johnny love me
   And why should I not love Johnny
   As well as another bodie

   To the tune of the old country dance the Bounty got under weigh [sic]. (McKee, 1989: 13)

   Since the source for this highly specific description is not given, and I have not encountered the reference elsewhere, there must be, at very least, a substantial question mark over the veracity of this passage.
6. The statement that these songs were "composed by Byrne" appears to be purely speculative rather than based on any contemporary reference.

7. See Ellis (1829: 218-310) for a description of musical and dance practices in the early 1800s.

8. See Ellis (1829: 311-344) and Oliver (1988: 100-105) for further discussion.

9. This, and all other quotations from Morrison's account, are taken from an unpaginated manuscript copy held in the Mitchell Library, Sydney.

10. Interestingly, while Morrison's journal details many of the items the party remaining on Tahiti were allowed to take ashore, Byrne's fiddle is not listed. There is however no evidence that Byrne's violin found its way to Pitcairn Island with the *Bounty*.

11. It seems likely that this followed some of the models offered by Cook's account of his previous voyage to Tahiti, published in 1784, which had also been imaginatively interpreted on stage in the form of a pantomime at the Theatre Royal in London entitled *Omai: Or, A Trip Round the World*. This included 'Tahitian dance' sequences performed to music by a Mr Shield.

12. Cited in Christian, G (1999: 167) – I have been unable to obtain further information on the Parisian production.

Chapter Two

NO EREWHON
The first Pitcairn Island settlement

Pitcairn was not the scene of a Utopia or an Erewhon. No social or political theories stimulated its founding. But it was an unconscious and spontaneous experiment nonetheless. The problems it illuminates are those of culture contact. This is a phenomenon as ancient and as widespread as the existence of culture itself ... On Pitcairn, we see an experiment in culture contact – the impact of European, or English civilization and Polynesian. It occurs, to be sure, on a small scale, but it is a reduction in degree only. Here we have a number of advantages for the study of the phenomenon. The situation has been simplified to its very elements. Most of the imponderables which affect other foci of culture contact and the complex reactions that obscure the design are absent on Pitcairn. (Shapiro, 1936: 137–139)

Soon after their arrival on Pitcairn the mutineers' escapist dream soured. By 1793 all the Polynesian men and five of the mutineers, including Christian, had been killed as a result of violent disputes. The women were far from innocent bystanders in this, colluding and assisting with various of the deaths and later plotting against the remaining mutineers. In 1797 the remaining mutineers made a still to produce alcohol and during an extended period of drunkenness William McCoy died in an accident and in 1799 Matthew Quintal was killed by Alexander Smith and Edward Young, the latter of whom died in 1800, leaving the population of the island as Smith, nine Tahitian women and twenty children, nineteen of whom had been born on Pitcairn. Smith's isolation and the fate of his fellow mutineers appear to have prompted a profound change as he turned to religion and endeavoured to be pastor and patriarch of the small community. While he does not seem to have been particularly blessed with musical gifts, his cultural influence appears to have been profound. Writing in 1882, to New Englander Captain Gibbons, Pitcairn Islander Rosalind Young recalled:

> *John Adams taught his small and young flock to sing, as best he could, as I have been informed by old Mrs. E. Young, 'Mama' as everybody here calls her ... After reading a chapter from the Bible, and a portion from 'Come to Jesus', they would turn to the end of their Bibles and sing in tremulous tones, one of the old psalms[1], the Scottish version, to the tune taught to them by their sailor father so long ago, in their early home on Pitcairn Island. As I write I seem to hear them sing again, the old quaint and plaintive tune to the Scottish version of the Second Psalm, but the following stanza is the one that seems imprinted on my memory – 'A sure decree I will declare/The Lord has said to me/ Thou art my only Son, this day/Have I begotten thee.' As they sung so often, I have since wondered if that could have been the particular psalm John Adams taught them to sing and love. (1882-1891: 3-4)[2]*

[NB Smith was known as John Adams after 1808.]

I. Emergent Pitcairn Identity

With Smith as its leader but with Tahitian women as its mainstay, the community developed a cultural identity and emergent creole language that blended Tahitian elements and aspects of British Christian religion and morality. In terms of music, any vernacular songs that the mutineers knew appear to have died with them. Similarly, Smith appears to have only taught the islanders aspects of the British hymnody he was familiar with. The Polynesian settlers had more of an opportunity to maintain their musical traditions, in that many of the Tahitian women retained a knowledge of song and dance. The only traditional Tahitian instrument that seems to have been present on the island during the initial years of settlement was a nose flute (either brought to the island or made there) that was used to accompany traditional Tahitian singing. Our information on this derives from reports of an unfortunate incident. In 1793 the Tahitian male Manarii[3], jealous of his compatriot Teimua, shot the latter dead while he was performing a flute accompaniment to a song sung by Teraura (also known by the English name Susannah). Following this tragedy – and the death of the other Polynesian men – the instrument seems to have disappeared from island culture.

Little is known about what music and dance practices may have taken place on the island between 1793 and 1807 but following the discovery of the mutineers' hideaway in 1808 by the *Topaz*, a stream of mariners visited Pitcairn and recorded observations of the community they encountered. The discovery of the *Bounty* mutineers and their offspring captivated Western Europe and North America for several decades and led to many fanciful representations in verse, picture and on stage. One of the more curious of the latter was a "new romantick, operatick ballet spectacle" (programme notes[4]) entitled *Pitcairn's Island* performed at the Theatre Royal in London in April 1816, with music and dance composed and directed by Oscar Byrne[5]. With a narrative entirely lacking in reference to the *Bounty* mutiny and music taken from contemporary European composers and "ancient British melodies" (ibid), the production was both fanciful and opportunistic.

During the 1810s visitors to Pitcairn were regularly entertained by performances of Tahitian-style music and dancing[6] and often reciprocated by reacquainting islanders with western music and dancing. David Ramsay, surgeon on the Australian ship the *Sydney*, which visited in 1821, noted that after dinner one night:

> *We passed the rest of the evening in dancing and singing. The women showed us the Otahetian dance, as also the men, they liked very much to see the English men dance.* (1821: np)

With regard to this brief description it is perhaps not too fanciful to conjecture that for the older Tahitian women, the sight of British sailors dancing might have rekindled memories of the *Bounty* crew's days on Tahiti. Conversely, the memoirs of western visitors to Tahiti also appear to have been on the mind of Captain Beechey, who visited the island in 1825 on HMS *Blossom* and specifically requested a performance of traditional Tahitian music and dance and later reported the following:

> *A large room in Quintal's house was prepared for the occasion, and the company were ranged on one side of the apartment, glowing beneath a blazing string of doodoe nuts; the musicians were on the other, under the direction of Arthur Quintal. He was seated on the ground, as head musician, and had before him a large gourd, and a piece of musical wood (porou), which he balanced nicely upon his toes, that there might be the less interruption to its vibrations. He struck the instrument alternatively with two sticks, and was accompanied by Dolly, who performed very skillfully with both hands upon a gourd, which had a longitudinal hole cut in one end of it; rapidly beating the orifice with the palms of her hands, and releasing it again with uncommon dexterity, so as to produce a tattoo, but in perfect time with the other instrument. A third performed upon the Bounty's old copper fish-kettle, which formed a sort of bass.* (1831: 82)

After having described the percussion ensemble in these appreciative terms, Beechey referred to the dance performance in a more muted manner:

> *To this exhilarating music three grown-up females stood up to dance, but with a reluctance which showed it was done only to oblige us, as they consider such performances an inroad upon their usual innocent pastimes. The figure consisted of such parts of the Otaheitan dance as were thought most decorous, and was little more than a shuffling of the feet, sliding past each other, and snapping their fingers; but even this produced, at times, considerable laughter from the female spectators, perhaps from some association of ridiculous ideas, which we, as strangers, did not feel; and no doubt had our opinion of the performance been consulted, it would have been essentially different from theirs. They did not long continue these diversions, from an idea that it was too great a levity to be continued long; and only the three beforementioned ladies could be prevailed on to exhibit their skill.* (ibid)

There are a number of interesting aspects to Beechey's account. His description of the percussion players emphasises their rhythmic skills and tightness and identifies Arthur Quintal as musical leader. This would seem to suggest that this ensemble had some degree of prior musical experience together and/or might have rehearsed or performed with some degree of regularity. Far from this percussion playing being some dimly recollected relic of Tahitian culture, it seems to have been a continuing practice in the 1820s. However, Beechey's descriptions of dancing are differently nuanced. He opens by (implicitly) contrasting the "exhilarating" percussion music with the performances of the obligated dancers, all three of whom he emphasises as *"grown-up"* (italics in original), which can be taken to mean of a mature age. This, in turn, might suggest that the dancers were three of the original Tahitian women who had accompanied the *Bounty* to Pitcairn. If so, age might be one factor to explain their restrained movements. There is also the question of what Beechey and his companions were expecting. If they had either previously seen or (as likely) read or heard about more risqué and/or athletic dances, they may well have been disappointed to see a more restrained performance. But while this is one explanation, another interpretation of what was occurring is suggested by Beechey's awareness that there were elements of the dance that were prompting "considerable laughter" from (specifically) female spectators.

It may well have been that the three mature female dancers were including gestures, moves or postures that satirised some aspect of their naval audience or of previous encounters between British sailors and Polynesian women (aspects of sexual suggestiveness, congress or rejection being available topics). Indeed, with regard to the possibility that the dances incorporated aspects derived from or imitative of British referents, it is possible that something more syncretic was being presented. As early as 1773, members of Cook's second expedition to Tahiti encountered forms of local dance that appear to have syncretically engaged with British naval dance traditions:

> [The Tahitian women] *performed a dance on the Quarter deck which we had not seen before, it might be perhaps to express their Joy on their safe arrival at this place, it was performed by two at a time – they did not jump up as in the common dance but used a kind of a regular Step & moved their Legs something like our sailors dancing a Hornpipe, they moved their Arms up and down, repeated a Song together, changed their places often, wriggled their backsides and used many lascivious Gestures.* (Samwell, D in Beaglehole, J [ed] 1967: 1222)

It is notable, with regard to the above, that aspects of both Samwell's and Beechey's descriptions of Tahitian and Pitcairn dances are echoed in accounts given by James Revell Carr III that in the 19th Century some Hawaiian dances included elements derived from the hornpipe. In particular, Carr refers to a dancer who "performed a hula in a style that combined 'ancient' (*kahiko*) dance steps with finger snaps and steps from the sailors' hornpipe" (2004: 4). But whatever the degree of syncretism involved in the dances that Beechey observed, there is also enough his account to suggest that aspects of Tahitian culture were being 'tempered' by performers in this decade and were increasingly regarded as risqué and indelicate. Under the

27

'born-again' Christian leadership of Alexander Smith (John Adams), the population increasingly evinced Christian piety and modesty.

Two significant outsiders, the Englishman John Buffett and Irish-born George Hunn Nobbs, joined the Pitcairn community in the 1820s. Buffett arrived in 1823 onboard the British whaling ship *Cyrus* and stayed on in response to Adams' plea to the captain to secure a teacher for the island's young people. Nobbs arrived in 1828 after a decade of adventuring in South America and Europe, seemingly inspired by a mission to lead the community. Following Adams's death in 1829 they, and Adams's unofficial successor Edward Young, vied for leadership of the community. Raymond Nobbs has identified that:

> *The piety that Adams instilled in the Pitcairn community was to become legend ... By the time of Nobbs' arrival ... Christian services had developed to such an extent that visitors to the island wavered between boredom at their length and repetitiousness, and awe of what they were witnessing.*

> *The devout attitudes and observances of the Pitcairners, admiringly reported to the outside world, invoked a wave of approval so forceful that it intensified the piety or religiosity (depending on the particular commentator) of its inhabitants. What was reported from Pitcairn served as a dramatic argument in support of some of the most cherished tenets of both organised religious institutions and believing individuals.* (Nobbs, 1984: 17).

The latter argument is supported by Nobbs's reference to an account written by Hancock (1947: 6-7), which summarised 19th Century Christian perceptions of the 'morality tale' of Pitcairn in the following terms:

> *Evil men (the mutineers) and evil women (the Polynesians) ate of the apple (of unlicensed sex) and fell into discord and bestiality too horrendous to be more than hinted at. When all seemed lost, the word of God appeared through the media of the ship's Bible and Prayer book, relayed by a regenerated John Adams (the Island Moses), lone survivor of the evil men. This brought the little Pitcairn remnant to salvation. Thereupon it became transmuted into an idyllic community, where Christian precepts prevailed, sex was subdued into sanctioned channels, and harmony reigned. Here was living, flourishing proof of the efficacy of the Christian ethic and the salvation which lay in the Gospel and in religious attitudes and observances.* (quoted in Nobbs, 1984: 17).

This particular vision of Pitcairn society was rocked in the early 1830s.

During Beechey's visit in 1825, John Adams raised concerns that the island was no longer capable of supporting the growing population and asked Beechey whether the British Government would consider relocating them to New South Wales or Van Diemen's Land (Tasmania). In 1827, following two years of discussion, the British Colonial Office responded with a markedly different initiative and asked Tahitian royalty to allow the Pitcairners to settled there. Despite Adams' death in 1829, this request was agreed to and, after due consultation, all eighty seven islanders were relocated to Tahiti in 1831. This venture was far from successful. Disease afflicted the migrants and within eight months sixteen of the party (close to 20 per cent) had died. The remainder returned to Pitcairn and re-established the community there. The visit served to distance many Pitcairners from any sense of identification with their Polynesian heritage, largely as a result of their perceptions of Tahiti's licentious socio-sexual mores and the enthusiastic consumption of alcohol they witnessed.

More upheavals were to follow. In 1832 an Englishman named Joshua Hill arrived on Pitcairn and set himself up as ruler of the island community on the strength of an invented mandate from the British Government. Despite his brutal and tyrannical regime he managed to retain power until 1837, when mounting resentment of his conduct moved him to quit the island. Little is known of the music and dance culture during his rule but given his strong puritanical streak it is likely that hymns constituted the primary form of musical performance and that dancing was not tolerated as a public form.

Following Hill's exit, George Hunn Nobbs – who had spent much of the period of Hill's administration off the island – assumed the mantle of community leader. During the next two decades he played a prominent part in island culture. Nobbs was particularly significant in promoting an English/British identity for the Pitcairn community. This was made manifest in the anthem that he wrote (at an unknown date), which was "sung on Pitcairn for many years as the national anthem" to the tune of *Rousseau's dream* (Nobbs, 1984: 113). The song's lyrics represent the celebration of the Queen's Birthday, an event that was to become one of the main festivities in the Pitcairn calendar, as in its opening verse:

'Mid the mighty Southern Ocean
Stands an isolated rock
Blanched by surf's commotion
Riven by the lightning's shock
Hark those strains to heaven ascending
From those slopes of vivid green
Old and young their voices blending
God preserve Britannia's Queen![7]

Although a significant proportion of Pitcairners recoiled from Tahitian culture and became more intensely religious under the guardianship of Hill and Nobbs, these influences were not sufficient to erase aspects of Tahitian culture. Writing about the Queen's Birthday festivities held on the island in 1848, for instance, Pitcairn Islander Rosalind Amelia Young noted that:

The daughters of the mutineers, being now themselves the grandmothers, entered with zest into the sports, and contributed not a little to the general entertainment by reviving many of the games learnt from their Tahitian mothers.

They introduced into their games and sports the beating of calabashes with sticks, performed with extreme precision, to which the players kept time, moving with noiseless step and easy grace that was pleasing to witness. Their performance was called the ihara[8]. Another native dance, the uri[9], was performed by Susannah, the girl of fifteen who came in

29

the Bounty, *now an old woman of seventy-four and blind in one eye. She displayed remarkable liveliness in honor of the Queen's Birthday.*

The merry players kept up the dancing to a late hour. What mattered if most of them danced with bare feet; that did not affect their light-heartedness and happiness. A drum and a tambourine supplied all the music they wanted. (Young, 1894: 102)

Visiting the island in 1855, Captain Freemantle reported that local women undertook tapa cloth manufacture. Given that tapa cloth making was a common skill amongst the female population of Tahiti at the time of the *Bounty*'s visit, it seems likely that the Pitcairn women's activity represented a continuance of the traditional Tahitian practice. If this was the case, then it may also have included a traditional Tahitian song since, as James Morrison observed during the *Bounty*'s stay on Tahiti:

[strips of bark were] *placed at equal distances about 6 feet asunder & at each of them two women work, having the Piece between them, beating it with square beetles to its proper breadth; this they perform by a Song given by one and Chorous'd by the rest and keep regular time and Shifting the Piece backwards and forwards till it is all beat out ...* (1789: np)

Traditional tapa cloth manufacture continued into the 20th Century (after the island's abandonment and resettlement) with Jacob Warren (born 1920) having clear memories of tapa cloth being made on Pitcairn through until the mid-1930s (pc 1999[10]). The extent to which the tradition of singing the Tahitian song with this continued is unclear, however, given the repetitive and tedious nature of the cloth manufacture, any habitual distraction, such as singing, might well have been welcome and therefore been communicated (and taught) to women by their older female relatives as they co-operated on the task. This practice may have been the type of Tahitian singing that some older Pitcairners have identified as continuing on until the mid-1900s (Meralda Warren, pc 1999)[11].

II. Hymns, Singing and Repertoire

By the 1850s hymn singing had been a staple of island life for over fifty years. In the early days this appears to have been unaccompanied. Some time around the 1830s-40s, an accordion[12] made an appearance on the island, provided by a visiting ship, and harmoniums[13] appeared in the following decade. Singing to such accompaniment in all likelihood served to consolidate singing styles towards western standard pitch and performance practices. This was not necessarily the case prior to the arrival of Buffett in 1823 and Nobbs in 1828. In the early days a regular form of worship was the chanting of the 95th Psalm to a tune John Adams had composed. Amelia Young described this as a "simple and plaintive air, which, slightly modified, was made to suit either common, short or long meter" (1896: 102). This approach is perhaps significant given that forms of chanting were standard in both Polynesian music of the period and Anglican recitation of the Psalms. The nature of the melodies and their performance is also open to conjecture. It cannot be simply assumed that the islanders sang in western 'equal temperament' tuning, for example. Given the styles of singing that the Tahitians had been familiar with on Tahiti, it is more than likely that there were at least some remnants of the use of micro-tones and pitch slides. In this regard, elements of their hymnody may have resembled some of the melodic approaches presented in albums of reconstructed Polynesian *himene* choral music such as Pascal Nabet-Meyer's (eponymous) recording of the *Tubuai Choir* (1993) (from the island that the *Bounty* mutineers first tried to settle on following their departure from Tahiti) and his earlier Rapa Itian recording *The Tahitian Choir* (1992)[14].

John Buffett attempted to expand the repertoire of early ensemble singing after his arrival in 1823, as Amelia Young has documented:

> *Buffett soon sought to introduce at least a change of tunes into the services of the church, and, being gifted with a good voice, he managed ... to lead the people a few steps further on. A book of church music given him at Tahiti supplied a variety of tunes, but nothing more was attempted than the simple air. Nor were the songs sung in unison.* (1896: 103)

Further development – and possibly further westernisation – of island singing styles occurred in 1850 when five passengers visiting Pitcairn onboard the *Noble* were obliged to spend 18 days on the island after their ship was blown off its anchorage during the night. Received with traditional hospitality, the visitors attended religious services. Young notes that one of the visitors, a Mr Carleton, who had some musical training, declared that the sound of the congregation singing "without regard to time or tune" was so "discordant and jarring" and "so grating on his ears" that it "nearly compelled him to take his hat and leave the house" (ibid: 104). Buffett responded to Carleton's critique by inviting him to teach islanders 'proper' western style hymn singing. According to Young, Carleton obtained a tuning fork from another visitor, Baron de Thierry (who fortuitously had one in his pocket at the time of being stranded) and selected a group of those islanders that he felt possessed musical talent and worked with them.

Carleton's companion Brodie recorded that fifty seven Pitcairners participated in Carleton's classes (1851: 41-42) and that:

> *The progress surpassed the most sanguine expectation of the teacher; on the fourth day from the commencement, they sang through a catch in four parts, with great steadiness; for people who had been hitherto unaware of even the existence in nature of harmony, the performance was very remarkable[15]. Both pupils and preceptor appeared to take equal delight in the task; and we heard them, after a fortnight's instruction, singing among themselves in the open air trios and quartettos, for the most part performed in chorus, during the greater part of the night.* (ibid: 29)

Brodie also added of the singing lessons that:

> *It is very gratifying to leave behind us some little memorial of our residence, even though it be of so airy a nature as this.* (ibid)

Young also reports that the results of the tuition were striking:

> *The pleasing results produced by harmony of sounds seemed to awaken*

in the hearts of the learners such eagerness and anxiety to do their best as to greatly encourage their teacher in his efforts ... in the short space of one week they accomplished a result beyond their highest hopes ... An old man used to tell how he was affected by the first sounds of harmony that he heard. He said: "The first tune I listened to was Devizes. Buffett was singing the air, and Mr. Carleton the bass. I stood by open mouthed drinking in the sweet sounds and thinking it must be like heaven". (ibid: 105)

Visiting the island three years later, Mr B. Toup Nicholas gave a particularly poignant account of island singing that suggests that Carleton's influence had continued:

In the evening, it being a beautiful moonlight night, we all met in front of a house where the organ-harmonium is kept. The Islanders then sang several hymns and touching melodies, one of which from its simple pathos, and from the exquisite manner in which it was sung, to the tune of "Long, long ago," I believe I shall never forget. (quoted in Murray, 1860: 291)

Nicholas then goes on to describe how the singers gave a stirring rendition of a popular Victorian sentimental song *The sailor boy's early grave*, the first verse of which comprised:

Shed not a tear o'er your friend's early bier
When I am gone, when I am gone
Nor, if the slow-tolling bell you should hear
When I am gone, when I am gone

Nicholas obviously found the rendition of the song particularly moving, since he recorded that:

The voices of the islanders are both powerful and sweet; and the thrill of rare and unexpected pleasure I experienced on hearing them sing the above song, was never surpassed, not even when listening to Jenny Lind[16]. (ibid: 256)

Nicholas also had the unfortunate opportunity to witness hymn singing at a funeral (that of Matthew McCoy), and provided a vivid and poignant sound picture of the event:

The Burial Service was impressively read by the Rev. W. Holman, after which a hymn was sung – or attempted to be sung – for the accents of the poor islanders were stifled by sobs; and amidst the sobs the body was lowered into the grave. It was a beautiful sunset; the tall, plume-like cocoanut trees waved gently above our heads. Borne upwards from the sea, mournfully, but not discordantly, came the sound of the breakers as they burst against the shore. (ibid: 255)

Fortescue Moresby, who visited the island shortly before the relocation to Norfolk in 1855, was also highly positive in his assessment of a church service he attended, noting that "the islanders sang two hymns in most magnificent style; I have never heard any Church singing that could equal theirs, except at Cathedrals" (quoted in Belcher, 1870: 221).

As several visitors to the island observed, the existence of original Pitcairn hymns was as surprising as the vocal competence of the choir. George Hunn Nobbs was the originator of these, which appear to have comprised original lyrics set to pre-existing and/or modified melodies. In addition to his Pitcairn Queen's birthday 'anthem' (discussed above), he wrote several other songs. One of these was *The Angel's lament*, of which George Hunn Nobbs commented that, "this was composed at the request of several of our little community, who wished to have one of their own [hymns] which they might sing to the pathetic air of 'Bonny Doon'" (cited in Murray, 1885: 306). The lyrics (reproduced in Nobbs, 1984: 130-131) are lengthy and dour and – aside to some possible allusion to the turbulent years of first settlement – have no obvious local reference and there is no evidence that the song was sung on Pitcairn on more than an occasional basis.

Nobbs wrote a very different hymn in praise of Pitcairn Island and its landscape entitled *Fenua maitai* (Tahitian for 'The Good Land'). Aside from its Tahitian title, repeated at the end of each verse, the song's six eight-line verses are in Standard English and blend description of the natural environment and local history and folklore, as in the opening lines of verse four:

> *By torch-light the haunts of the white bird exploring*
> *Perched high on the "big tree's" aerial bridge*
> *How quick beat each heart, as the death-wail came soaring*
> *From the ghost that still lingers on "Talaloo's ridge!"*[17]

Despite its number of verses and multi-syllabic lines, Thomas Murray noted that the song was sung in 1850, on the sixtieth anniversary of the community's establishment and describes it – and/or its performance on that occasion – as "a singularly wild effusion" (1885: 308).

It is unclear whether the two best-known hymns associated with Nobbs, *The Pitcairn anthem* and *Gethsemane* – commonly credited as co-composed with Driver Christian, were written on Pitcairn or after the relocation to Norfolk Island. Aspects of the songs' lyrics and subsequent history lead me to suspect the latter, and for this reason they are discussed in Chapter 3. The evidence is, however, inconclusive. Raymond Nobbs (1984: 129-131) also credits his ancestor with writing two other hymns (*Evening hymn* and an untitled one with an opening line "I will not encumber my verse"). It is also uncertain whether these were composed and/or performed on Pitcairn or Norfolk Island, since no written record of their performance in either location remains.

Yet least the extended discussions of island hymn singing and religiosity offered above suggest a saturation of the community's socio-cultural life with Christian worship, it is important to emphasise that visitors to Pitcairn in the 1850s witnessed other sides of island culture. Brodie's account of his 1850 visit, for instance, indicates that the island's population had also rediscovered the most prominent musical characteristics of the *Bounty's* voyage to Tahiti:

> *Edward Quintal brought his fiddle; he had picked up some hornpipe and*
> *reel tunes by ear on board ship, which he really played with great spirit,*

33

and the true artistic twang, not omitting the stamp and wriggle, or the grind upon the fourth string. Some of the islanders danced very well, not waltzes certainly, but reels. The women never dance[18]. We three, Carleton, Taylor and myself, danced a Scotch reel, which threw the spectators into ecstasies. The women shrieked with laughing. (Brodie, 1851: 21)[19]

The (previously discussed) reel and the hornpipe were Scottish-derived solo dances that were modified by sailors to incorporate various gestures and movements imitating everyday maritime actions (such as looking out for land, saluting an officer, hauling ropes etc.). While there is no direct evidence to support the contention, it is possible that the Pitcairners tacitly understood these dances as a male 'heritage' form dating back to the *Bounty*, a connection that their dancing reaffirmed and maintained (much as styles of Polynesian dance were largely a preserve of female Pitcairn islanders, learnt from their aunts and mothers, at this time).

* * *

In the early 1850s change was in the air. There was substantial agreement on Pitcairn that the population, which now exceeded 175 adults and children, was too large for the island to comfortably sustain. While several older islanders retained bitter memories of the earlier abortive relocation to Tahiti, the British Government's offer to grant the Pitcairn community land on the former penal colony of Norfolk Island, off the east coast of Australia, convinced many of the merits of their evacuation. In 1856, following a majority vote by the islanders, the *Morayshire* arrived to transport the population to their new home. While the Pitcairners had to leave much of their material culture behind on the island, their intangible assets of language and memory were more easily transported. They made good use of such cultural knowledge to alleviate the tedium and anxiety of their sea journey by celebrating the Queen's Birthday onboard the *Morayshire* with festivities and dances[20].

Notes

1. As Christian music scholar Robin Ryan has identified, this reference is somewhat confusing as the psalms do not appear at the end of the Bible (pc January 2005).

2. Thanks to James Revell Carr III for supplying me with this (pc December 2004).

3. Also known as 'Menalee' and 'Minarii'.

4. Held in the Mitchell Library, Sydney.

5. There is no evidence to suppose that this Oscar Byrne was any relation to Michael Byrne, fiddler on the *Bounty*.

6. For all that these offered an immediate point of connection to Tahiti and the *Bounty* crew's sojourn there, they do not appear to have always been appreciated. Captain Henry King, visiting in 1819 for instance, noted that he witnessed "an Otaheitian dance, which consisted of various writhings and distortions of the body, by no means obscene yet in no respect pleasant" (quoted in Silverman, D [1967: 225]).

7. The remainder of the lyrics are as follows:
   Who are these whose aspirations
   With such ardour greet the ear?
   Sons, whose sires wrought consternation
   Daughters of the Mutineer

Yet those sires were ne'er disloyal
Though they curbed a tyrant's sway
Their children with affection loyal
Hail Victoria's natal day!
Ha! that flash in yon grove illuming
Long impervious to the sun
How quick report comes booming
From the ocean's rescued gun
Now the bell is gaily ringing
Where yon white-robed train are seen
Now they all unite in singing-
God preserve our gracious Queen!
(Lyrics as reproduced in Nobbs, 1984: 113.)

8. The name that Young gives the performance is that of a Tahitian bamboo instrument struck with sticks, possibly the traditional accompaniment to the dance she describes.

9. I have been unable to ascertain what kind of dance this may have been.

10. Recollection stated by Jacob Warren in conversation with his daughter Meralda Warren via shortwave radio (Norfolk to Pitcairn Island), May 1999, in response to the author's inquiries on the subject.

11. Meralda Warren recalls Bernice Christian and others relating this in the 1980s.

12. This is the early form of the instrument; the piano accordion was not manufactured until the 1860s.

13. Essentially a pipe-less organ, with air being pushed to sound-producing reed blocks via foot-operated bellows.

14. There is some debate as to whether Nabet-Mayer's recordings of such ensembles represent an 'authentic' representation of traditional Polynesian vocal music hybridised with western hymnody or an exaggerated version of the latter, with over-emphasised pitch slides to half and micro notes. Whatever the case, the recordings at least suggest what earlier hybridised vocal performances might have sounded like.

15. This characterisation may tend to overstatement.

16. Lind (1820-1887) was a reknown Swedish singer who became feted in Britain after performing in London in 1847 and also spent her later years in the city principally singing at concerts for charitable causes.

17. The full text of the poem is reproduced in Nobbs (1984:112).

18. The writer was presumably unaware of the occasional performance of Tahitian-derived dances.

19. Quintal's skills appear to have developed in the previous five years since Amelia Young had noted of the 1848 festivities that "The island boasted one fiddle, but no one considered himself sufficiently expert in the use of the bow to volunteer his services" (1984: 102)

20. Gregorie, G (1856) *Journal*, RUSI/NM/138 N.M.M. (referred to by Nobbs, 1984: 50).

Chapter Three

A HOME AWAY FROM HOME
The establishment of the Pitcairn community on Norfolk Island (1856–1900)

The establishment of the Pitcairn community on Norfolk Island, with relatively easy access to both Eastern Australia and New Zealand, soon attracted visitors eager to meet the Pitcairners whose existence and Christian piety had attracted so much international interest over the previous decades. As a result, there are a number of eyewitness accounts that attest to various aspects of the island population's music culture in the years immediately following settlement.

I. Vocal music and hymns

In July 1856, Frederick Howard, a midshipman on *HMS Herald*, sent to Norfolk Island from Sydney to await the arrival of the *Morayshire*, wrote to his sister of a "singing meeting... like those they had twice a week on Pitcairn", held in one of the large rooms at Kingston, which the Pitcairners put on:

> *having got together about 60 men and women, and divided themselves into 4 parties* [presumably, sections for four part harmonising] *they commenced to sing glees, which were sung so well that it quite surprised me. The first thing they sang was, "school days" a very simple tune of itself, but from the way it was sung sounding very sweet. They sang glees and anthems for about 2 hours one after another, and I think I could have listened all night without tiring. The room was well adapted for such singing being large and lofty, and I could shut my eyes and fancy I was near the choir in some cathedral – I never recollect having my senses enthralled to such an extent by any music. I have heard some first class singing at Sydney, both professional and amateur.*
> (Howard, 1856: np)

He went on to conjecture that the effect of the music on him was not primarily due to "the excellence of the performance" (in itself):

> but rather the simplicity of both the singing and the singers, and perhaps the knowledge that they did not sing for effect but rather for their own amusement and that of their visitors[1]. (ibid)

Visiting in 1863, Thomas Hood noted that:

> All, both young and old, seem passionately fond of music. They have a singing class every Wednesday; and we listened with great pleasure to the glees and sacred music performed in a good time. Both men and women appear to have full, rich-toned voices[2]. (1863: 244-245)

The proto-society that established itself on Norfolk Island was shaken in December 1858 by the decision of group of twelve Pitcairners to leave Norfolk and return to Pitcairn to live. Writing nearly forty years after the event, drawing on the Pitcairn community's memories of it, Amelia Rosalind Young detailed that:

> The parting was sad. One last gathering in the church where they had worshipped for two years, one last mingling of their voices together in the parting song, which was falteringly sung, while sobs choked the utterance and dimmed the sight, and then the final prayer was uttered in tremulous tones and with tender earnestness by the lips of the faithful pastor, Mr Nobbs, commending the departing company to God's care. (1894: 138)

The "parting song" referred to by Young appears to have been a hymn specifically written by George Hunn Nobbs to mark the occasion. The hymn was also sung again in December 1863 when a second party left the island to return to Pitcairn, in similarly emotional circumstances. While the music appears to have been lost, the hymn's final verses declared:

> For those who in the flesh remain
> Though absent from our sight
> For their remembrance we'll retain
> Affections pure and bright
> Although parted, severed, far away
> Perchance to meet no more
> For their prosperity we'll pray
> And love them as before
>
> Again dissevered is the tie
> Brethren and sisters part
> The mournful separation nigh
> Pervades with grief each heart
> Here now, beneath this sacred roof
> Fresh blessings we implore
> Beneath our tears the fervent proof
> 'We'll love you as before'
> (ibid: 163)

A further, and even more tragic, event occurred in the following year when Nobbs's son Edwin and his companion Fisher Christian were killed at

Santa Cruz by locals while accompanying Bishop Patteson on an Anglican Melanesian Mission expedition to the island (see Chapter 4 for further discussion). In memory of his son he wrote a hymn entitled *At home again*, which was sung to the music of the tune *Ewing (Jerusalem the Golden)* (Nobbs, 1984: 103). The lyrics of its opening verse summarised its theme:

O Lord, the heathens' madness
Has caused our tears to flow
Yet still, amidst our sadness
This thought assuages woe
There's naught on Earth progressing
That's hidden from thy sight
Correcting, as in blessing
"Shall not our God do right?"

There seems little doubt that hymn singing and, particularly, the singing of hymns that had been written on Pitcairn and Norfolk, was an important affirmation of the community's identity.

Along with his own compositions Nobbs is also credited with composing two hymns with the assistance of Driver Christian, *Gethsemane*, and the music for the hymn now commonly known on Norfolk as *The Pitcairn anthem* (or, on occasion, *Come ye blessed*, after its initial line). Christian was born on Tahiti during the Pitcairners' abortive settlement there in 1831 and was twenty five years old at the time of relocation to Norfolk Island. One common folkloric memory, repeated to me in several versions, was that he had intense inspirations that occurred to him in visions. His great grandson, Gilbert Jackson, for instance, has recalled that his grandmother, Evelyn Christian (Driver's daughter), informed him that Driver "saw visions of music on the walls of his home and then went and wrote it down" (interview 1999).

Gethsemane, as the title suggests, is a hymn that refers to the Biblical Garden of Gethsemane and recounts an incident whereby the song's protagonist encounters a vision of Jesus descended from Heaven, relating how he died for the redemption of mankind. While there are no local references that identify Norfolk Island, elements of the opening verse – most particularly, the reference to "fields" – are more suggestive of the more expansive landscape of Norfolk Island than that of Pitcairn and might suggest that the song was composed after 1856:

While nature was sinking in stillness to rest
The last beams of daylight shone dim in the west
O'er fields by pale moonlight wandered abroad
In deep meditation, I thought on my lord

The hymn, a pentatonic composition, sung in 3/4 time, to a similar melody to that of *Auld lang syne*, is a sombre and plaintive hymn that has remained an essentially sacred song, in contrast to *The Pitcairn anthem*, which has been sung in a variety of ceremonial and social contexts. The latter's versatility is all the more surprising since its words are taken from The Bible's Matthew 25: 34-46 and its introductory chant and pious lyrics do not immediately suggest a secular application:

Then shall the King say unto them on his right hand:

Come ye blessed of my father
Inherit the kingdom prepared for you
From the foundation of the world

I was a'hungered and ye gave me meat
I was thirsty and ye gave me drink
I was a stranger and ye took me in
Naked and ye clothed me
I was sick and ye visited me
I was in prison and ye came to me

Inasmuch as ye have done it to me
Of the least of these my brethren
Ye have done it unto me
Ye have done it unto me

Given that there is no evidence that the song was performed on Pitcairn Island after its re-settlement by Pitcairners returning from Norfolk Island in the 1850s and 1860s, it is possible that the song was written after 1863[3].

Along with writing original hymns, Driver Christian is also credited with writing alternative music for a series of well-known hymn lyrics, such as *Awake my soul*, *Bethlehem (While shepherds watched their flocks by night)* and *Put thou thy trust in God* that continued to be performed on Norfolk Island (on occasion, at least) until the 1990s. This practice merits comment since, as Christian theomusicologist Mark Evans has emphasised:

> *while rewriting lyrics to popular tunes was common practice* [in the period in question] *writing new music to existing hymn lyrics was a more specialist or 'advanced' activity normally undertaken only by those who recognised the required contextual change.* (pc 2004)

Although the factors that motivated Driver Christian's musical revisions remain unknown, the activity, in itself, indicates his creative investment in sacred music. The readiness of islanders to adopt and perpetuate his versions also suggests their sense of hymn singing as expressive of their community identity and piety.

Following the traumatic events of the early 1860s, and the initial shock of the establishment of the Melanesian Mission on the island in 1866 (discussed in the following chapter), the fledgling community began to settle and establish routines distinct from those of Pitcairn. The nature and quality of singing, and particularly communal performance, continued to attract the admiration of visitors. In 1865, for instance, Herbert Meade, a naval lieutenant, visited the island along with Bishop Patteson, on board the *HMS Curaçoa*. Recalling his first night ashore, he commented that:

> *After supper we adjourned to the singing-room, where we found nearly every grown-up person on the island ... The chanting and glee singing, which was led by Driver Christian, and unaccompanied by an instru-ment, was pronounced to be really very good by the Bishop and those of our party who understood music.* (1871: 181)

Bishop Selwyn also passed favourable comment while visiting in 1872.

During a visit to the Melanesian Mission facility on Norfolk Island he also held a confirmation service for the Pitcairn-Norfolk community at which George Hunn Nobbs' granddaughter Catherine Nobbs played the harmonium and "the hymns were particularly well-sung by nearly the whole congregation, one of them to the tune *Cambridge new*, said to have been a great favourite with Bishop Patteson" (1872: 18). Bishop Selwyn also attended a service that he described in the following terms:

> *At 8p.m. the greater part of the adult population assembled in a fine room of one of the deserted Government buildings, according to their custom, and sang hymns and other songs until 10 o'clock. Their voices are particularly good, with a sweetness of their own, and they have been trained and are well led by Mr Driver Christian.*[4] (ibid: 14)

In 1875 the musical life of the church and community was enhanced by the arrival of George Bailey, an Englishman, from Devon, who migrated to New Zealand in the early 1870s. Bailey was appointed by the Melanesian Mission to come to Norfolk Island to assemble and fit the organ in the St Barnabas chapel (which was then about to commence construction). Soon after his arrival, he met and married Evelyn Wellesley Christian and settled on the island. A blacksmith by trade, Bailey proved a valuable addition to the island community as a choirmaster, and performer and teacher on the organ and fife[5]. Bailey's impact on the public performance culture of the island was evident by the end of the decade. In December 1880, Bishop Selwyn visited to celebrate the consecration of St Barnabus. The occasion was one that was marked by various kinds of musical performance both at St Barnabus Chapel itself and around the island. On December 4th, for instance, a great picnic was held at the Rossiter family farm that "The Fife and Drum Band of Kingtown attended" (unattributed, 1880: 18). The band was also in attendance four days later, with additional musicians, at a large-scale picnic at Long Ridge that was entertained by "a string and fife and drum band and a harmonium" (ibid: 24). It is also likely to have been the same band that accompanied the departure of Selwyn from Kingston pier playing the melodies of popular Victorian songs *The girl I left behind me* and *Home sweet home* as Selwyn departed (Elcum, 1885: 361). Bailey went on to play and lead ensembles performing at a variety of locations and also had a significant role in fathering four offspring, Charles, Charlotte, Mariah and Thomas, all of who were to be prominent performers in the period 1900-1950 (see discussions in Chapter 6).

Further confirmation of the islanders' love of hymn singing and general musicality was provided by the Reverend R. Comins, of the Melanesian Mission, in 1879. In that year Comins was approached by George Hunn Nobbs to assist devotion during Lent, and he toured the island giving "cottage lectures" in the evenings. Commenting that these were "well attended", he noted that:

> *Almost every house has a small harmonium and someone who can play it, and as everyone can sing and nearly everyone can read music, the services are bright and interesting without being unsuitable to the season.* (quoted in Nobbs, 1984: 93)

Comins was also pleased to note that the islanders' devotion to worship was so marked that they chose to attend services on one evening rather than partake in an alternative attraction:

A small vessel, a sort of yacht was here and determined to give a grand dinner and dance in the evening to all their Pitcairn friends. This took place ashore of course, in a large room [presumably in Kingston] *used for such purposes. Now I had a cottage lecture that night and I almost doubted whether I should have congregation, for the Pitcairners like a good dinner as well as most people, and they are exceeding fond of music and dancing, but when I reached the house it seemed to me to be fuller than usual and I recognized many young people who I knew were enthusiastic dancers and who must have exercised some self-denial to have chosen the cottage lecture in preference to the entertainment provided for them by their yacht friends.* (ibid)

Comins's remarks indicate a duality in the early Pitcairn community on Norfolk that a series of later visitors also observed (in various contexts), an enthusiastic and accomplished commitment to hymn singing (in both religious and social contexts) and a love of dancing and sociability in general.

II. Dancing

Although Polynesian dances were performed on Pitcairn up until the mid-1800s there is no evidence that these dances were ever performed by members of the Pitcairn community who relocated to Norfolk Island on the *Morayshire* in 1856. As Chapter 7 discusses, present-day Polynesian dance traditions on Norfolk derive from a revival of the form in the 1930s. However, another style of dancing took root in the new location and provided a continuing diversion for young and old.

Following his description of Pitcairn singing in 1856 (discussed above), Meade also noted that the evening ended with dancing:

George Evans and Caleb Quintall play the violin very well, and we soon got up Sir Roger de Coverly, which was danced with great glee. After that Meyer [a colleague of Howard's] tried to get up the polka but they could not manage that, but danced a kind of elephant waltz with each other that we could not match. (1856: np)

Meade's reference is an intriguing one, since it suggests that by 1856 some members of the community were familiar with western styles of dancing. Since the polka only rose to prominence in England during the late 1840s, following its popularisation in Paris, the Pitcairners' lack of knowledge of it is not surprising. The reference to "a kind of elephant waltz" is not so derogatory as it might first appear, since there were several compositions with similar titles written in the mid-late 1800s (such as *White elephant waltz* [1884]), which appear to have accompanied dancing with a more elevated stepping pattern than standard waltzes. Although their repertoire may have initially been limited, by 1863 Hood was commenting that the women's "love of dancing, inherited from their Otaheitian mothers[6], is as great as the girls of Spain" (1863: 244-245).

A considerably more detailed account of cultural experiences was provided by Herbert Meade, a naval lieutenant who visited the island in 1865 on the *HMS Curaçoa*. His account offers a greater insight into the hedonistic nature of the community and the welcome it afforded to visitors than many of the more overtly religious travelers to the island whose accounts are referred to in this chapter. During his visit he stayed with John Adams who, he noted, supplied the guests with "a few bottles of ale" for their "refection" during their stay (1871: 181). He later recalled that:

> *Singing and dancing are the principal amusement, and they certainly go in for both* con amore *... After supper we adjourned to the singing-room, where we found nearly every grown-up person on the island.* [After a communal singing session] *the seats were cleared away, most of the girls slipped off to make some alteration in their simple dress, – a fiddle wielded by a most muscular musician soon followed, and a rattling dance was kept with hardly a moment's interval from 9 till nearly 3.A.M.* (ibid)

While the fiddler's identity is not revealed, various performers suggest themselves. Caleb Quintal or George Evans are contenders, since they were reported as performing on violin for dances in 1856 – indicating that there was a small group of fiddlers active in the early decades of Norfolk's Pitcairn settlement.

Meade's account also relates his perception of the charms of the female participants in the dance. While he punctuates his somewhat breathless appreciation of Norfolk Islander women's physique and demeanour with an abrupt and highly pointed moral qualification (lest the reader take an incorrect inference of an amorous undercurrent to the dancing), his account has substantial similarities to the descriptions of the pleasures the *Bounty* crew took from the female form during their visit to Tahiti:

> *What fun we had! We all agreed next day that it was worth a half dozen regular balls lashed together, and that we had never seen so many pretty girls in one room before ...*

> *Their principal attraction lies in their eyes and teeth, which are perfect; their plump, healthy, well-shaped forms, which have never been de-formed by stays and to which crinolines are as yet a rare novelty, and lastly to the free gait and elastic step which they inherit from their Tahitian ancestresses. Besides the advantage of feeling that you really have your partner's waist, instead of a bundle of whalebone and steel springs, the girls have a jolly, free, unaffected sort of way about them, which is very pleasant, but to which I will only say that the grossest of mankind could impute no evil.*

> *At first they would only dance such dances as the 'Triumph' and 'Sir Rogers' and a marvellous test of activity and wind named 'Sixteens', but we soon substituted valses, galops &c. which they danced very fairly, in spite of their protestations that they had never danced them before, and did not know how.* (ibid: 173-175)

Of the specific dances referred to, the Sir Roger de Coverly and Triumph are brisk-paced dances that date from the late 17th Century and which involve two lines of couples facing each other and executing a series of moves between the lines (similar to the US Virginia Reel). The Sixteens appears to have been a brisker couple dance (of unknown formation).

'Elise', a New Zealander who visited the island in 1883 onboard the *Coral Queen*, provided an account of local dancing as experienced by a female visitor:

> forward came a tall young fellow with fair hair and moustache, and blond complexion, who, bowing low, requested the honour of my hand for the cotillion. Amazed I certainly was, for I entertained the idea that their dancing must necessarily be of a native type. But the cotillion! Really I hardly knew it myself. However, it would not do to plead ignorance so my hand was placed in that of Mr. Francis Nobbs, and we took our place gravely at the head of the quadrille, for it was not, as I had feared, the old style dance[7]. A master of ceremonies conducted the affair, and it was performed quite accurately. At the close, however, there was a queer pause before the final bow and I had the curiosity to enquire the reason. Amid much stammering the explanation was given that it was customary for the gentleman to kiss his partner, but in deference to the stranger, the rule was for the nonce, held in abeyance. Dance after dance followed, and as restraint somewhat wore off, acquaintanceship ripened and soon a request was made that I would teach them a new dance. And gladly I imparted to them the intricacies of the Varsoviana, then just introduced to Australia, and 'Pop goes the Weasel", not yet considered out of society's pale. I am sure they learned these dances much quicker than ordinary folks, for in a very little while they had them quite correct. At midnight the frolic closed and under escort I reached home completely tired out. ([1883]/1938: 5)

III. Religion and Social Transition

During the decades following the Pitcairners' re-location, the Norfolk community experienced a series of changes, largely as a result of the influences they were exposed to by contact with outsiders. This brought changes to patterns of religious belief, song repertoire (particularly hymns) and social customs. One influence arose from Norfolk Island's position on the southeastern Pacific whale migration route and its contact with the whalers who exploited this.

From the late 1850s–1890s, whaling ships, mostly from the United States, and particularly New England ports, frequently visited the island. The officers and crew of these often came ashore during such visits. Many of the whaling ships calling during this period also carried their captains' wives[8]. As Joan Druett has elaborated, "it was quite common for the [captain's] wives to be left on shore for a few weeks" when whaling ships called at safe and "civilised" islands or ports, and "Norfolk Island, having a mission, was popular for this" (Druett, 1991: 113). Indeed, so many were the whalers operating in the region around Norfolk Island, that several US whalers' wives were often in temporary residence at any one time. Druett records one instance, in late 1886, when three wives (Mrs Chase, Fisher and Potter) were staying on the island. Fisher recording in her journal that she attended various parties and dances, most notably a lavish ball thrown for

Lord Dudley (ibid: 116). During their stays, these women communicated much of their culture to the local population, especially their talents at sewing, cooking and music[9]. With regard to the latter skill, they appear to have been prime agents in introducing US hymns. Their musical skills often included harmonium playing, since the (small, portable and easily collapsible) instrument was a regular accessory in the captains' quarters of whalers in the mid-late 1800s[10], and were often brought ashore when their (usually) female players spent time away from the ships. On Norfolk Island, at least[11], these were regularly left on the island when their owners departed, as either gifts for the wives' hosts and/or recompense for accommodation.

Such influences provided competition with the island's dominant Anglican culture. Methodism also received a boost with the arrival of Alfred Phelps in 1879, a lay-preacher who arrived as a member of the crew of the US whaling ship *Canton* and stayed for three years before returning in 1884 and opening a Methodist church. Active Methodist member and amateur historian Bob Tofts has described the rise of this denomination as having a major influence on island life, reconciling the drift towards the polarities of a relatively austere Anglican worship and hymnody and an (increasingly distinct and heavily secularised) social culture through its more impassioned and unrestrained style of worship and hymn singing (interview 1999).

Along with Methodism, another religious phenomenon also occurred in the 1880s. As Anglican cleric C. Elcum reported, at this time several islanders felt themselves to have received religious "visions" and have been inspired by a "spirit of prophecy" (cited in Nobbs, 1984: 99). Following the visit of a Seventh Day Adventist preacher, F. Belden in 1891, the Seventh Day Adventists also began to operate, under the initial pastorship of Alfred Nobbs. The existence of these rival churches served to displace the significance of a single weekly service as a focus of island religious life and community singing in favour of a series of variants.

By the mid-1880s established religious music was increasingly accompanied and complemented by a range of music practices that formed part of a lively social culture. Illustrating the flux of Norfolk Island society and culture experienced by the first and second generations of local-born Pitcairners, the final years of the 19th Century also appear to have offered other changes to local life, since the subject and incidence of covert alcohol consumption and pre- and extra-marital sex became a subject of concern for the church and the administration[12]. An invaluable window into the social life of this period is provided by the publication *The Norfolk Island Pioneer* (*NIP*) that was produced between May 1885 and December 1886. Some sense of the co-existence of religious and social musical practices can be gleaned from its pages, where reports of hymn singing and sacred music concerts were interleaved with notices and reviews of dances. The paper is also significant for commenting on changes in public support for civil occasions. A report of a rather sparsely celebrated Queen's Birthday holiday in 1885, for instance reported that "If the day's sports were not cheering, the dance in the evening was quite a galaxy of youth and beauty on the light fantastic" (*NIP* n2 15.6.85: 3).

Another item reported the somewhat muted celebration of the 29th anniversary of the Pitcairners' arrival at Norfolk Island on the *Morayshire* (an occasion now known as 'Bounty Day' or 'Anniversary Day''), noting that, for undisclosed reasons, "there was not on this occasion any marching" and commenting that "the band was not up to much" (*NIP* n2 15.6.85: 3). This report contrasts with the paper's reports on the energies expended on "the usual dance" in the evening. In her 'Social Notes' column, 'Mary Jane' noted that the "dresses and the music [provided by Willie[13] and Hugo Quintal] were good" but that "there are some who from misbehaviour or otherwise get extradited and who on occasions like this 'cut in' as it were and shock the nerves of my more delicate sisters" (ibid). She also included similar comments about lively behaviour ("scamping") in a report on a ball held by the island's medical practitioner:

> The dancing commenced at eight, and continued with but a short intermission for supper, until half past twelve; the music, under the able direction of Mr. Bailey, was good, there was apparently, however, a little scamping[14] after supper. Of the guests, few were married couples, the majority... being young dancing folks, who appeared to enjoy themselves amazingly. (*NIP* n2 15.6.85: 3)

In her description of a dinner held by Mrs Rossiter to welcome the return of her son, Mary Jane also notes that there "was no dancing in the house, but the young people managed to purloin the hrrmonium [sic] out on the grass and it was tortured to some purpose judging from the mirth and noise afterwards" (*NIP* n8 14.11.85: 4).

This type of behaviour was evidently so noticeable that it attracted comment from the pulpit, 'May Jane's' column (now renamed 'Gossip'), recounted that an (unnamed) minister "lifted up his voice... in holy anger and pious grief against such sinfulness" as that evident at island dances (*NIP* n3 20.7.85:4). But whatever her concerns about "scamping", "cutting in" or the "torture" of "hrrmoniums", 'Mary Jane' clearly held different views to the minister, being moved to write a description of the wedding of Mr Heywood Quintal and Miss Elizabeth Clow ("of Auckland") in May 1885 which included reference to the celebration dance in the evening being "not so felicitous: fenced in on one side by an evangelist meeting, and in front by a choir practice" and adding that "I fear there was little enjoyment to be derived under these saddening auspices" (*NIP* n2 15.6.85: 3).

In 1885 Fax Quintal began to appear at island dances, acting as M.C and performing on the accordion. 'Mary Jane' commented on his debut at a ball held in September 1885 to farewell the Special Commissioner, Mr Wilkinson: "a new hand, Mr. Fax Quintal ... in a low sweet voice announced the different movements, which, if not an improvement, is certainly a new departure" (*NIP* v5 28.9.95: 4). A report of a party held by the "Chief Magistrate and his lady, to the friends of their grandson, who is about to leave the island" (n5 28.9.85: 3) also reported that: "[a]fterwards the drawing room was cleared out for dancing, and an antiquated accordion got underweigh [sic], the manipulator, professor F.Q. [ie Fax Quintal] keeping the pot boiling until midnight" (ibid).

1885's festive season was evidently a lively one, with *NIP* noting that, "the Longridge Choral Class under the leadership of the Rev. C. Bice" gave a concert on December 22nd "in the large room of the Kingston Club" (n9 21.1.86: 2). 'Mary Jane' noted that the programme "consisted principally of Carols, capitally well rendered by the class, and several numbers well executed by the Norfolk Island String Band" (ibid) and also reported a concert on December 30th at which the string band also performed and at which a magic lantern presentation was given (ibid). Other events included a singing concert at the Kingston Club on Christmas Day and a New Year's Eve dance at the same venue.

There was a gap in publication between January – October 1885 (followed by a misnumbering of the next issue as v1n11 – not n10 as per sequence) due to "differences between Mr. Menges [of the Kingston Cub] and the publishers" (n11 October 1885: 1). Two distinctly different additions to the island's cultural life to have emerged in the interim were the Longridge singing group's rehearsal of Handel's *Messiah*, intended for performance at Christmas, and the presence of a "Mr Martin" at Kingston Club concerts, where he entertained audiences with ventriloquism and comic singing (ibid: 3).

The final issue of the *NIP* included a poem by Alic. Martin entitled 'Ode to the Pine Trees' that reflected on island life, history and landscape. Its final verse offered a particularly evocative description of the island's natural soundscape and the vocal quality of winds and breezes:

And when the scented breath of Even's balmy breeze
Returns at morn, so fresh across the seas
When thrillingly to it thy bosom heaves
And when it stirs thy soul to sing a plaintive song
As it goes throbbing, trilling, humming sad along
Thou'lt sing them sweetly, softly o'er the slumbering dead
Melodiously whisper to the soul that's fled
To souls that are around, though not in seeing
That have put on a better, more exalted being
Spread thou soft shadows over slumbering men
Sigh a soft requiem over them now and then
Thou'lt murmur often with the sighing sea
And shade their graves for ever in futurity

The sombre tone of the verse served as an epitaph for the project of *NIP* as a local journal of social life and comment. The publication's demise also deprived the future historian of an invaluable source of information on island culture, since there are minimal reference sources on the island's social and cultural life over the following three decades.

Notes

1. Despite his generally positive characterisation, Howard went on to profess a general fondness for the male voice and to comment that two of the female singers, "married ladies of a certain age", tended towards "screechiness in the upper parts" (ibid). Despite this bias he also notes, later in his letter, that during his stay he "got some of the girls to sing by themselves, which they did very nicely, one named Dorcas Young having a very sweet voice" (ibid).

2. Hood also repeats the contention that Carleton's visit to Pitcairn in 1850 was the cause of the singers' competence.

3. Although it might also be the case that if the song was written and known on Norfolk Island prior to the departure of the two groups of Pitcairners, it was simply not popular enough amongst them to be retained.

4. Selwyn also repeats the claim that the islanders were taught singing by Hugh Carleton on Pitcairn in 1850 (ibid).

5. A large woodwind instrument.

6. This aside suggests that the author was familiar with the narrative of the *Bounty* crew's experience of traditional Tahitian dancing.

7. The cotillon, the "old style dance" that Elise refers to, was a form of square dance popular in the early 1800s that repeated identical figures. The cotillion – in the spelling used by Elise – was a version popularised in the USA in the mid-1800s that featured a greater variety of figures (hence the need for the "master of ceremonies" referred to to call the figures) and which traditionally ended with a pleasantry of some kind delivered to the female dancer by her male partner.

8. See Druitt (1991) for a detailed history of this particular, and historically limited, practice.

9. It was during this period that the practice of holding Thanksgiving celebrations was introduced into Norfolk Island, where it continues to the present.

10. See Druitt, (1991: 36) for a detailed description of one such cabin.

11. I have not come across reference to this elsewhere, though it may also have happened in other locations.

12. See Nobbs (1984: 95) for elaboration.

13. The schoolmaster.

14. In this context 'scamping' appears to be a mild term of reproach for impolite or otherwise boisterous behaviour.

Chapter Four

A COMMUNITY OF VISITORS
Music and the Melanesian
Mission on Norfolk Island

Introduction

During the early 1850s, as plans were put in place to shut down Norfolk Island's penal establishment, various bodies and individuals expressed an interest in taking over the island. The London-based Pitcairn Island Fund Committee eventually succeeded in pressing their claim to establish a new home for Pitcairn Islanders there. One of the other notable interested parties was the Anglican bishop of New Zealand, George Augustus Selwyn. Following a visit to Norfolk Island in 1853 Selwyn identified it as a suitable site to re-locate the Melanesian Mission, then based in Auckland. The Melanesian Mission was a training school for Melanesians from the Solomon Islands and the central and northerly islands of (present-day) Vanuatu. The Mission's Auckland centre was established by Selwyn shortly after his appointment in 1841 but was deemed increasingly unsuitable due to its distance from its students' homelands and its cool climate. While he was unsuccessful in his initial bid, Selwyn continued to covet Norfolk as a base and, if anything, his interest was intensified by the introduction of the Pitcairners to the island.

As early as the 1820s members of the Anglican establishment in London perceived that the Pitcairners' partial Polynesian descent would give them an advantage in communicating, interacting with, converting and ministering to fellow Pacific Islanders. This was one factor behind the abortive relocation of the Pitcairn population to the outskirts of Pape'ete in 1830 (Nicolson, 1997: 114). However, this experience had the effect of alienating the Pitcairn community from their Tahitian roots and, instead, led them to emphasise the English aspect of their English-Tahitian ancestral identity. Perceptions of Pitcairners serving as pan-Pacific missionaries were also problematised by the community's lack of contact with Melanesians prior to its relocation to Norfolk Island. Unless any Melanesians were employed on boats visiting Pitcairn in the early 1800s it is unlikely that Pitcairners had encountered any (and may have only been aware of them from tales of 'savagery' and cannibalism emerging from initial European merchant and missionary contacts with the region).

Shortly after the Pitcairners' relocation to Norfolk Island, John Coleridge Patteson was appointed as the first Anglican missionary bishop of Melanesia and began recruiting in the region. Moral piety and desire to be good citizens of the Anglican Church and British Empire led the Norfolk Island community to volunteer Edwin Hunn Nobbs (George Hunn Nobbs's son) and Fisher Young to the missionary cause. They joined the Melanesian Mission in 1861, trained in Auckland and went on to serve with Patteson. In 1864, during their first mission to The Solomon Islands, Nobbs and Young died as a result of injuries sustained during an attack by inhabitants of Santa Cruz island. Their deaths had a profound impact on the fledgling Norfolk Island community[1], emphasising the dangers of the region they inhabited.

During the late 1850s and early 1860s Bishop Selwyn continued to press colonial authorities to allow the Anglican Church to establish a mission base on Norfolk Island. With the Santa Cruz deaths fresh in their minds, members of the Norfolk Island community strongly opposed such plans. Indeed, the Norfolk Island community's first meeting with Melanesians provoked recoil rather than a sense of pan-Pacific affinity. The encounter occurred when Bishop Selwyn visited the island in 1856 and brought ashore a small party of Solomon Islanders, adorned with nose rings and with punctured and distended ears. This vision of another indigenous Pacific identity (even more disturbingly different from that of 1830s' Tahiti) was not one welcomed by the *Bounty* descendants establishing their new home amongst the stone buildings built by convict labour. When this initial contact was followed up by discussions between the Anglican mission and Norfolk Islanders, the community's leader, George Hunn Nobbs, expressed his strong opposition:

> *I do not think, my honoured friend, you will at all attribute this opposition to a want of sympathy for the dark places of the earth, which are full of cruelty. I will contribute cheerfully of my substance, or in any other feasible way assist in promoting the entrance of the Word of Life into the regions of Moloch; but the evils which will arise from the personal introduction of an incarnate code of idolatry and degradation among us, are so unmistakably palpable, that I may not yield even to the eloquent arguments of the bishop of New Zealand.* (quoted in Nobbs, 1984: 84)[2]

Sir John Young, the second Governor of Norfolk Island, concurred with Nobbs and argued in 1862:

> *I cannot conceive of anything more likely to demoralize the population and turn it from the higher type of race it now assumes back to that of mere South Sea savages ... I cannot but think that the introduction of a number of half-savage youths at the period of life when their passions are least under control would be in the highest degree pernicious, and indeed fatal to the prospects of the community.* (ibid: 86)

Undeterred by the extreme language and sentiments of such statements, the Governor of New South Wales rewarded Bishop Selwyn's dogged campaign in 1866 by granting the Melanesian Mission 418 hectares of land on the western side of the island. The allocation of parts of the island to the Mission abruptly alerted the Pitcairn community to their lack of control over the island they now inhabited. The prospect of the introduction of a new group of settlers and visitors of different cultural origins also caused further alarm (Hoare, 1969: 89). The first of these arrived in October 1866 when the Rev J. Palmer and sixteen young Melanesian men arrived and began clearance and construction work in the Mission grounds. Initial constructions were completed by early 1867 and the Mission began processing Melanesian trainees soon after. In 1880 construction of the centrepiece of the Mission, a large, ornate British-style church named St Barnabas, was completed.

The arrival of the Melanesian Mission had a complex impact on the Norfolk Island community. Raymond Nobbs has identified that:

Figure 1: St Barnabas

While they were generally cordial to the newcomers, the resentment over the alienating of what they regarded as their land often flowed onto their attitude to the Mission itself. (1984: 90)

And, more profoundly:

The overriding effect of the establishment of the Mission ... was a reinforcing of the Pitcairners sense of loss of identity, self-determination and isolation. (ibid)

While the Pitcairners may have experienced the first of many disillusionments with their new political position, the enclave of Norfolk Island ceded to the Mission facilitated a series of cultural interactions that, while largely separate from the Pitcairn/Norfolk Island communities that are the principal subject of this book, form a distinct episode in both the history of Norfolk Island and Melanesia.

I. The Mission and Island Life

Due to the tensions and apprehensions discussed above, the Mission essentially operated as a separate community from the Pitcairn-occupied remainder of the island. However, there were some occasions when members of both communities came together. One of the most notable early meetings was for the ordination of three Melanesian scholars, Henry Tagalana (from the islet of Ara, in the Banks group), Robert Pantutun (from Mota) and Edward Wogale (from Qakea, an islet close to Vanua Lava, Great Banks Island) in 1872. This service, presided over by Bishop Selwyn, took place off Mission lands, down at Kingston in the newly completed All Saints chapel, in the presence of invited Pitcairners, including George Hunn Nobbs, and Mission students who travelled down for the occasion. As Bishop Selwyn later commented:

I had drawn up a programme for the service before leaving New Zealand, and brought with me a number of copies printed in Mota and in English for the use of the mixed congregation. Had Mr Nobbs been all his life accustomed to arrange for such 'functions,' the preparations for the "decency and order" of the service could not have been better made; and the programme was followed in every particular. (1872: 17)

Selwyn described the service as follows:

The clergy entered the church by the west door, the three junior members of the Mission staff, viz: Messrs. Bice, Brooke, and Jackson going first, each leading in one of the Melanesian candidates for deacons' orders. Psalm LXXXXIV. (in English) was chanted as the clergy walked up the church to the chancel. The seats in front were occupied by the Melanesians (140 in number), and the rest of the building was filled by Norfolk Islanders. The service began with a hymn in Mota, very heartily sung by the Mission scholars. Then followed the sermon, preached by Mr Codrington, first in Mota then in English, a very simple and touching address, which was listened to most attentively by all the congregation ... The Litany was said (in Mota) by the Rev. C. Bice; the commandments and the Epistle were read by the Revs. C. Brooke and R. Jackson; and the Gospel by the Rev. Henry Tagalana. The venerable pastor of the

51

quondam Pitcairn Islanders, the Rev. G.H. Nobbs, assisted me at the administration of the Holy Communion, as did also the Rev. G. Maunsell, and the newly ordained deacons; the communicants numbering over a hundred. Whilst the clergy were communicating, Hebar's beautiful hymn, 'Bread of the world in mercy broken' was softly and sweetly sung by the congregation. (ibid: 17-18)

Another such opportunity to meet in a large, organised setting occurred in 1880 during the visit of Bishop Selwyn to celebrate the consecration of St Barnabus. The occasion was one that was marked by various kinds of musical performance both at St Barnabus Chapel itself and – as discussed in Chapter 3 – elsewhere on the island. In addition to hymn singing, several of these performances included secular material. On the evening of November 26th, for instance, a visitor observed that:

there was a concert in the school-room. The Melanesians sang rounds and choral songs to the tunes used commonly in our day schools in South Australia very prettily, and in perfect time and tune. The Maori clergymen sang native songs, to the delight and uproarious mirth of the company. Mrs Mitchell, a most accomplished vocalist, Miss Maunsell, and Mr Elcum, with others, added much to the entertainment of the evening by exercising their vocal talents. (unattributed, 1880: 18)

In addition to their daily duties with students, the Mission staff also staged occasional (public relations) events for the broader island population. One such occasion was reported in the *Norfolk Island Pioneer* in the following terms:

A very recherche entertainment was given at St Barnabas by our Missionary neighbours, on the 5th inst. It took the form of a concert, and was largely attended: the guests on arrival were chaperoned by the Revds. Palmer and Bice who, notwithstanding the large attendance, performed their onerous duties most efficiently. The arrangements inside were most appropriate, the decorations being chaste and elegant, the Chinese lamps giving a finishing touch to what otherwise was a bright and festive scene. The program was principally vocal, the prominent executants being Miss Maunsell, The Rev. Mr. Brittain and Mr. Wilkinson whose efforts were evidently much appreciated judging from the applause. (NIP 18.5.85: 3)

The Melanesian students at the Mission had a low-key presence at such occasions. This was a reverse of the case with standard, weekly worship at the church, where students played the leading roles, as is attested to in various period sources.

Visiting the Mission in November 1872, Bishop Selwyn provided a vivid account of Melanesian participation in Anglican worship at the Mission:

Soon after 7p.m. the bell summoned us to chapel. The lights in the windows reminded me of winter evening 'chapel' at Cambridge; but vespers at S Barnabas is a very different service from that to which we were accustomed at Trinity Hall. On entering the building, which is of wood and unsubstantial, we found it nearly filled by Melanesians, dressed in trousers and flannel shirts, sitting quietly on long benches

*arranged across the chapel and along the side walls; the latter being
set apart for the clergy and other teachers, and for females. The service
consisted of part of the Evening Prayer, said (in Mota) by the Rev. R.
Jackson, who appeared to be very familiar with the language, saying
the prayers almost by heart. The* Magnificat *and* Nunc Dimittis *were
chanted by the whole congregation, in a manner that quite astonished
me; indeed I never heard the canticles sung with more spirit, or more
devotionally by any congregation. Each word was distinctly pronounced
and with the proper emphasis. The harmonium accompaniment, played
by the Rev. C. Brooke (to whose skill and perseverance the excellence of
the singing is due), was just what an accompaniment should be, and so
seldom is in our churches, – a support to the singers, exact in time, with
expression, and subdued in tone. The chants moreover were particularly
well chosen, suited to the voices of the Melanesians, and appropriate to
the words sung. The precision and spirit of the chanting, together with
the almost metallic ring of the boys' voices, recalled to me the inspiriting
tones of the band of an English cavalry regiment.* (1872: 7)[3]

While the Rev Brooke performed on the harmonium on this occasion,
Melanesian scholars were also trained on the instrument and frequently
performed at services. Following the installation of one of the chapel's most
prominent features, an ornate, expensive pipe organ made by Henry Willis
and Sons of London[4], selected students were also taught to play this
instrument. A visitor to the island in late 1880 noted that of the 199 students
"about ten can play the harmonium, more or less, and two play the organ"
(unattributed, 1880: 24). During a visit in 1892 H. Montgomery reported
that the organist accompanying the service was John Pantutun, from the
Torres group of islands, in the north of the present day nation of Vanuatu.
Montgomery described his playing (and appearance) in the following terms:

*most striking it is to watch a Melanesian in the beautiful little church,
a boy [sic] with frizzly head and bare feet making full use of the pedals,
and playing with taste and feeling the music of most of the great
composers of sacred music.* (1908: 121)

Writing in 1909, another visitor to the Mission gave a similar account,
stating that the organ "is always played by a Melanesian, and played
surprisingly well too … a couple of boys [sic] stand beside him to help with
the stops, and lead the singing" (Coombe, 1909: 27); and added

*When one organist's course of training is ended, and he goes back to the
Islands, there is a little anxiety as to who will succeed him; and perhaps
for a few days we may have to sing unaccompanied, to the precenting
of a white man; but within a week, Mr. Bailey, our blacksmith and
master of music … pronounces that one or two more are ready for the
post, and all goes smoothly again.* (ibid: 27-28)

Such transitions were also problematic in other ways since, as Montgomery
had commented in 1908:

*It can easily be realized what a deprivation it is to these native organists
when they return to their homes as teachers and are debarred from the
use of musical instruments, for no harmonium has yet been invented*

which will stand the damp and insect pests of these tropical islands.
(ibid: 121)

Various observers also noted that some Melanesian students (at least) retained and enjoyed traditional cultural practices during the phases of their induction into European-Christian customs, conventions and behaviour. Indeed recognition of the value of indigenous customs – or, more accurately, those that were not actively antithetical to various aspects of Christianity – was a distinguishing aspect of the Melanesian Mission. This was manifest in the Melanesian Mission's adoption of the Austronesian language Mota as the principal language of instruction. Mota was chosen following initial fruitful contact with inhabitants of Mota and other islands in the Banks group (in the north of present day Vanuatu). The Melanesian Mission published translations of parts of the Bible in Mota 1864[5] and rapidly produced Mota language versions of well-known hymns (Hilliard, 1978: 38).

There were also work songs, specifically written in Mota to encourage the completion of tasks. One heavily didactic song, identified by Coombes as sung "to the old air of 'Buy a Broom'" (1909: 31), translated into English as:

Sweep the house, you fellows! The bell will ring directly
Run–run–run–run! Or you'll have to stand up!
There's the bell! It's school, you fellows! Let's go at once!
Whoever comes late will soon be standing out
Perhaps it's already written up, "Stand!" for it is late
Woe be to us if we arrive late!
Don't dawdle, you! It is the Bishop's rule
"Every late-comer shall stand!" (ibid)

This promotion of Mota as a language of religious service also spilt over into another form of repertoire diffusion, that of teaching students Mota language versions of British popular songs. During the 1880s the teaching and performance of such material became a regular practice. This usually occurred on Wednesday evenings and continued for over twenty five years. Visiting in the early 1900s, Florence Coombe observed:

Wednesday is always a half-holiday and song-singing takes the place
of evening school. We chiefly use the good, old-fashioned melodies, such
as "Auld Lang Syne", "Away with Melancholy", "Oh dear, what can the
matter be?" and so forth[6], putting simple Mota words to the air. All
Melanesians are music-lovers, but native music is not like the European
kind, and every accidental is at first a stumbling block. However they
quickly learn to sing well in parts, unaccompanied, and seem never to
weary of doing so. (1909: 53-54)

II. Melanesian Culture on Norfolk Island

With regard to the above discussion, it is significant to note that the Mission did not seek to obliterate the indigenous customs and traditions of its students, but rather allowed them expression within the schedules of regular weekday training and weekend work and worship. Weddings between students and major festivals were particular times when these emerged. In 1868 for example, a double wedding ceremony was held which was followed by sports (including a cricket match) and afternoon tea, culminating in "a native dance by a big bonfire" (Armstrong, 1900: 103). Christmas 1868 was also accompanied by various forms of worship and recreation that Armstrong described in the following terms:

[The day] *opened with the Angel's Song[7] in Mota at 12.5 A.M., at the Bishop's door, sung in the clear moonlight by Dr. Bice and some twenty Melanesians. Then at 7 the celebration in the chapel, all radiant with ever-greens, arums, pomegranites, oleanders, and lilies ... And after the bright joyful Matins and Hymns, games, races, cricket and a big feast, the whole ending up, after Evensong, with native dances and snap-dragon[8].* (ibid: 104)

Visiting the Mission for the consecration of St Barnabas chapel in 1880, Anne Ruddock produced a detailed description of the "native dancing" performed by the students at the time of her visit:

After enjoying chapel, on Saturday ... we went to see the boys dancing some native dances. That of the Opa boys had figures resembling a quadrille, and the latter part of Sir Roger de Coverly. The Solomon Islanders was the best however; they went through all the different motions used in rowing a canoe, making a grunting noise sometimes, diversified by other curious sounds. I was very much amused by seeing how some very small boys would persist in pushing into the row of bigger boys, and trying to do as they did. One of the mission party told me that on their own islands they get so excited that they go on all night. (1880: 493)

The island of Opa – also formerly known as Aopa (or Aoba), now more usually referred to today as Ambae, is in central island group of present day Vanuatu. The island, and, indeed, the area in general, was subject to frequent contact with Australian agencies from the 1870s on. In addition to members of the Melanesian mission, proselytizing and seeking trainees for the Norfolk Island centre, Australian 'blackbirders' also visited the Island, ships seeking to recruit and/or kidnap Melanesians to work in the Queensland sugarcane fields. The two western dances referred to provide some suggestion as to the nature of the Opa dance. The quadrille began as an 18th Century French dance in quadrangle formation performed to a lively accompaniment. With a series of sets (originally five, more commonly three by the late 1800s) and brief pauses, couples would perform various set movements and change positions[9]. As discussed in the previous chapter, the Sir Roger de Coverly is a brisk-paced dance that involves two lines of couples facing each other and executing a series of moves between the lines. The final section comprises a march where the end couple separate, dance back down the outside of the line and go through an arch of hands, the second couple taking their places as new leads and the process then repeating.

The second dance referred to by Ruddock is a group dance, of a general type widespread throughout Melanesia, based around the imitation of the action of paddling a canoe, dancers alternating paddling motions to either side. In the absence of further detail it is impossible to deduce which local variety of the dance it may have been (see the discussion of Tikopian culture below for a description of one variety of this dance form).

The dances Ruddock refers to might also have been among those that were described as taking place on the evening of December 4th 1880 following a large-scale picnic at the Rossiter family farm:

> a large bonfire and a good display of fireworks ... were appreciated by the delighted audience of the Melanesians. Native dances and Maori songs and dances in character, given during the evening, excited much interest and amusement. (unattributed, 1880: 18)

It is possible that the "Maori" songs and dances referred to were performed by Maori staff from the Mission (who were prominent in the first fifteen years of the Mission's establishment on Norfolk Island). An alternative explanation is that the term "Maori" was used by the writer in an expanded sense to refer to Polynesian (as opposed to Melanesian) performance by students.

Over twenty five years later, Coombe also noted that on particular occasions:

> there are native games too, in which imagination plays a great part, and it is not easy for a white mind to follow the thread. Queer little native songs accompany the games, and they are pretty to watch, even though it is hard to know (till you are told) that these are ghosts in a banana plantation, or those are birds shot by arrows. (1909: 62)

As with the above descriptions of dances, it is difficult to ascertain precisely where these games and songs originated.

In addition to these written accounts, one surviving photograph[10] (Figure 2) gives some idea of the material culture associated with music and dance performance. The (undated) photograph shows a group of students carrying spears and shields. Given the size of the group, their appearance and arrangement for camera, they look likely to have been posed for the photograph and it is difficult to identify any aspect of the dance that they may have been assembled to perform.

Along with the documentary evidence of the photograph and written

Figure 2: Student performance (occasion and date unknown).

accounts referenced above there are also three (ostensible) relics of indigenous music practice at the Mission that have been identified on (present-day) Norfolk Island. The first is a conch shell discovered in the early 1990s by local fossickers exploring the site of the old Mission. The conch shell had a hole bored in, of the type used as a musical/ceremonial instrument in various Pacific cultures[11]. Since conch shells are not found in coastal waters off Norfolk Island, it seems likely that this was an object brought to the Mission by recruits or missionaries. Given the lack of mention of conch shell performance in any written account, it could have been used for signaling or else have served another purpose (such as an ornamental souvenir acquired by Mission staff).

The other relics are even more problematic. They comprise two small drums displayed at the (privately owned) Bounty Folk Museum in the 1990s and early 2000s. As Figure 3 shows, these are a single-handled, approximately 50cm high hour-glass shaped drum and a small hand drum featured as part of a corner display together with a copy of the image reproduced as

Figure 3: Melanesian Mission display at Bounty Folk Museum (1999).

57

Figure 2. The small drum is the most anomalous part of the display. Along with its intact, good-condition membrane (suggesting that it is far less than the minimum eighty years old necessary for a Mission artifact), it is of a type unknown to the western Pacific region and looks more like an African instrument[12]. The second instrument is a *kundu*, a Melanesian drum commonly found in Papua New Guinea but not in any areas of Melanesia that the Mission was active in. This similarly suggests that the instrument did not originate from students at the Mission, since the Mission's most northerly limit was the northern part of the present-day Solomon Islands group, where the instrument has not been recorded. As with the conch shell, there are several explanations for the instrument's presence in the display. One is that, like the smaller drum, it does not originate from the Mission but from another source. Another is that it was an artifact from the Mission, either brought to (or made on) the island by a student from outside the Mission's usual area of recruitment, or else was a souvenir traded from or acquired in Papua New Guinea.

Whatever the purpose[13] – and outcome – of the Melanesian students' visits to Norfolk Island, it is clear that during their stay they interacted with members of communities that they would have had little contact with in their home environments. They also had the opportunity to hear, see and – in some cases – participate in different performance repertoires. The Mission thereby facilitated a degree of inter-regional pan-Melanesian interaction on Norfolk Island that appears to have been historically unprecedented. While research of the topic has been beyond the scope of this volume, it is also possible that, in addition to teaching Melanesian students' aspects of western hymnody and keyboard skills, the Norfolk Island experience may have facilitated a degree of repertoire exchange, expansion and/or development in the song and dance cultures the students returned to.

III. Echoes and Outcomes

The Melanesian Mission on Norfolk Island began to decline in importance in the early 1900s as missionary training activities were increasingly established in the Solomon Islands and the Mission's site was largely dismantled in 1919. Aside from St Barnabus chapel itself, the Mission – and the cultural activities of Melanesian students on Norfolk's soil – has largely receded from the memory of contemporary islanders. In five years of research (1999-2004) the only oral historical recollection of Melanesian presence on the island was one told to me at second hand, an arresting, intriguing image that I have not managed to illuminate, that of a Melanesian dancing a traditional dance with a live tern tied to his head[14]. This vivid fragment aside, the Melanesian students' fenced off graveyard area at St Barnabus, replete with island names on simple crosses, is their only public memorial. And even this hides a sleight of hand; the crosses were recently relocated to their present location from the actual graveyard in order to make them more visible – and photogenic – close to the chapel.

As Chapter 7 relates, the beginning of a conscious embrace of a pan-Pacific identity for Norfolk Islanders, predominantly focused on Polynesian aspects, did not occur until the in the 1930s and did not acquire significant

Figure 4: Present day location of gravestones and markers of deceased Melanesian Mission students in grounds of St Barnabas chapel.

political momentum until the 1980s, when Norfolk Island began to be represented at Pacific Arts Festivals. As subsequent chapters explore, this continued in the 1990s with the development of the island's multi-cultural arts festival (which hosted Maori, Aboriginal and Polynesian performers in the late 1990s and early 2000s).

One notable connection between Norfolk Island and the cultures from which students at the Mission were drawn occurred in 1999 when Norfolk Island Polynesian-style dancer and dance educator Karlene Christian (whose work is discussed in the Chapter 7) contacted the Mapungamanu performance troupe, an ensemble dedicated to preserving the culture of Tikopia. Tikopia is a small volcanic island, about ten square kilometres in area, located to the far south of the present-day Solomon Islands group. While geographically part of what is generally considered southern Melanesia, the population culturally and linguistically belongs to the western Polynesian group. In the late 1800s and early 1900s the population numbered around 1000, dispersed in coastal villages, who were involved in fishing, farming and gathering growing vegetables and fruit. According to Firth (1970) traditional Tikopian beliefs centred on various ancestors and gods who were venerated in order to ensure successful fishing, health etc. While the island began to have occasional contact with westerners from the early 1800s on, indigenous culture remained dominant well into the 20th Century. Members of the Mapungamanu ensemble are largely drawn from the Tikopian community that has relocated to Makira province (in the central Solomons), since the 1950s due to overcrowding and lack of employment opportunities on their home island.

Karlene Christian's interest in the troupe stemmed from an account of their work published in *Pacific Islands Monthly* magazine (Walker, 1999) that emphasised the troupe's endeavours to preserve their culture. Perceiving an affinity between the projects of late 20th Century Norfolk Island cultural activists such as herself and Mapungamanu, she wrote to the troupe. The troupe's manager, Julian Treadaway, warmly received her communication since (unbeknownst to Christian – and contemporary Norfolk Islanders in general) several Tikopians attended the Melanesian Mission on Norfolk Island. Raymond Firth and Mervyn McLean have described the initial result of increased Tikopian interaction with other cultures in the late 1800s and early 1900s as cultural "reference to overseas voyages to lands of the white man" and in song texts "by inclusion of various words from 'pijin' English" (1991: 12). One song Firth heard at a dance festival on Tikopia in 1952 is particularly relevant for this study. The song he referred to was sung to a *matavaka* dance and its theme was Norfolk Island (referred to in the lyrics as "Narfark" [ibid: 101]) – which Firth understood the composer to have visited[15]. Firth describes the *matavaka* as one of the dance styles he most frequently witnessed on Tikopia. As the use of the common Polynesian word *vaka* (canoe) suggests, the dance belongs to that pan-Pacific genre of 'canoe paddling' dances discussed in the previous section. Firth describes a *matavaka* performed on Tikopia in 1929 in the following terms:

> *A solid group of people, knees bent, swaying bodies, heads bending to this side and to that, feet moving in time to the rhythmic beat ... The undulating mass of heads and bodies resembles the heaving of the sea, the waving hair, its flying spray. The unchanging rhythm as a background to the cadences of the song produces a sort of intoxication, to which people yield themselves, swaying to and fro with an intent look, their gestures becoming more and more violent as the beat begins to quicken.* (ibid: 77)

Along with such specific inscriptions of Norfolk Island in songs and dances the main impact of the Tikopians' training with the Melanesian Mission was the introduction of Christian hymns to the island. As Firth and McLean detail, these hymns were sung in Mota in the early 20th Century[16] and the musical form "was one of European melodic line, but sung in a Pacific mode, with much portamento and some modification of intervals, and without instrumentation" (ibid: 12)

Reflecting the history of Tikopian engagement with the Melanesian Mission in the late 1800s and early 1900s, several Tikopian families still bear surnames derived from the words 'Norfolk' or 'Norfolk Island'. Interested to re-open cultural contacts, Treadaway responded to Christian by inviting her to visit Makira and expressed a desire for the Mapungamanu troupe to visit Norfolk Island. However, in the late 20th Century, with the demise of the Melanesian Mission's regular sea routes from Melanesia to Norfolk (and Auckland) on the *Southern Cross*, the costs of travel have – in a paradoxical illustration of the nature of 'progress' – become prohibitive for such contacts and neither visit has yet occurred.

While the music and dance culture of the Melanesian Mission on Norfolk Island has far greater links to both the internal history of the Mission and the external cultures of those island communities from which it drew scholars and to which it sent missionaries; it remains a part of Norfolk Island's heritage – forgotten or not – as an intangible counterpart to the monumental stone buildings left over from the penal era which loom large in the landscape and tourist image of the present-day island.

Notes

1. And on Pitcairn too, where Young's parents had returned shortly after his enlistment.

2. Nobbs soon shifted his ground and by 1859 actively supported the establishment of the Mission on Norfolk Island. See Nobbs (1984: 84) for discussion of the reasons for this reversal.

3. The Melanesians present at the mission at this time were from Florida, San Christoval, Ambryn and Leper's Island (Selwyn, 1879: 9).

4. Maidment, J (1981) notes that Willis and Sons were a minor, albeit significant, manufacturer and exporter of organs to Australia in the late 1800s, and comments that "the Willis instruments were largely concentrated in Maitland, near Newcastle"(1981: xii).

5. The Melanesian Mission published a translation of the full text of the New Testament in 1885 and a complete version of The Bible in 1912.

6. Hillard also identifies *John Peel* and *For he's a jolly good fellow* as being adapted into Mota (1978: 224).

7. It is possible that this song is the George Hunn Nobbs composition *Angel's Lament* referred to in Chapter 2. If this is the case, its translation to Mota and performance by Melanesian students represents a significant gesture of solidarity between the Mission and Nobbs following Nobbs's early resistance to the Mission's establishment on Norfolk.

8. A popular card game of the time.

9. Introduced to Jamaica in the early 19th century, the quadrille became localised as a Jamaican folk dance form.

10. Research in specialist locations such as the Kinder Library in Auckland, which has a sizeable holding of Melanesian Mission material, has not revealed further images of the kind discussed.

11. Information supplied by Robert Tofts, interview with the author, 1999.

12. Don Niles, Institute of Papua New Guinea Studies, pc May 2002.

13. One of the principal problems the Melanesian Mission had to contend with was that many students "went to Norfolk Island in the expectation of instant wealth" (Hillard, 1978: 165) and anticipated advancement within their communities upon their return, these being their primary motivations to attend.

14. While bird feathers, carcasses and carvings often form part of ceremonial headware, I have not been able to find any reference to live birds being used in dancing in this manner amongst Melanesian communities.

15. As with any oral culture, many topical songs are only in circulation for a relatively short period and their specific meanings may become obscure with the passing of time. Reflecting this, Firth notes that, "the audience were largely ignorant of what the theme was [and] as to whether 'Narfark' was a country" (Firth and McLean, 1991: 101).

16. English language texts replaced Mota in from the 1930s on, as the Melanesian Mission's policy of dropping use of Mota as a pan-Melanesian *lingua franca* spread throughout its mission operations.

Chapter Five

RE-ESTABLISHMENT
Pitcairn Island from 1858 to
World War Two

In 1858 sixteen islanders departed Norfolk Island, via Tahiti, to re-establish the Pitcairn settlement. This group was followed by a further party of twenty-seven who arrived back in 1864. The second group included Simon Young who, with the support of George Hunn Nobbs, became the leader of the new community. While the early experiences of the first (re-) settlers remains obscure, the history of the settlement in the thirty years after Simon Young's arrival was documented with admirable clarity by his daughter Rosalind Amelia Young in a book published in 1894. Her account includes several detailed discussions of aspects of music, musical instruments and instruction on Pitcairn. She provides a somewhat paradoxical picture of a small community on an isolated island, with no means of generating (financial) income, who nevertheless achieved a degree of musical resources, instruction and abilities which were more extensive than many larger, less-isolated communities in the Pacific region. The explanation for this paradox, as discussed below, involves factors such as the musical inclination of the islanders, their contact with the ships that visited them (with considerable frequency) in the late 1800s, and the degree of support for their community shown by patrons in the United Kingdom and United States.

The first party of Pitcairners to leave Norfolk Island, comprising sixteen individuals from two families, returned to Pitcairn in 1859. Amongst their number was Moses Young, an accomplished fiddle and fife player, who organised some singing lessons soon after returning, with somewhat mixed results, Rosalind Young commenting that:

> *Having drilled his little class in "do, re, mi, fa, so, la, si, do" and learning the skips ad infinitum, he made a sudden advance to a few of the old standard church tunes, and succeeded in reviving, for the benefit of his youthful learners, the old tunes of Truro and Clarendon, and teaching them an entirely new tune besides. He did not accomplish more of his laudable undertaking, probably because his pupils did not give him the*

needed encouragement, or else he himself checked their ardor (by being critical of their performances). (1894: 153-154).

Aside from this brief reference there appears to be no other record of music on the island in the first five years of the re-settlement.

The second party of returning Pitcairners provided a notably cacophonous announcement of their arrival:

It was night when the little ship reached the end of her voyage, a beautiful night, calm and clear, and the unsuspecting folks on shore did not dream of seeing on the morrow the long absent faces of relatives and friends, and were preparing to retire to rest when a musket's sharp report from over the water broke the stillness. On board all was excitement and bustle, muskets firing, the young men hallooing and burning flash lights to attract the attention of those on shore ... The perfect Babel of sounds soon succeeded in rousing, not the peaceful inhabitants only, but their terror as well. (ibid: 165)

The islanders' anxiety was not abated until the following morning when they realised the identity of the ship's party and welcomed them ashore. The new arrivals began to create an infrastructure for the administration and education of the islanders. Simon Young took on the role of pastor and schoolteacher and, in the latter capacity, set about developing the children's singing abilities. In this he was assisted by the musical education that several of the children had received on Norfolk Island, with ten of his fifteen students being already able to read music. Rosalind Young recorded that after her father led the children "through the simplest airs" he taught them "with great success, to sing in four parts, and the fact that out of a class of fifteen ten were able to read music by sight, gave him great encouragement in that branch of his work" (ibid: 174). The singing abilities of the children and their parents became a significant source of pleasure for the community in both formal worship and social gatherings, particularly given the absence of other significant cultural diversions. While the repertoire of the islanders at this time has not been documented, it seems safe to assume that it comprised essentially the same hymns and popular tunes observed to be in use on Pitcairn in the period immediately prior to evacuation and on Norfolk Island in the period immediately following settlement in 1856. One of the first citations of new material is the adoption of George Hunn Nobbs' hymn *O Lord, the heathens' madness*, written by him to commemorate the deaths of his son Edwin and Fisher Young while on service with the Melanesian Mission (see Chapter 3 for further discussion). Young records that the hymn was sent from Norfolk Island, arriving some years after their deaths and was "soon learned and frequently sung" (ibid: 178).

Exposure to fresh repertoire and singing styles was provided in June 1868 when *The Ashburton* visited, en route from Australia. Amongst the passengers on board were members of an opera troupe led by Fred Lyster and Minnie Walton who sang a selection of material, and, in response, were entertained by Young's pupils singing some of the part songs they had been taught. Singing during this period appears to have been exclusively unaccompanied. But the situation changed significantly in 1876 when the community was gifted two keyboards by separate benefactors.

The first was an old harmonium given to an (unidentified) young woman to whom the ship's doctor from the HMS *Petrel* appears to have taken a particular liking for during a brief visit to the island. The gift, though appreciated, was tempered by its condition. Young described the instrument as "weak-lunged and out of tune" (ibid: 198) necessitating that it be dismantled, cleaned and repaired before use. It was put to use in training children how to play the keyboard but hardly had time to establish itself as a community resource before it was superseded by a more impressive instrument. This second keyboard to arrive was a gift from the people of San Francisco who had read of the (materially/technologically) impoverished nature of Pitcairn Island life in newspaper accounts which followed the return of the crew of the *Khandeish*, who had been shipwrecked near Oeno Island and subsequently supported by Pitcairn Islanders for nearly two months before being picked up by the British ship *Ennerdale*. San Franciscans donated sufficient funds for a Mason and Hamlin organ, and other goods, to be purchased and shipped to the island.

Young provides a detailed account of the instrument's arrival on the US ship *St John* and the impression it made on Pitcairners:

> The organ was brought by Captain Scribner. Directly on its being landed it was lifted on the shoulders of a few strong men and borne by them up the steep path, nor was the precious burden set down until they reached the little thatch-roofed church, where it was placed beside the reading table. All the inhabitants, old and young, gathered around while Captain Scribner played, "Shall We Gather at the River?" Every voice joined in the song, and when it ended, repeated expressions of thanks were given to the kind friend who brought it, and through him to the generous friends who sent the handsome gift … It was a new and very delightful experience to them to listen for the first time to the tones of a perfect-keyed instrument … when the new organ was opened, all who wished had the gratification of trying a few chords on it, and enjoying the power of the instrument, an experience as delightful as it was new. (ibid: 198-199)

Along with his demonstration of keyboard technique Scribner also helped established *Shall we gather at the river?* as an enduring hymn in local repertoire. The hymn was written by US pastor Robert Lowry in 1864, based on Revelation 22:1-22. Some clues to the cause of its popularity may be gained from its watery lyrical theme:

> Shall we gather at the river
> Where bright angel feet have trod
> With its crystal tide forever
> Flowing by the throne of God?

In the late 1870s the island was not only tolerably resourced in terms of keyboards, but also enlivened by the musical performances of visiting ships' crews, and, on occasion, naval bands. Given that the island had a population of around ninety in the late 1870s, the scale and impact of ships such as the HMS *Shah*, with a crew of some eight hundred, which visited in September 1878, must have been considerable. The captain invited islanders on board, where a range of musical pleasures were available:

> *On deck the band were playing, while in one of the rooms below one of the officers was seated at a piano, making music for a company of admiring listeners. In the gun room the crowd of young officers had gathered the schoolchildren together, and persuaded them to sing some of their songs and glees, they in return singing some of their bright lively songs.* (ibid: 203)

The sheer size of the ship, its crew and the range of musical performances on offer must have provided an experience whose impressions would have lasted long after the vessel departed. The ship was commanded by Admiral De Horsey, who was sufficiently impressed by the temperate lifestyle and behaviour of the islanders to petition the Navy and Crown to assist and support Pitcairn. One result of his petition was the provision of a third keyboard, delivered by HMS *Opal* in 1879, a Clough and Warren's organ, made in the United States. This was purchased for the island by Admiral de Horsey, along with other goods, from a twenty pound donation provided by Queen Victoria herself[1].

A further visit from a British navy ship, the HMS *Cormorant*, in December 1887, also provided a significant musical diversion for the islanders. As Young recalled:

> *Captain Nicolls gave an invitation to all who so wished to visit his ship and enjoy a pleasant entertainment on board ... The captain presided at a large piano, while at his side stood one of his officers, accompanying on the violin, which instrument contributed largely to the music, two or three more being skillfully played by as many of the ship's company. The cheers that greeted every fresh performance were heard on shore, and when the first star of evening appeared, the islanders sang for their closing piece, "Twilight is Stealing o'er the Sea". Then all rose to finish the evening's enjoyment by singing "God Save the Queen", after which the island boats, with their human freight, started homewards, and the Cormorant steamed away to her destination, bidding good-bye with her siren whistle.* (ibid: 236)

The Pitcairners' closing song is significant in island repertoire for not being a hymn but, rather, a 19th Century US sentimental song[2] that subsequently entered a number of regional repertoires[3]. Its lyrics were clearly apposite to the Pitcairners' heritage, as in verse 1:

> *Twilight is stealing over the sea*
> *Shadows are falling oe'r the lea*
> *Born on the night winds, voices of yore*
> *Come in from the far off shore*

and, particularly, the opening lines of verse 2:

> *Voices of loved ones, songs of the past*
> *Still linger 'round me while life shall last*

The song appears to have had an enduring appeal on Pitcairn since Harry

Shapiro also noted that it was still performed on the island when he visited in 1934 (1936: 270).

In response to the regular visits of ships, and, more specifically, their farewelling, Amelia Young wrote a composition entitled *The goodbye song* some time in the late 1880s or early 1890s. Young's original lyrics comprise:

Now, one last song we'll sing – Goodbye, goodbye!
Time moves on rapid wings – Goodbye!
And this short year will soon be past
Will soon be numbered with the last
But as we part, to all we'll say –
Goodbye, goodbye, goodbye
But as we part, to all we'll say –
Goodbye, goodbye, goodbye

We gather now to say Goodbye, goodbye!
We can no longer stay – Goodbye!
Thanks for your love and constant care
And kindness that we kindly share
We part but hope to meet again
Goodbye, goodbye, goodbye!
We part but hope to meet again –
GOODBYE, goodbye, goodbye

The song appears to have been introduced into the local repertoire fairly immediately after its composition and continues to be sung when a visiting ship departs from Pitcairn (or, often, when the island's longboats are leaving on fishing trips or visits to nearby Henderson, Ducie and Oeno islands).

1890 marked the 100th anniversary of the *Bounty's* arrival at Pitcairn and the founding of the island community. A hymn was composed for the occasion (presumably by one of the Youngs), the first since re-settlement. The song recalled the history of the first settlement and how its initial turmoil was pacified by Smith's embrace of the Bible, as its second and third verses stated:

To this fair land our fathers sought
To flee the doom their sins had brought
In vain – nor peace nor rest was found
For strife possessed th' unhallowed ground

Darkness around their path was spread
Their crimes deserved a vengeance dread
When, lo! a beam of hope was given
To guide their erring feet to heaven[4]

Unlike Young's *The goodbye song*, this hymn does not appear to have entered the islanders' regular repertoire and is not performed today.

1890 also marked a moment when the island switched, apparently en masse, from Anglicanism to the Seventh Day Adventist (SDA) faith. The first SDA missionary had visited the island on the HMS *Pelican* some four years before, and had succeeded in interesting many of the islanders in the (then) relatively new religion[5]. An SDA team arrived in November 1890 on board a missionary vessel, named *Pitcairn*, led by Elder Gates who arranged a mass baptism of the island's population, who henceforth celebrated the Sabbath on Saturdays. Gates remained on the island after the conversion and was joined in February 1893 by a young missionary, Hattie Andre, who came to teach school[6]. The SDA brought with them a complex millenarian faith with a set of complicated prohibitions and disapprovals. Amongst these was a renunciation of dancing and a deep distrust of anything but strictly approved church music – returning Pitcairn to a cultural austerity similar to that of the middle-period of the island's settlement, when religious leaders such as George Hunn Nobbs and Joseph Hill strongly discouraged dancing, levity and any form of perceived 'licentiousness' in general. In her tract *Patriarchs and Prophets*, SDA founder Ellen G. White declared that:

> *Many of the amusements popular in the world today, even with those who claim to be Christians, tend to the same end as did those of the heathen. There are indeed few among them that Satan does not turn to account in destroying souls. Through the drama he has worked for ages to excite passion and glorify vice. The opera, with its fascinating display and bewildering music, the masquerade, the dance, the card table, Satan employs to break down the barriers of principle and open the door to sensual indulgence. In every gathering for pleasure where pride is fostered or appetite indulged, where one is led to forget God and lose sight of eternal interests, there Satan is binding his chains about the soul.* (1890: 459/240)

Despite the SDA's strictures against dancing, a number of members of the community, particularly older women, appear to have continued traditional dance practices. Pitcairn Island singer Meralda Warren (whose work is discussed in Chapter 12) recalls Bernice Christian relating how Tahitian-style dancing (and also a particular dance performed on Bounty Day round a 'maypole'[7]) continued up until the 1940s (pc 1999). The survival of these practices represents a significant resistance to the SDA's cultural suppression of previous island culture.

The early SDA church had complex and somewhat contradictory approaches to music-making. While it decried popular social music (as suggested in White, above) some early leaders embraced instruments such as the organ, melodeon and guitar as accompaniments to hymn singing, while others rejected such modern technologies outright (Ward, online: np). Also, despite White's rejection of profane popular culture, several early SDA hymns simply substituted the words of famous songs (such as Stephen Foster's 1851 *Old folks at home* [also known as *Way down upon the Swannee River*] and Dan Emmett's 1859 composition *Dixie*) with more spiritual lyrics (ibid). A particular concern of the early church was that participation in popular social music making was a distraction from righteousness. The duality of music is clearly articulated in a recent 'Philosophy of Music' document written by a committee of the SDA General Conference and featured on the SDA's official website, which quotes extracts from and summarises White's writings, stating that:

> *"Music when not abused, is a great blessing; but when it is put to a wrong use, it is a terrible curse"* ... *Music, which may move us to the*

most exalted human experience, may be used by the prince of evil [ie Satan] *to debase and degrade us, to stir up lust, passion, despair, anger, and hatred.* (2003: np)

While there is little record of the music sung or otherwise performed on the island in the decades immediately following the SDA's establishment on Pitcairn, it is likely that SDA hymnody dominated.

Between 1890 and 1910, the island's main contact with the outside world occurred in the form of occasional visits of British and US Navy vessels[8]. However, the situation changed drastically with the growth of Pacific cruise lines operating in between World Wars One and Two. As Spencer Murray has characterised:

Popularity of the island as a stop-over began to return ... with the opening of the Panama Canal on 15 August 1914. The "Big Ditch" lopped 7,000 miles off a voyage between the Atlantic and the Pacific which served to encourage trans-ocean commerce ... Freighters furrowed the Pacific in growing numbers and Pitcairn was not far off their track. Best of all, the canal bought ocean liners to cruise between the Americas and Australasia, each carrying hundreds of passengers. Some firms arranged routes and itineraries specifically to include Pitcairn ... Pitcairners greeted the hordes of visitors with outstretched arms – arms offering carvings, fruit baskets, woven hats (etc.) ... Trading must have been spirited indeed when, in 1937, Pitcairn's population peaked at 233 individuals. (1992: 108)

While sales of produce injected some cash into the local economy, the dominance of the SDA church in island affairs and culture ensured that a significant proportion of this was directed into SDA expenses on Pitcairn or the support of SDA missionary activity further afield.

The Australian film maker Charles Chauvel wrote a detailed account of Pitcairn society after visiting the island in 1932 to shoot sequences for his film *In the wake of The Bounty*. Pitcairn's austere, pious culture provided a sharp contrast to the Tahitian culture that Chauvel had experienced immediately prior to arriving. Chauvel describes a culture in which SDA prohibitions on alcohol, tobacco, stimulants (such as tea) and pork are strictly held; where "[a]ll literature except religious books and tracts and a panic-stricken sheet called 'The Signs of the Times' are censored" (1933: 131) and where "[d]ancing is not allowed, and only religious records and nursery rhymes are encouraged on the gramophone" (ibid). The latter comment accords with Fullerton's observations in 1923 that:

There is a gramophone on the island. One of the young men was anxious to get a Columbia one-inch spring; another was eager for the record of the hymn, "There are lonely hearts to cherish". (1923: 98)

Chauvel's' qualification about gramophone use is significant, while only the two forms of music may have been actively "encouraged" at the time, the presence of gramophones on Pitcairn in the 1920s and 1930s, left by and/or purchased from passing ships, offered a point of entry for new musical material, and a context (ie the domestic situation) where choice of track and listening could be exercised with diminished risk of interference or censure.

Chauvel noted that one outsider resident on Pitcairn at the time of his visit, referred to by him as "the *Retriever's* captain, a polished Englishman" (ibid: 136), possessed a collection of musical recordings in his room in "one of the Christian families" houses, which he played regularly – presumably in hearing of the family itself. As some indication of the value some islanders' ascribed to gramophone ownership (and maintenance), one of the vintage gramophones from this period was reported to be still in use in the late 1970s, a wind-up 78rpm phonograph owned by Roy Clarke[9], who had a substantial set of recordings obtained from various sources[10].

Chauvel's account of island life not only confirms previous reports of the prevalence of hymn singing (and the near-abandonment of singing of the British national anthem, given the sway of the US dominated SDA faith) but also provides a useful insight into the other material which had either lingered since early settlement or been introduced by passing ships and/or gramophone records. As he described:

> Some of our jolliest evenings were spent with the Edwin Christians, where we were always joined by old Uncle Ben and Fred Christian ... After a menu of soup, fish, chicken, goat, yams, "pilli"[11] and arrow-root[12], we would gather round the organ while Edward Christian played accompaniments to hymns and old songs of England such as "Sally Horner" and "Ben Bolt," while the sea would be there with "Rolling Down to Rio"; and Uncle Ben, spurred to naughtiness, would suggest "John Brown's Wife drinks Whisky In Her Tea" and others that are seldom, if ever, sung on Pitcairn to-day. (ibid: 152)

There are a number of significant aspects of this account, not the least that the performance of such secular material – and, in particular, mildly risqué tunes such as the latter – took place in a social group that included the island's SDA pastor, Fred Christian, apparently without comment or censure. This suggests, at very least, a degree of laxity and/or occasional tolerance to what Chauvel characterised as the "dreary backwash" of the island's SDA-dominated social and cultural life (ibid: 131). Despite Chauvel's description, two of the specific songs referred to originate from the USA. *Ben Bolt* is a sentimental, nostalgic ballad popularised in 1848 and it seems likely that *John Brown's wife* is a parody of the American Civil War song *John Brown's body*. While I have not been able to identify the origins of *Sally Horner*, *Rolling down to Rio* is one of the *Rolling down/Rolling home* variants – one of the most popular sea shanties of the 1800s[13].

Despite this colourful account, the majority of musical life on Pitcairn in the pre-War era remained within the more solemn Christian tradition described earlier in the chapter. Visiting in 1934, for instance, Harry Shapiro described a typical Friday night with the Young family in the following terms:

> We were twelve adults and eight children, gathered for family prayers. We began with a hymn. Then Andrew [Young] read a passage from the Old Testament, followed by an eloquent prayer couched by Edith

[Young] *in fine Biblical style. This was succeeded by the singing of hymns again – about half a dozen old favorites were sung. A particular favorite would be called for by someone and the whole party would oblige, Aunt Ann* [McCoy] *sat through it all with a beatific expression which became even more ecstatic when a hymn she had requested was sung ... When the sound of our singing ceased, we could hear similar hymns from other houses where identical family groups were gathered.* (1936: 271)

In addition to domestic singing, the practice of ceremonial musical farewells was also well-established in the 1930s, and was found particularly moving by visitors such as Chauvel, who wrote that:

My wife was able to come to the railing with me to hear the islanders sing for us their favorite hymn, in which we had joined so often – "In the Sweet By and By We Shall Meet on That Beautiful Shore"[14]. (1933: 157)

Shapiro described his departure from the island on New Year's Day as follows:

More than seventy islanders, men and women, came out to the Zaca in two whale boats and in two canoes ... We went back on deck where the ship's victrola was being played. But the islanders preferred to make their own music, singing "Happy New Year" and a number of other songs. [Following a rowing race] *[a]fter the rowers were back on board again and had regained their breath, they once more broke into song. This time they started with "We Shall Meet by the River"*[15] *and continued to sing hymn after hymn until all the general favorites had been exhausted.* [After they left the Zaca] *the islanders once more lifted up their voices in song. Our parting view was of boat-loads of natives standing up to pour their voices into the air.* (1936: 285-286)

Frank West, a British sailor who visited the island in 1931 also had similar recollections and emotions:

The lowering sun shone on the Islanders, as they took themselves over the side into their longboats, ten or fifteen in each. Now, as they pulled away, they waved their farewells and then began to sing the well loved hymns of my childhood, in strong voices and beautiful harmonies. Then, as the sun sank below the horizon leaving the sky and island in a deep, rapidly changing glow of light, we followed as the boats in silhouette pulled hard to make a safe landfall. We could hear the faint strains of the singing as they carried across the water, until they faded with the dusk and we saw and heard them no more. (quoted in *PM* March 1995: 3)

West also added the query:

I wonder if these island men had any idea of the beauty of that sea and sound as they pulled on their oars to return to their womenfolk in the safety of the remaining daylight, or of the lasting, and at the time, deeply moving, emotional effect they and their nature had combined to inspire? (ibid)

The outbreak of the Pacific phase of World War Two in 1941 plunged the island into greater isolation as cruise ships and trading boats ceased to call, leaving the islanders to their own resources and the dominating influence of the Seventh Day Adventism they had embraced some fifty years previously. While the language, heritage and perceived affinities between the two communities continued to link Norfolk and Pitcairn Island in the imagination of their inhabitants, the years following the re-establishment of Pitcairn were ones in which the two small societies developed along different paths. The tiny Pitcairn community remained dominated by the austere tone of early-mid 20th Century Seventh Day Adventism. By contrast, Norfolk Island culture was diversifying, inspired by the energies of a revived Polynesianism and an embrace of a series of popular cultural forms.

Notes

1. Further gifts followed as a result of Horsey's appeal, many arriving on the HMS *Osprey* in 1880, including two boats and many books.
2. I have been unable to locate a text of the original version, nor any reference to its date of publication.
3. Such as the Appalachian region, where the song was later performed and recorded by the Ritchie family after World War Two.
4. Full lyrics are reproduced in Young (1894: 239-240).
5. The SDA church was formally inaugurated in 1860, opened its first theological college in 1871 and soon after began sending missionaries overseas.
6. Shortly after Andre's arrival an outbreak of diseases followed the visit of the HMS *Hyacinth*, killing twelve people and temporarily incapacitating many more.
7. A garlanded and be-ribboned pole used by dancers performing at 'traditional' May Day celebrations in England in the 19th-20th Centuries (and earlier).
8. This was a marked reversal of Pitcairn Island's frequent visitations in the 1830s-1850s. The number of whaling ships calling at Pitcairn declined markedly in the period 1860-80, principally due to kerosene replacing whale oil as standard lamp fuel. British and US navy ships comprised the principal visitors in the later decades of the 19th Century.
9. Who settled on the island in 1906 at the age of sixteen.
10. These were described by him in an article entitled "I Learn of My Death" published in the *Pitcairn Miscellany* in August 1978, written by Clarke, at that time the island's oldest inhabitant, at the age of eighty four.
11. Grated kumera and yams, cooked together.
12. The varied nature of this repast suggests that Chauvel is referring to special meals/feasts here, rather than regular daily fare.
13. See Hayward (2002: 5) for further discussion of the song.
14. See Chapter 9 for a discussion of the hymn and its origins.
15. The author is most likely referring to the previously mentioned hymn *Shall we gather at the river?*

Chapter Six

A TIME OF TRANSITION
Performance culture on Norfolk Island (1900-1940)

I. The Early 1900s

One of the few reports of island music in the final decade of the 19th Century is provided in an aside in an unpublished diary written by William Quintal in 1899–1901[1], which notes that Handel's *Messiah* was again being rehearsed for public performance. One of the few visitors in this period to record their observations was novelist Beatrice Grimshaw, author of many Pacific romances. She wrote that:

> *The voices of the Islanders are remarkably low and musical. They are the voices of those whose ancestors for many generations have never known hurry or anxiety; of people dwelling in 'a land where it is always afternoon' – of a gentle, dreamy folk, living slow, sweet lives as changeless as the empty sea that rings around their island home.* (quoted in Clarke, 1986: 157)

Such sources, and informed speculation, led historian Merval Hoare to characterise Norfolk Island life around 1900 in the following terms:

> *Life was leisurely and work not too demanding; there was time for picnics and excursions to the outlying islands. Dances, conversaziones, and magic lantern pictures provided evening entertainment. Choir practice was still an important affair, and the islanders, who were renown for their sweet voices and harmonious singing, coped with such difficult compositions as Handel's oratorios.* (1978: 99)

The visit of naval ships to the island continued to be a major source of cultural contact and communication from 1900-1920 and islanders welcomed visitors by holding picnics, outings and end-of-stay parties for their guests. Similarly, the occasional visits of tourist steamers also provided a stimulus for the local economy, an early taste of the tourist industry that came to dominate the island's economy from the 1960s on. A more gradual shift in the population and cultural and social character of the island was affected by the gradual rise in the number of Australian and New Zealand settlers from the early 1900s on, many of whom brought various possessions, including instruments, onto the island.

Atlee Hunt, the secretary to the Australian Department of External Affairs, who visited Norfolk in January 1914 to compile a report on the island, produced a significant set of observations of Norfolk Island life and culture. The document numbered the population at 985 persons, 568 of whom were male and 417 female. It identified 42 as Pitcairn-born, 554 as persons born on Norfolk Island, 193 Melanesians temporarily residing on the island while studying at the Melanesian Mission and 150 others of unspecified nationality (Hunt, 1914: 15). The latter category was identified by Hunt as comprising "white missionaries and mission helpers"; employees of the Pacific Cable Board; and "a number of people, mostly Australians and New Zealanders, officials, storekeepers, pensioners, tradesmen &c., who have settled on the island from time to time" (ibid: 15-16). Hunt also reported that the island was served by a monthly steamer service, on the Burns Philp route Sydney – Lord Howe Island – Norfolk Island – New Hebrides (present day Vanuatu) (and return) and by half yearly visits by the steamer Southern Cross, from New Zealand, maintained by the Melanesian Mission.

With regard to social aspects of island life, Hunt reported, with a polite censoriousness, that:

> They are a pleasure-loving folk. Work is placed aside readily when the chance offers a picnic or other form of amusement, and they gladly put off til tomorrow, or, preferably, til next week, what ought to be done today. This "hilli" to use the Tahitian term common among them is noticeable even to themselves, and is much lamented by the wiser men[2]. (ibid: 17)

and added that:

> As might be expected they are extremely conservative. The methods of their forefathers are to them the only right and proper rules of life. "The custom of the island" is a phrase to be heard in opposition to suggestions involving innovations of any kind. (ibid)

As Hunt identified, this conservatism also extended to cultural practice:

> They are intensely fond of music but commonly limit their expression of that art to the rendering of hymns and simple songs, keen and expert at dances, their proficiency excites the admiration of visitors[3]. (ibid)

In his comments on education on the island, he also reported on a school concert he had attended which "showed a measure of skill and music culture quite equal to what one would find among children of the same age in Australia" (ibid: 18). The latter appears to have been substantially assisted by a factor noticed by Hunt in his observations on island buildings and facilities:

> Many [homes] contain pianos, and more, sewing machines. It has been said that when a man has a piano and a sewing machine for his wife

and daughters, and a sulky [horse drawn cart] *for himself, his desires are fully satisfied.* (ibid)

and that:

Social purposes are met by a public hall [The Rawson Hall], *which, originally a convict-built farm building, has been altered to meet the requirements of public meetings, dances, concerts &c.* (ibid: 20)

There are several interesting aspects to these compact references to the island's music culture. One concerns musical repertoire and its relation to religious commitment (and religiosity) since, as Hunt laments:

The people of Pitcairn were brought up on the Bible and the Prayer-book; their devout religious observances were a feature of life much commented on by visitors. It is to be feared that, though attendance at church and Sunday-school is still fairly constant, the Norfolkers have in this regard departed considerably from the ways of their fathers. (ibid: 19)

While Hunt is vague about the manners in which the islanders had "departed" from their ways of their fathers it seems probable that consumption of alcohol is one aspect being alluded to here. While Hunt addresses no particular comments to this phenomenon, aside from expressing the opinion that the liquor sales restrictions should be continued (ibid: 26), scrutiny of the island administration's accounts for the year 1912-13, as presented in Hunt's Report (20-21), reveals that 8 per cent of the administration's total annual expenditure (which included substantial costs such as salaries, the school, post services etc.) was expended on alcohol purchases for sales through the administration bond store.

The schoolmaster supervising the school concert so favourably reviewed by Hunt was Gustav Quintal who wrote a number of hymns, one of which, *Oakleigh*[4], continues to be performed to the present. *Oakleigh* comprises a fervent plea for divine blessing over four verses with particularly vivid imagery in the second verse:

Wash us in thy crimson tide
Cleanse us Lord from sin
Let thy blood to us applied
Make and keep us pure within

In this regard, the hymn's sentiments clearly align with the "devout religious observances" of the older community rather than the more recent laxity that Hunt perceived. While the hymn is rarely sung in anything but formal worship contexts, it is often considered as one of the 'fringe' locally associated hymns (discussed in detail in Chapter 9).

Quintal retired in 1914[5] but the school evidently continued to maintain standards since in May 1915 visiting (New South Wales) school inspector W.E. Black observed that:

Music is one of the outstanding features of the school. The voices are rich and full and give evidence of careful training. (quoted in Mercer, 1987: 13)

Australian Bertha Murrell, who resided on the island during an extended visit in 1914-16, provided various references to music in her diaries (edited and published in 2001). One of the most intriguing entries details a visit to Benjamin Brancker Nobbs's residence in December 1915 where eighty two year old Susan Fletcher Nobbs (who came to Norfolk Island on the *Moray-shire* as a young child) entertained the guests:

> Her wonderful memory supplied old tales full of interest and her playing on her old beloved autoharp and singing old songs, not a word forgotten, fills one with amazement (2001: 54).

The reference is intriguing not only for its identification of the autoharp but also by reference to "old songs". Given that these were specified as "songs" rather than "hymns", it leaves open the possibility that these were secular songs of a type that went unreported elsewhere.

Other entries in Murrell's diary record her participation in a "singing society" (ibid: 60), of which no further details are recorded, and she notes on two occasions that Kerrin Buffett was an accomplished (but untrained) singer (ibid: 49, 54). Murrell identified Dinah Anabella Christian ('Aunt Amy') as the Anglican organist in 1915 and gave her the backhanded complement that "I have heard much worse playing in Victoria" (2001: 51). Murrell also provided favourable remarks on the musical abilities of the islanders in general, such as her description of a concert at Rawson Hall on August 19th 1915:

> Our popular archdeacon Oakes, in conjunction with two tourists, enter-tained the whole population at a social ... The first part was a very fair concert, most of the performers being Norfolk Islanders, who, without doubt are truly musical, working men and women playing and singing as only people of the better classes do in less favoured lands. Supper came soon after ten, then until midnight there was a dance. (ibid: 47)

As Murrell also noted, public functions were a common occurrence. In 1916 two fund raising dances were held for departing soldiers, on February 12th and 24th. Murrell described the latter as follows:

> Went to the patriotic concert to raise funds for the benefit of N.I. soldiers[6], 56 pounds was subscribed. An impromptu dance finished up the evening, at which the Administrator's party and the cable people danced. The absence of class distinction is a feature of Norfolk Island conditions. Every one seemed happy, all danced, old and young, yet the tears were ever near the surface, not a soul present but had some near and dear one at the war. (ibid: 59)

As Murrell's diary relates, Blanche Rossiter's residence, in the central part of the island, was the principal tourist venue during the 1910s, hosting up to six adults at any one time (usually in summer season). Occasional musical entertainment was supplied by Rossiter's teenage niece, Daisy Rossiter (later Buffett), who was a pianist who often performed ably from memory[7].

Murrell, whose diary displays an exquisite sense of middle class propri-ety, includes a particularly striking account of the visit of a group of twenty Australian parliamentarians in December 1914. Four of them boarded at Rossiter's Guest House and were described by Murrell as "an awful example of the Labour crowd" (ibid: 24). She continued her critique of the group's manners and decorum, describing a New Year's Eve ball held by the Administrator. After commenting on how dark she perceived the skin colour of many of the island attendees to be, she noted that:

> Our parliamentary guests threw themselves into the fun with gusto, a certain Mr. Anstey vividly recalled visions of a Hampstead Heath Bank holiday[8], to watch his antics, dancing with a very dark blooded lady, finally careering round with arms about eachother's necks left nothing to be desired to complete the Coster picture[9]. (ibid: 25)

This description parallels those accounts of island dances and dancing discussed in Chapter 3 and suggests that such occasions retained the liveliness they had exhibited in the mid-late 1800s. Murrell's description of her own send-off from the island also attests to communal liveliness and spontaneity:

> There was speech making by dear old "Aunt Susan", Mrs Fletcher Nobbs ... in her own clever style ... Speeches over and large handsome bouquets duly presented, all joined in a big ring – over 100 people – to sing "Auld Lang Syne". Then the climax of surprises came when four of the tallest and strongest women suddenly hoisted us shoulder high singing "He's a jolly good fellow". "God Save the King" ended the happiest of farewells ever given to departing friends. (ibid: 62)

Musical life on the island appears to have continued in its established pattern after the end of the First World War, with the school, church and dances providing its public mainstay. In 1924, under the headship of Jacob Barnes, the staff and pupils of the school mounted a (full costume) version of Gilbert and Sullivan's *Mikado* (see photographs in Mercer, 1987: 19). A school inspection by H.D. McLell noted that, "a gift for musical expression is inborn in these pupils" (ibid: 20). Music continued to be a key element of the curriculum and extra-curricular facets of the school in the 1920s and 1930s, and was further enhanced by the appointment of Arthur Morris in 1938, who had prior experience as an organ, piano and flute player in Sydney, and had also conducted choirs and worked in community theatre (ibid: 25).

In 1920 Lieutenant General John Parnell, who had previously been commandant of the Australian military college at Duntroon, was appointed as administrator. Parnell encouraged the formation of a local brass band for civic-ceremonial purposes that appears to have begun rehearsing and performing in 1921. Given the cost of acquiring a set of brass instruments, it is likely that Parnell was either responsible for equipping the band or else involved in securing funding from other sources. Information about the longevity and performing career of this ensemble is sketchy, and the principal documentation of the band is photographic (see Figure 5). Parnell departed Norfolk in 1924 and there is no evidence of the brass band performing at ceremonial functions after this time. The brass instruments and the skills acquired by the players were however channeled into social music-making and band members Hugo Quintal, Swain Quintal, Brancker Nobbs, Tiwi Nobbs and Bert Starr went on to become prominent local performers.

Figure 5: Ceremonial brass band (c1921–1922)
(l–r – back row: Hugo Quintal, Swain Quintal, two unknown performers, John Parnell [patron], Brancker Nobbs, unknown performer; middle row: Tiwi Nobbs, John Buffett, Bert Starr, Reginald Buffett, George Nobbs; front row: Oswald Nobbs and Noel Menzies.)

During the 1920s-1930s, social dances, usually held at Rawson Hall, were particularly popular. In the main these were organised as fundraisers for community projects[10] rather than as commercial ventures. In order to attract maximum patronage, these events were usually carefully decorated (an aspect which would attract community discussion and/or press comment in its own right) and were occasionally themed. As Ruby Matthews later recalled, in published reminiscences of her youth on the island:

> *What did we do for fun? There were balls – any excuse for one too! They were held in old Rawson Hall ... We had a fine orchestra for these occasions Hugo Quintal, George Nobbs and Bert Starr each played violins and Swain Quintal at the piano. We didn't pair off. Everyone danced with everyone else. We danced 'The Lancers', 'The Chatish', square dances and the old-time waltz – and others. (NIN, May 1967: 32)*

Many of the island's more adept pianists also found employment performing the music for silent film screenings, which were increasingly popular following their introduction in 1925 until the early 1930s, when they were gradually replaced by synch-sound films (ie 'talkies').

For much of the period prior to World War Two, attendance at (usually) weekend night entertainments held at venues such as Rawson Hall were all the more special – and 'eventful' – for those patrons residing outside of the immediate Burnt Pine area due to the poor state of roads, total absence of street lights, highly limited ownership of motor vehicles and lack of any form of public transport. Up until the 1940s, horses were still a regular form of transport for patrons (either individually ridden or pulling a small cart with several passengers)[11].

From the early 1900s through to the early 1950s, members of the Bailey family provided the core of one of the island's most popular musical ensembles. Founded by George Bailey, who died in 1936, and maintained (in various combinations) by Charles Bailey (cello), Charlotte Bailey (piano), Mariah Bailey (piano) and Thomas Bailey (violin), the group performed at public dances and at soirees at family houses. Bernie Christian Bailey has described the latter in the following terms:

> *The musical evenings they would play at were quite common occurrences. The family and friends would get together, quite often have supper, and enjoy the music. People would listen and appreciate them, not so formally, like a proper chamber music concert in a hall, but they would pay attention. Someone might also get up and sing later on, Gilbert [Bailey – brother of the band members] was a regular singer, he'd sing popular songs sometimes ... to round things off.* (interview 1999)

While there are few period accounts of the ensemble's repertoire, a collection of Bailey family music remains in the possession of Bernie Christian-Bailey, much of it purchase-dated and/or with its owner's name written on the front cover. Assuming that much of the material was actually played by the ensemble (and the tattered, well-finger state of much of it suggests so), the ensemble appears to have had a wide repertoire, ranging from classical material (such as Chopin *Études*), light classical pieces (by composers such as Sousa and Eric Coates) through to exotic mood music (including Archibald Joyce's *Vision of Salome* [1911]), popular songs (such as *The Policeman's holiday* [1911] and *Boys of the Dardenelles* [1915]) and British and Irish regional songs (including the albums *Most Popular Irish Songs* [1905] and *The Family Songbook* [1898]). Dance tunes are also prominent in the collection and while many of these are waltzes, livelier material is also present in the form of albums such as *Kerr's Collection of Reels and Strathspeys, Highland Scottisches, Country Dances, Jigs, Hornpipes, Flirtations &c.* (c1910). The presence of the latter offers a point of continuance of those dances previously described as performed to violin accompaniment on Pitcairn Island in the 1850s and on Norfolk Island in the 1860s.

II. The 1930s

The 1930s saw a number of innovations to Norfolk Island culture. These included the commencement of regular programmes of synch-sound films, the return of a newspaper, in the form of the *Norfolk Island Times* and the *Norfolk Island Weekly Times*, and the formalisation of various drama and concert initiatives through organisations such as the Music and Drama Society. The newspapers published a series of (often highly detailed) accounts of concert repertoires and performers that give a clear picture of the nature of entertainment on offer during the decade.

One strand of public performance on the island concentrated on the presentation of classical, light classical and parlour songs for the edification of 'polite' island society. This aspect of the island's music culture was boosted by the extended visit of concert pianist Frederick Hyde and vocalist Edith Allen-Taylor in 1933. The duo performed two piano and vocal recitals and organised a fundraising concert for an X-Ray facility in June 1933 that included various local performers. *NIT* provided a detailed report of the event:

> The X-Ray Concert on Thursday evening was a most successful affair, both from the point of view of the entertainment provided and of the financial results. Mr Hyde and Mme. Taylor are to be complimented on the organisation of an excellent programme which went without a hitch, one item following on another with no delays. The opening duet, Liszt's Rhapsody No. 2 (Daisy Rossiter and F.J. Hyde) was received with great enthusiasm, and the encore "Three Fours" (Coleridge-Taylor) was delightful.
>
> A new singer with a very true voice was introduced in Rawson Hall in Nellie White whose numbers "At Dawning" and "Love's Garden of Roses" were very popular. The pianoforte solo Polka by Smetana and the encore Valse Sibelius by F.J. Hyde were both brilliantly executed, though the upright piano did not give the soloists the same opportunities as the grand used at the previous concert. An old favourite was welcomed again in H.E. Quintal, whose song "I am Fate" (Hamblen) and encore "When I go Home" received rounds of applause.
>
> Edith Allen-Taylor sung two delightful numbers, "The Bitterness of Love", (Dunn) and "Birthday Song" (MacFadgen) with a popular encore, "Five Little Picanninnies". Daisy Rossiter's Solo study (Chopin) showed the popular artiste's virtuosity to an enthusiastic audience, and the encore number was equally admired. Edith Allen-Taylor and F.J. Hyde sang two beautiful duets, "Awake" (Pellissier) and "Crucifix" (Faure), and the popular and amusing "Singing Lesson" was given as an encore.

Following the performance of a short play entitled 'The Dear Departed':

> The entertainment concluded with the musical items from Nellie White, "Little Brown Owl", perhaps her best number, and encore "I Love the Moon"; H.E. Quintal "Have you News of My Boy Jack", a powerful number with encore "My Wishes for You"; Daisy Rossiter and F.J. Hyde duet "Automne" (Chaminade) and "Irish Tune" (Markham Lee). Edith Allen-Taylor gave two songs, "The Little Silver Ring" (Chaminade) and "Who is Sylvia" (Schubert), a particularly delightful performance, with "Cuckoo Clock" as an encore. Mr. Hyde had a busy evening at the piano providing a very important part of the programme, i.e. the accompaniments. Miss Daisy Rossiter is also to be congratulated on her accompaniments as well as her solo work. (NIT 28.6.33: 3-4[12])

Community singing also continued to be popular and occasional concerts mixed on-stage entertainment with audience participation items. A concert at the newly constructed Methodist Hall in February 1934, for instance, featured instrumental quartet and solo pieces performed by members of the Bailey family and others, vocal items by Wesley Christian, Carty Christian and Raymond Nobbs "interspersed with community singing items when lusty voices nearly raised the roof". (NIT 21.2.34: 6)

Other regular and occasional performers provided lighter and more musically varied items for public performances, as can be ascertained from the following account of a variety concert for the Girl Guides and Rangers held at Rawson Hall in June 1935 (which produced a return of thirteen pounds seven and sixpence for the troupes – a not inconsiderable sum for the time):

After the arrival of the official guests and the playing of the National Anthem an excellent programme began with the signalling of the word "Welcome". A chorus "Coming to the Orchard" by Guides and Rangers followed; Penelope Christian amused with her recitation "Anthony Washes"; and the "Floral march" by Guides and Rangers carrying garlands of poinsettias showed that much hard work had been put into the several intricate movements. Mr. Charles Bailey filled a gap in the programme with a pleasing cello solo and later on his rendering of "Home Sweet Home" received well earned applause. Vi Christian gave a pianoforte solo of considerable merit and Madeline Grande proved popular with her recitation "The Careful Messenger". A chorus "A Song Down Every Roadway" followed and the Gymnastic display of the guides showed how splendidly fit they all were, doing great credit to the Instructor Mr. Ken Whisker. Phil Stevenson and Vi Christian in a Dutch Song and Dance Number were excellent, and little Enid Quintal and Marie Bailey were quite charming in their duet "No John, No". The final item of the first half of the programme caused the heartiest laughter of the evening, Gwen Bailey, Audrey Robinson, Vi Christian, Dora Buffett, Phil Stephenson, Mary Gordon and Betty Frogley and Olga Robinson in eccentric male and female attire worn back to front, and with masks on the backs of their heads executed the various movements of the Quadrille to the delight and vast amusement of the audience, – altogether a really funny and clever burlesque. Ruth Edwards recited "Naughty Paul" very pleasingly and in a one act play "Amelia's Mistake" Gwen Bailey, Phil and Ruth Stevenson and Dora Buffett showed versatility. The Guides and Rangers contributed "Song of the Guides" and the "Canoe Song" led by Vi Christian, and Penelope Christian, Madeline Grande, Audrey Robinson, May Adams, Fay Bataille, Marie Bailey and Enid Quintal, with actions in the costumes of Maori Maidens were delightful. The display by Charlie Nobbs on the horizontal and parallel bars was brilliant and the ease with which he completed several very difficult positions proved his perfect fitness and an ability which many of us envied. The final item was the signalling of the words "The End" which concluded an excellent and most creditable concert. Miss Joan Bailey proving a most able accompanist to the various vocal items. (NIT, July 1935: 2)

The inclusion of a Maori-costumed 'Canoe song' item is not as radical a departure from standard repertoire as might first be perceived[13]. Maori and Maori themed songs – many of which were written by non-Maori composers – were popular on both sides of the Tasman in the 1920s and 1930s. One strong candidate for the 'Canoe song' referred to is a composition by London-based New Zealand stage composer Wainright Morgan, written in the early 1930s and known as *See the vessel glide (the Maori canoe song)* which was popular in Australia and New Zealand (and which remains in the repertoire of New Zealand bagpipe bands through to the present).

Along with the presence of a Maori item in the abovementioned variety show, during the 1930s a number of other new musical forms that had established themselves in Australia and New Zealand also began to make inroads into the island's cultural life.

III. Modern Musical Styles and Performances

During the 1930s published advertisements and reviews began to make a clear distinction between the established style of island dances and music and newer styles. The former were usually referred to as 'old time' while the latter came to be referred to as 'jazz'[14]. In this usage, the term 'jazz' was an umbrella one for a range of styles from jazz itself through to various forms of brisk tempo dance music. 'Jazz' ensembles on the island were often somewhat ad hoc and featured unusual instrumental line-ups. An ensemble performing "brightly rendered" dance music at the July 1932 Planters' Association Social and Dance comprised Marcia Nobbs (piano), Harry Horner (saxophone), Adrian Nobbs (trombone), Bert Starr (violin) and G. Lee and G. Dunkley (mandolins) (NIWN 29.7.32: 6). The arrival of jazz music and associated styles of lively dancing did not go uncontested though.

Harvey Brooke ('Brookey') Christian was one of the best-regarded dance pianists of the decade. He learnt piano as a child on the island and went on to work as a silent film accompanist in New Zealand before returning to live on Norfolk Island in the early 1930s. He played at dances frequented by young and old at venues such as Rawson Hall but made his dislike of 'hot' styles of music and dancing evident. If he observed things to be getting too lively on the dance floor he would stop his performance and instruct his audience to behave with more restraint, making statements such as "no more of that jumpy-jumpy" (Gilbert Christian, interview 1999). Eileen Snell has also recalled that in later decades "he'd get up and take a broom and waltz round the stage with it" to show the dancers what they should be doing (interview 1999). He continued playing at dances until the 1950s and remained a strong advocate of 'old time' styles and social niceties.

The label 'jazz' – and various local interpretations of it – became a particular selling point for concerts in the early 1930s, targeting a more youthful and hedonistic audience than standard old time dances. One event held in November 1932 advertised itself as a "Jazz Carnival!" which it specified as a "real night of gaiety and a real dinkie die jazz orchestra – Full jazz programme – by special request" (NIWN 21.10.32: 9). A line at the bottom of the ad stated that, "people patronising this are specially requested to appear in Carnival or Jazz Caps"(ibid). The mysterious reference to specialist headgear was clarified in an ad in the subsequent edition of the newspaper (28.10.32: 5) showing the "jazz caps" to be a tall conical hat with a pom-pom on the top. The line up for the event comprised Marcia Nobbs (piano), Harry Horner (saxophone), Bert Starr (violin), F. Nobbs (saxophone), J. Rennie (drums) and A. Greenwood (banjo).

It seems likely that the performers combined traditional performance practices with self-conscious musical and sartorial eccentricisms to create their 'jazz' feel in a similar manner to that of early Australian jazz performers (see Whiteoak, 1999). In particular, the "jazz carnival" referred to above appears to draw on both the island's tradition of fancy dress dances and novelty performances and such musical eccentricisms as that provided in June 1932 as part of a performance of the pantomime 'Sing a Song of Sixpence' at Rawson Hall, which included at least one member of the "dinkie die jazz orchestra". A review of the concert noted that:

> The histrionic ability of the performers was given ample scope in the "Village Concert Hall Scene"; "Our Own Silver Tuber Band" produced a marvellous harmony of discord, and Mr Peachblossom's (Harry Horner) saxophone being set a shart or three high added very effectively to the ingenious variations. Mrs. Dolly Long, on the piano, did her very best on behalf of the local piano-tuner, and Mr. George Lee and Mr. Walter Moy with newspapers for music sheets produced "notes" unsuitable for publication. "Our Own Madame Reject" in an operatic number rent the air with super-operatic violence, and her efforts at caricature "brought the house down". (NIWN 24.6.32: 10)

The "jazz carnival" also bore more than a passing resemblance to the entertainment offered at a fundraiser for improvements to Rawson Hall that was held under the patronage of the Administrator, Captain Pinney. This was advertised as "Pageant Dancing – Varied and Beautiful Costumes – A Delightful Extravaganza" and added that "A pleasing variety of Fancy Dances ... will hold you Spellbound" (unattributed period account quoted in NI 5.11.65: 10).

During the late 1930s a number of forms of North American derived popular music began to be performed on the island. One of these, pseudo African-American style 'minstrelsy', was something of a 'throwback' in that it established itself considerably later than its peak of popularity in Australia. In May 1939, NIW published a report of a concert in which "Nigger Minstrels led by Mrs. Carr occupied the second half of the programme with an extensive selection of southern melodies and humorous interludes." (NIW 3.3.39: 3). In June of that year a similar set opened a Church of England organised concert at Rawson Hall – "Negro spirituals, tunefully sung by a glee club" (NIW 9.6.39: 4). A similar, although more elaborate, item occurred at the same venue in a Halloween theme ball in 1940, when the "opening feature of the evening was a Cake-walk by negro minstrels, followed by a tableau of departed spirits" (NIW 12.7.40: 7). 1939 also saw the advent of a local ensemble variously referred to as the "Mouth Organ Band" or "Norfolk Island Harmonica Band", which provided "several songs in harmony and were much appreciated for their mouth organ renditions" at a Girl Guide benefit concert in March (NIW 24.3.39: 3) and also appeared at a dance in aid of the Mount Pitt Queen competition in August. While these two forms enjoyed brief vogues, a third style of music, hillbilly, was of greater significance for the development of popular music on the island in the mid-latter 20th Century.

As discussed in Whiteoak (2002) and Smith (2003), hillbilly music began to achieve prominence in Australia in the early 1930s and was popularised by expatriate New Zealand performer Tex Morton and Australian Smoky Dawson. The first public performances of this style on Norfolk arose out of Boy Scout concert events run by Leclerq Clare. According to Leo McCoy, who played acoustic guitar and harmonica at the events, the first occurred as a cowboy theme entertainment around 1935 that was performed on stage with a campfire effect created with a pile of wood illuminated with a red light. Along with McCoy, the young performers included Jackey Ralph Quintal on accordion, Jimmy Olsson and Harvey Logan on fiddles, Roy Quintal on banjo and Gwyneth Finley on lap steel guitar. The band based their musical style on recordings by 'singing cowboys' such as Gene Autry and Roy Rogers and sang songs such as *Home on the range* (first published in 1873) and, later, *When it's springtime in the Rockies* (1938). Keen to emulate the echoic effects of recorded hillbilly yodeling, McCoy would go and practice down in a valley near his home where the natural echo would enhance his delivery. The boys in the band were taken on a tour of rural areas of New South Wales in 1938, including Tamworth and Lismore, where they performed several informal concerts, making them the first local musicians to perform overseas as a Norfolk Island ensemble. A review of a performance at the Methodist Hall in February 1939 described the "songs and choruses by the Hill Billy Boys" as "tunefully rendered and well received" (*NIW* 3.3.39: 3). The ensemble broke up soon after when members left to join the Australian military or moved to the mainland following the outbreak of War.

In addition to these innovations in musical style, technology began to affect local music culture in the 1930s. In cinema, the arrival of synch-sound film gave audiences exposure to a range of musical styles. Live pianists continued to feature before and during the intervals in film screenings – Cathy Allen, Girlie Christian, Harvey Christian, Marcia Nobbs and Bert Starr were regular and popular performers. The musical content of films also introduced new sounds, ranging from the inventive eccentricisms of the Disney *Silly Symphonies* animation that screened on November 4th 1933 through to the *hapa haole* Hawaiian music that featured in the *Hawaii Calls* movie that screened in December 1939. Pre-recorded music also began to feature as an increasingly common element in domestic entertainment and

Figure 6: Hillbilly band (c1936)
(l–r – standing: Roy Quintal, Leclerq Clare, Harvey Logan, Leo McCoy, Noel Menzies, Jimmy Olsson; seated: Gwyneth Finley and Jackey-Ralph Quintal.)

organised soirees. The Bailey family, for instance, were well known for their extensive and regularly updated phonogram collection. Radio broadcasts from Australia, New Zealand and further away also began to affect music tastes and for special events, such as the 1935 New Year's Eve ball at Anson Bay, music for dancing was provided by an amplifier attached to a radio set (*NIT* 4.1.35: 1). However, as the following chapter relates, perhaps the most significant innovations in Norfolk Islander music and dance were those that were occurring in Sydney amongst the young islanders who were constructing new networks of friendship and affinities with a variety of Pacific cultures.

Notes

1.   Currently lodged in the Alexander Turnbull Library in Wellington, New Zealand.

2.   NB this section of the copy of Hunt's report I managed to access was partially obscured by a stain and there may be minor errors in wordage in my extract here.

3.   While I have not been able to uncover specific documentation supporting the contention, this particular statement, and its wording, seems to suggest that it refers to the dance that would undoubtedly been held by the administration to farewell Hunt.

4.   The title, which does not occur in the hymn lyrics, inscribes a family association, 'Oakleigh' also being the name of the family residence.

5.   The final page of Hunt's report, a "List of Officers at Norfolk Island, and Salaries paid to same" shows Quintal as the only local teacher, alongside two others (Miss Deveril and Miss Mallet) and the headmaster A. Matthews, who were appointed and paid by the New South Wales Government (ibid: 30).

6.   Who, she notes in her diary entry of February 16th, comprised 7 per cent of the population (2001: 59).

7.   An observation made in Murrell's diary December 5th 1915 (2001: 54).

8.   A reference to public holiday festivities on London's Hampstead Heath that were regarded by some members of 'polite society' as intolerably boisterous.

9.   'Coster' is an English term for a street vendor that was often used in the 18th and early 19th centuries as a derogatory term to describe low class individuals or practices.

10.   Such as the island's various churches or bodies such as the Farmers and Grower's Association.

11.   As Bob Tofts has noted, it was commonly felt at the time that many patrons using this form of transport relied on their horse's familiarity with their return track in order to compensate for their rider's tiredness and/or inebriation at the end of an evening (interview 1999)

12.   Paragraph breaks condensed from the original.

13.   Page 223 of Alice Buffett's compendium *Coconuts to Computers* (2004) also includes an (undated) photograph of fifteen young local performers in Maori-style clothing posed in front of a painted 'Marae' style backdrop which Buffett has captioned 'Maori play'. While I have not been able to find out any more information about this presentation, the appearance of several recognisable performers suggests that the photo was taken in the late 1930s (and that Maori themed entertainment thereby continued in vogue during the decade).

14.   Covering both bases, several dances included both forms, the A&H Society's 1933 dance was advertised as featuring; "Jazzing, Lancers, Novelties and Oldtime Dancing" (*NIT* 18.3.33:4) and a benefit concert for the All Saints church roof fund in July 1935 advertised that "Two orchestras will be in attendance" – ie old time and jazz (*NIT* 10.7.35: 4)

Chapter Seven

A DANCE WITH HISTORY
The re-Polynesianisation of Norfolk Island performance culture

During the 1930s Norfolk Island experienced an economic depression that many felt was inadequately understood and mismanaged by the island's Australian administration. One outcome of this disillusionment was a revival of interest in aspects of Polynesian culture and the rebellion of Fletcher Christian and the *Bounty* mutineers against the harsh regime of Captain Bligh. This renewed interest was sparked by two complementary factors: the international re-popularisation of the *Bounty* saga in novels and films and the experiences of islanders displaced to Sydney in the 1930s and 1940s. As the following sections relate, Norfolk Islanders responded to these phenomena in a manner that produced a re-Polynesianisation of aspects of their performance culture – and, indeed, cultural identity – most apparent in the realms of dance and music.

I. The 1930s and the revival of interest in the *Bounty* Mutiny

While memories of Pitcairn Island and the *Bounty* mutiny may have faded as the last members of the Norfolk community who had arrived on the *Morayshire* died, external agencies revived interest in this heritage and, indeed, re-presented it to Norfolk Islanders in a particularly glamourised version. The agencies in question were those of the authors and filmmakers who produced widely circulated representations of the *Bounty* saga in the 1930s. A factor common to these representations is that they valourised Fletcher Christian and the mutineers, demonised Bligh and produced vivid, alluring representations of the welcome Tahitians provided for the *Bounty* crew. While there had been a number of scholarly articles and books published on the *Bounty*, Pitcairn and Norfolk Island since the discovery of the Pitcairn Island community in 1808, the 1930s was significant for re-presenting these areas in the popular media of novels and cinema.

In Australia, the revival of interest in the *Bounty* saga was evident as early as 1916 when Raymond Longford made his (now lost) film *The Mutiny of the Bounty* in collaboration with actress Lottie Lyell. Studio sequences for the film were shot in Sydney and exterior scenes were – according to production notes – shot in New Zealand and on Norfolk Island[1]. Due to the paucity of written records of Norfolk Island culture at the time, there is no indication of what impact the filming of a version of the *Bounty* story may have had locally[2]. However, it would not seem unreasonable to speculate that if locals were aware of the production it would have reminded them of continuing Australian public interest in the historic roots of their community. The second film on the topic, Charles Chauvel's *In the Wake of the Bounty*, shot in 1932 and released in 1933, provided a further reminder.

Chauvel's production combined a dramatic re-enactment of the *Bounty* mutiny with footage of a visit to contemporary Pitcairn. The film further valourised the mutineers by casting the highly photogenic young Tasmanian adventurer Errol Flynn in the role of Fletcher Christian[3]. In addition to its depiction of the mutiny, the film was notable for its representation of the welcome accorded to the *Bounty's* crew in Tahiti. While various accounts had provided written descriptions of the women and dances that had entertained the British sailors, Chauvel staged an elaborate audio-visual representation of the reception provided for the mariners. This was a focal point of the film and one that required some ingenuity to produce. Chauvel's desire to film traditional Tahitian dances of the kind performed for the *Bounty* crew was hindered by the major disruption of Tahitian culture caused by Christian missionaries and the increasingly multi-racial composition of Tahiti during the 19th and early 20th centuries. These factors had been particularly prominent in and around Pape'ete, where the film sequences were shot and, as a result, traditional dances and ceremonies were rarely performed in the area by the early 20th Century[4]. Chauvel responded by securing the assistance of Taro[5], a 'fixer' who had previous worked on Friedrich Murnau's 1931 film *Tabu*, who obtained the services of a group of young women from nearby villages. As Chauvel later recalled:

> *Within a week a sunripe ballet of beautiful girls was at our location on a golden beach in the district of Faa, eight miles from Papeete, being led through primitive dances by little Germaine, Tetia, Momo and Juillet … and for each dance before the camera [the girls] turned out bedecked always in fresh frangipani, as Lulu had special women detailed to keep making new wreaths of the blossom. As each village has a different interpretive dance, it took a number of days to train all the girls to execute the same routine of dancing. (1933: 58)*

One of the significant aspects of Chauvel's account is that the four women identified as instructors – Germaine, Tetia, Momo and Juliet – were well-known dancers at Pape'ete nightspots such as the Blue Lagoon Hotel, where they performed highly mediated versions of traditional Polynesian dances targeted at a clientele that substantially comprised Europeans, North Americans, Australasians and members of the local bourgeoisie. There is an obvious paradox regarding the role of these semi-professional dancers in instructing village girls in the performance of traditional dances. As Moulin Freeman has asserted:

Because of the drunkenness and impropriety of bar-girl dancers in Pape'ete, dance from the 1920s to the 1930s had a stigma that prevented widespread participation, particularly for women. (1998: 875)

This paradox is further intensified by the subsequent perception of these dance scenes as semi-documentary footage of Polynesian traditional culture.

The film's Polynesian sequence is introduced by a look-out sighting the island and a chorus of seamen exultantly taking up the cry of "Tahiti!" that introduces a series of scenes that exemplify the clichéd, western male fantasy of beautiful and pliant Polynesian women that was established in the 1700s and that persists to the present in tourist marketing of Pacific destinations[6]. Following the sailors' cries, the image and sound then take us into the island world with shots of a young Tahitian male hurriedly climbing a tall palm tree to look out at the *Bounty* on the horizon and a young, barely clad female looking out from the shore and calling her companions to join her. A group of young men promptly appear, carrying a canoe above their heads in which is seated a young female. A voice-over sequence, spoken by the character of Michael Byrne, reflecting back on *Bounty* days, declares:

Brown gods, sculptured in a primitive clime carry great canoes to the waterfront. Princess Tikea decked with garlands of frangipani passes on her way to greet the men of the Bounty.

The idyllic island scene represented in these images and voice-over is accompanied by the standard 1930s' (western) musical signifier of Polynesianness – a hapa haole Hawaiian-style instrumental performed on lap-steel guitar and ukulele[7]. The cameo of Polynesian female plus Hawaiian music served as an instant indicator of the sensory pleasures soon to be provided to the mariners. As further canoes are shown paddling out from the shore the music shifts from these lilting sounds to a more frenetic, festive music to illustrate the feverish activity as boats swarm out to greet the ship. Drawing on sounds more appropriate to the modern, mixed cultural context of 1930s' Pape'ete than 18th Century Tahiti[8], the soundtrack features a fast-tempo, klezma-esque instrumental piece[9]. Cutting back to the British tavern setting in which Byrne's reminiscences commence the film, we are then shown Byrne in fond recollection, standing and raising his glass, inviting his companions:

Come let us drink to those Tahiti days, to those girls ... Ha, ha, ho ... What girls, what days, what nights ...

The film then cuts to the landscapes of the inner island and sequences of barely clad young women frolicking and posing in pools and under waterfalls, to the accompaniment of a light-classical string melody (fittingly entitled, '[In] a Little Garden (You Made Paradise)'[10]. These scenes were so blatantly voyeuristic that they attracted controversy in Australia when the chief censor, Creswell O'Reilly, demanded cuts before allowing the film to be premiered in Sydney[11]. The narration confirms the western fantasy by proclaiming:

Mischievous brown girls whose innocent souls were one [indistinct] *laughter, played the hours away in cool mountain pools. Their voices sang to us a song of freedom and we listened, thinking like misers, we could snatch for ourself this most priceless of all man's wishes.*

This statement, and the lingering eroticism of the images, is immediately followed by scenes showing many of the same girls dancing.

This sequence begins with a shift from the gentle music of the landscape scenes to a fast-paced *ote'a* rhythm[12] and a close-up of a male Tahitian drummer playing on a vertically positioned drum with his hands. The image then pulls back to show us a group of around twenty young female dancers entering a clearing, clapped on by *Bounty* sailors. After a cut that shows us the drummer accompanied by three other males playing small wooden slit-gongs, the women are shown arranged in three rows performing a series of Polynesian dance moves, more or less in synch with each other[13]. Through a slightly puzzling cut, the same dancers are then shown dancing in a single line along the seashore, as the rhythm continues. A brief sequence of some young boys imitating the girls' routine in the clearing follows, and they scatter as a *Bounty* sailor (played by Chauvel's local 'fixer' Taro) enters the frame carrying a female dancer. Letting her down, they then commence dancing as the rhythm continues, performing a couple dance traditionally known as the *'ori tahiti* but now often referred to as the *tamure*[14]. The specific *tamure* danced in the film utilises the potential of the form to:

exhibit flirtatious interplay [where] *dancers move as close as possible without touching, the man adding small, forward pelvic thrusts, the woman adding large, sideways swipes of the hips, aimed at her partner's pelvis, and urging his gaze toward her hips.* (Moulin-Freeman, 1998: 874)

As further couples join in the dance, and some exit the frame together, the sequence fades out. In addition to its function as part of the spectacle of Tahitian cultural life, this dance scene serves to provide an allusion to the amorous activities that Chauvel chose not to depict on screen (but referred to in print[15]). Following this sequence the image then cuts to the caption:

After months of enchantment the order to leave Tahiti sorely rent the heart of sailor and dusky maid.

superimposed over a dark, night-time shot of a solo Tahitian female dancing next to a fire to the accompaniment of a sad Polynesian song signaling a farewell to the island. After close-ups of a notice posted by Bligh that no women were to be allowed on ship, the Polynesian sequence ends with the sad farewells of couples and women waving from the shore as the *Bounty* departs.

I discuss these scenes in some detail since the representations of female physique and dance (along with supporting landscape shots) provide the *totality* of the film's representation of Tahiti (with nary a breadfruit in sight or dialogue), distilling the *Bounty* crew's Tahitian sojourn to focus on the energetic innocence of (young) Tahitians and the erotic inter-racial desire and contact between *Bounty* sailors and Tahitian women.

Following its release, the film was screened around Australia before being withdrawn from distribution after the Hollywood studio MGM bought out Chauvel's rights in order to clear the path for their own version of the story – *The Mutiny on the Bounty* (1935). While Chauvel's film was screened on Norfolk Island in the mid-1930s[16], the impact of Chauvel's representations upon Norfolk Islander perceptions of their ancestry and cultural identity appears to have been produced by a composite phenomenon. This comprised the impact of the film on those Norfolk Islanders (on Norfolk Island, in Sydney or elsewhere[17]) who had seen it in person, the information passed on to others about the film (both directly and via press reports) and the publication of Chauvel's associated book *In the wake of "The Bounty"* (1933). Chauvel's book included his own account of the mutiny, his comments on the filming of the location sequences on Tahiti and Pitcairn and a number of production stills, several of which comprised images of individual Tahitian dancers and dance sequences.

Chauvel's book leant further weight to assessments of the allure of Tahitian women, dance and lifestyle as a key factor in precipitating the mutiny. Indeed, in passages such as the following, he provides as intense summaries of the mythic-exotic appeal of Polynesia as any writer on the topic:

> *It is not difficult to conceive the state of Tahiti in the days when the young* Bounty *sailors arrived there, to fall under the spell of its tropic temptings. The Tahitians worshipped at the shrine of Venus, believing and practicing from an early age the most unrestrained excesses. Nature has been over-indulgent in the South Seas ... Through long centuries of easy living they became inveterate idlers ...*

> *With sweet scents from exotic flowers they perfumed their bodies and, dancing abandonedly to the beat of drums and to the tune of flutes, they interpreted the joys of warm nights and indulgent nature.* (1933: 30-31)

By linking the Tahiti scenes directly with the quasi-documentary representation of everyday life and characters on Pitcairn (in both the book and film), Chauvel underlined the manner in which the contact between British sailors and Tahitian women engendered the Pitcairn community. The sequences of Pitcairn life were also significant for Norfolk Islanders by providing them with the first opportunity to glimpse the faces, culture and island life style of their sister community (at a time when contact between the two communities was negligible[18]).

While in Tahiti in 1932, Chauvel met up with the US writer-adventurers Charles Nordhoff and James Norman Hall, who went on to be responsible for raising the international profile of the *Bounty* saga and its aftermath through the publication of their fictionalised trilogy *The Mutiny on the Bounty* (1932), *Men against the Sea* (1933) and *Pitcairn's Island* (1934). Nordhoff and Hall had met in the US Air Service during World War One and shared interests in writing and travel. Following the publication of their account of wartime adventures, *The Lafayette Flying Corps* (1920), the US magazine *Harpers* engaged them to write a series of travel stories. In order to produce these, they relocated to Tahiti, where they wrote their first book on a Pacific topic, a romantic travelogue entitled *Faery Lands of the South*

Seas (1921). Remaining in Tahiti, Nordhoff married a Tahitian, Pepe Teara, and continued to write about the region in books such as *The Pearl Lagoon* (1924). At Hall's suggestion, the duo researched and wrote *The Mutiny on the Bounty* and published it in 1932[19].

The book comprises a narrative of the *Bounty* mutiny told from the point of view of an invented character, Roger Byam, drawing on accounts provided by Bligh and evidence submitted to the court martial of the mutineers. Unlike Chauvel's film, Nordhoff and Hall's novel avoids any reference to the festivities that greeted the *Bounty* crew upon their arrival on Tahiti. It confines its references to Tahitian dance and the allure of female Tahitian dancers to a brief section when the Byam character is the only member of the *Bounty* crew who attends a gathering at Tetiaroa. Drawing on Bligh's accounts of the events he witnessed, Byam contrasts two particular dances. The first is a humorous dance, performed by barely clad women, that is described as "so unbelievably wanton that no words could convey the least idea of it" (108) that raises "a hurricane" of laughter amongst its audience. The second is one identified as a "couple-dance" called the *hura*, that is described as being performed by "upper class" women "of the most exquisite loveliness", dressed in "flowing draperies of snow-white cloth" and headdresses (109). These descriptions polarise the dancing styles on offer into a low-class explicit, shocking comedic form as opposed to a refined, demure and stately upper-class one.

The Mutiny on the Bounty became a runaway success for its publishers and Australian historian Greg Dening has estimated that it was read by twenty-five million people in the three years following its publication (1992: 355). The book's popularity stimulated an interest in the *Bounty* mutiny and subsequent history of Pitcairn and Norfolk Island that was taken up by amateur and professional historians (resulting in a stream of further publications that has continued unabated to the present). Notable public enthusiasts for the *Bounty* history in Australia included the Rev W.H. McFarlane, who gave public lectures in various parts of Australia in the period 1933-36[20] and historian Harold Rabone[21]. In December 1934, shortly after the first screening of Chauvel's film, Rabone visited Norfolk Island to give a public lecture on the topic.

The response to Rabone's presentation was notable. The attendance at his first lecture, on Tuesday December 11th, was large ("in spite of bad weather", *NIT* 12.12.34: 1) and a second presentation was held on Thursday 13th. Islanders not only consumed the historical information on offer, they also participated in its presentation and turned the event into an affirmation of Pitcairn-Norfolk ancestry and historical continuance. As the (unattributed) lead report in the *Norfolk Island Times* stated (of the first presentation):

> The lecture was interspersed with vocal and instrumental items supplied by artistes of Pitcairn descent. Miss Rossiter supplied the accompaniments for these items and also for the community singing which was a pleasant feature of the evening. Mr Hugo Quintal gave an item to his own accompaniment which was very greatly appreciated. The old Pitcairn Hymn "The Ship of Fame" was sung with great enthusiasm by the audience, the solo being supplied by Mr. Carty Christian. (ibid)

Both the event and account are significant for their assertion of Pitcairn-Norfolk identity, following a lengthy period when there had been minimal emphasis on this aspect of Norfolk Islander society (at least in published accounts of island life and subsequent historical studies). While the unspecified "items" referred to above were likely to have been ones drawn from the standard British-Australian repertoire discussed in the preceding chapter, the *Ship of Fame* (and other "Pitcairn Hymns" advertised in handbills for the evening) appear to have served as anthems for Norfolk-Pitcairn identity and (in this time and context, at least) indicate the readiness of Norfolk Islanders to evoke their histories and heritage in public. (See Chapter 9 for further discussion of the hymns.)

The popularity of Nordhoff and Hall's book led Hollywood film director Frank Lloyd to buy the rights for the novel and its two sequels[22]. Lloyd's film, produced for MGM Studios, starred US actors Charles Laughton as Bligh, Clark Gable as Christian and Hawaiian actress Margaret Mamo Clark as Christian's Tahitian consort Mauatua[23], was shot in Tahiti and California and released in 1935. Neither the comedic "wanton" dancing nor the stately *hura* referred to in Nordhoff and Hall's novel are represented in Lloyd's film. Instead, dance is used in a metaphoric, allusive manner in a key scene, Christian's first passionate encounter with Mauatua. This sequence occurs in the film at the end of an afternoon that Christian has spent in Mauatua's company, swimming with her, the (fictional) Byam and his Polynesian female friend. Summonsed back to the ship by Bligh, Christian glimpses a group of Tahitian men and women performing a formation dance, the men dancing vigorously while the women perform more restrained movements. Tearing himself away from this scene to return to the *Bounty*, he turns and sees Mauatua. Their eyes lock, they move together, embrace and kiss. The film then cuts to a sunset image of women performing a seated dance to a fast rhythm and ensemble vocals passage. This, in turn, cuts to a nighttime shot of Mauatua looking into Christian's eyes, before lying down on the ground, inviting him to her. The film then cuts to a frenetic dance, performed to throbbing drums with dancers brandishing flaming torches. A further cut then reintroduces us to the lovers, now in repose, eyes blissfully locked as a 'heavenly' choir soars on the soundtrack. The use of different dance tempos to allude to stages of passionate congress is hardly subtle but serves to cross associate the two activities in a manner complementary to the linkages established in Chauvel's film.

The film won critical acclaim and an Academy Award for Herbert Stothart's score but little appears to have been written about the location recorded Tahitian music that appears in the scene discussed above. The film's soundtrack album refers to the sequence as "Native Festival Music" and identifies its components as "Te Manu Pukurua/Torea/Tahitian drums" but the precise source of the music used in these scenes remains unclear.

Lloyd's *Mutiny on the Bounty* was first screened in Norfolk Island in December 1938. Norfolk Island film historian and archivist Roy Smith has recalled that it attracted considerable interest (interview, June 1999) and this claim is supported by the correspondence on the film published in the

NIW (30.12.38: 5) following its first screening on December 24th. The film, subsequently re-screened on the 31st, was described in the paper as:

> the most famous picture which has ever been brought to Norfolk Island, and which, of course is of particular interest to the people here. (ibid)

and, in the preceding week, had been introduced as a "wonderful opportunity ... afforded the residents of Norfolk Island to decide for themselves" (ie decide whether Bligh or Christian was the villain of the piece) (*NIW* 23.12.38: 4).

Given the publicly modest nature of Norfolk Islanders during this period, the film (like Chauvel's earlier version) represented a Pacific culture very different from that of Norfolk Island. The representations of Tahitian dancers and eroticism as the defining aspect of the *Bounty* crew's contact with Tahiti (which engendered the Norfolk community), in particular, must have drawn attention to the difference in socio-cultural mores between the two cultures[24]. All the more so perhaps, since the film's Norfolk Island premiere occurred on Christmas Eve and the evening concluded with pianist Harvey Christian accompanying audience carol singing (with the words projected on the screen). While there appears to have been no discernible impact on standards of public dress and/or performance culture on Norfolk in the 1930s, a major development, convergent with the images and associations of the *Bounty* texts described above, was taking place amongst the Norfolk Island community who resided in and/or passed through the Australian city of Sydney in the 1930s and 1940s.

II. Norfolk Islanders in Sydney

During the economic depression on Norfolk Island in the early-mid 1930s several Norfolk Islanders of Pitcairn descent, and a number of more recent settlers, travelled to Australia in search of better prospects. Many of these relocated to Sydney. From a peak of 1,231 in 1933[25], the population of Norfolk Island declined throughout the decade. This population drift intensified in the late 1930s with the outbreak of World War Two. With the rise in tension in the Pacific immediately prior to Japan's entry into the War a number of families relocated to Australia (or New Zealand) en masse. Further depletion arose when the main body of Norfolk Islanders who enlisted in the Australian military departed between 1941-42. Norfolk Island author Gil Hitch has calculated that these factors resulted in the island's population dropping to around 700 by September 1942 (1992: 35).

Many of the Norfolk Islanders who relocated to Sydney in the mid-late-1930s were welcomed and assisted by earlier migrants, such as the Menzies and McCann families, who resided in the inner city. In addition to this informal support group, a Norfolk Island Friendship Club was established and met at various venues in the late 1930s. Gil Evans has characterised it as:

> a place for Norfolk Islanders to meet and talk ... and there were occasional dances where a Sydney dance band would play. (interview, May 1999)

Around 1940 the Norfolk Island Friendship Club declined in importance as a number of Norfolk Islanders began to regularly frequent The Polynesian Club[26]. As subsequent sections of this chapter discuss, the 'Poly Club' (as it became known) provided a highly significant input into the history of Norfolk Islander music and dance culture. The Polynesian Club of Sydney was founded in late 1935 and, like the Norfolk Island Friendship Club, grew out of an informal, family activity. As founder member Leonard Moran recounted:

> My parents home [in the suburb of Woollhara] had been a meeting place for Polynesian people for more than 25 years. When it was no longer available, I determined to found the Club, so that men and women of Polynesian blood would have a meeting house in Sydney where they would always be welcome and at home. (1942: 31)

Aided by Maori chieftainess Waikanga Tipene[27] and Pacific enthusiast Eric Ramsden, the Club first met in a flat in Potts Point and went on to organise a series of meetings at other venues before securing a regular premises on George Street. Differences of opinion about the purpose and direction of the Club led Ramsden to leave and concentrate his energies into the Pacific Islands Society[28]. As an unattributed article in *PIM* succinctly described:

> If you want to see pretty girls and colourful dances and haunting songs of Polynesia, you may go to the Polynesian Club. If you want to meet the solid, somewhat older people who are the backbone of Pacific administration, culture and commerce, you will find them in the Pacific Islands Society. (1942: 14)

Membership of the Polynesian Club brought Norfolk Islanders in contact with individuals from various other Pacific cultures. A mainstay of the club's activities was entertainment by members and visitors, who would sing, play instruments and perform dances. Older members of the Club were willing to help new members acquire performing skills and learn their repertoire. Despite their lack of prior experience with the form, a number of young Norfolk Islander women quickly established a reputation as skilled and charismatic dancers.

Australian journalist Judith Tudor described a typical evening at the Polynesian Club in the following terms:

> The Polynesian Club met [in] an unpretentious clubroom, a piano, a violin, half a dozen ukuleles and guitars plus the abundant personalities of its members, infused a spiritual warmth into the atmosphere ... At the close of the evening the lady members of the club entertained the guests with Polynesian dances; a tiny lass, Hinemona Mahomet, with all the charms of her Polynesian forebears, gave a special kopikopi and Mrs Goodman (formerly of Tahiti) a hula which soon had half the men of the company out there on the floor accompanying her. (1943: 30)

A series of (irregularly published) reports of Polynesian Club functions in *PIM* provide insights into the specific dances learnt and performed by Norfolk Islander women. The October 1941 issue of *PIM*, for instance, reported that a reception had been held at the Polynesian Club for Prince Jione Gu, youngest son of Queen Salote of Tonga, where:

Lady members entertained the gathering with Polynesian dances, including the "Ma'ulu'ulu" and "Lakalaka", popular in Tonga. Miss Ivy Buffett, of Norfolk Island, performed the "Tauoluga[29]" and Chieftainess Waikanga Tipene danced the "hula ku'i Hawaii". Maori members performed several new forms of "Haka taporahi". (27)

In 1941 members of the Polynesian Club began performing open-air concerts in Sydney's Martin Place, war-related fundraisers (for organisations such as the Red Cross) and other entertainments for Australian and visiting overseas soldiers. Norfolk Islanders Ivy Buffett and Cora Young were regular and enthusiastic dancers in such events and were also joined on occasion by Aldin Buffett, Dora Buffett, Barbara Christian, Hagar Christian, Sheba Menghetti, Helen Quintal, Vina Quintal, John Young and Verle Young. Together with this pool of nine identified public performers, occasional items in *PIM* report that sixteen other identified Norfolk Islanders[30] attended the Club during the late 1930s-early 1940s. Given the highly infrequent listing of specific names, it can be safely assumed that the number of Norfolk visitors was considerably higher[31].

Figure 7 records the line-up for a public performance held in aid of Sydney University's Vice Chancellor's War Fund, held at the University Union Hall in July 1941. The Polynesian Club's dancers appear to have had two principal costumes, the traditional tapa cloth-derived patterns and garment shapes (as shown in the photo) and the conventional grass skirt

Figure 7: Polynesian Club dancers performing at Sydney University (l–r – back row: Katarina Darley, Estelle Darley, Cora Young; middle row: Koni Darley, Dora Buffett, Noni Hawkins; front row: Nua Binskin, Ivy Buffett, Hane Edwards)

and abbreviated top associated with Hawaiian-style hula dancing in the 1930s-1940s. The costume displayed in the photograph reflects both the demure nature of a public performance at the university and the style of dance being presented, identified in the original *PIM* photo-caption as "an Ellice Islands posture dance 'fa'atele'" (July, 1941: 50).

A description of a performance later in the same year provides a list of dances that emphasise the diverse repertoire:

> *a wide variety of Polynesian dances, done in authentic costumes, was presented. A programme of no less than 20 items included many Maori songs and dances, Tahitian songs, posture dances of Samoa... posture dances of Wallis Island, Futuna and Funafuti; and various farewell songs of Polynesia. (PIM, December 1941: 2)*

Together with the dances described above, the public performance at Sydney University also included "the kava ceremony of Tonga" (ibid). Kava ceremonies were a specialty of the Polynesian Club. An article in *PIM* in 1936 described the Club's first formal kava ceremony, arranged for the visiting Tongan Prince Tugi, in the following terms:

> *For the first time in the history of Sydney, the ancient Polynesian ceremony of the making and presentation of kava was performed.*[32] (June, 1936: 10)

For Norfolk Islanders, kava drinking was an entirely new practice. What is perhaps surprising is the manner in which Norfolk Islanders were regularly identified in press reports as those participating in the kava ceremony. A photograph published in *PIM* in 1941, for instance (under the caption 'Island Polynesians'), shows Cora Young, Helen Quintal and (Tongan) Truda Cameron preparing a bowl of kava for circulation amongst those present (April, 1945: 9). Combined with the dancers' (social and public) performances of Polynesian dances, their dress in traditional Polynesian clothes and the participation of a variety of Norfolk Islanders in the Polynesian Club's musical, dance and social activities and interchanges; their participation in kava drinking ceremonies indicates a degree of (willing) re-Polynesianisation on the part of a number of Norfolk Island attendees.

One notable contact facilitated by the Polynesian Club involved a reversal of roles. In the mid-1930s the two *Bounty* films (described in Section I above) asserted the impact and erotic allure of Tahitian women, and particularly their dancing, as a fundamental cause of the *Bounty* mutiny and, with that, the founding of the Pitcairn and, later, Norfolk Island communities. Given this, the acquisition of Polynesian dancing skills by Norfolk Islander women was not simply a fashion, it was a practice that acknowledged and reaffirmed what might be termed a central 'foundation myth' of Pitcairn/Norfolk identity (later celebrated in Susan Pedel's song *Dar Bounty shake* – discussed in Chapter 11). In addition to performing for appreciative audiences of Australian civilians and service personnel, the grace of the Norfolk Islander women's accomplishments was also appreciated by another group. During the War Norfolk Island dancers frequently found themselves performing at the Club for visiting Tahitian sailors. In May 1941, for instance, the Club provided "an open house" for visiting

Tahitian members of the Free French navy. A report in *PIM* noted that, "Club ladies from Norfolk Island, headed by Misses Ivy and Dora Buffett, Cora Young and Vina Quintal helped entertain their distant kinsmen" (June: 41). A May 1944 *PIM* report of a Polynesian Club evening also noted that a visiting Tahitian-Australian serviceman Peter Cowan "was greeted with cheers when he joined in the "ori Tahiti" with Cora Young, of Norfolk Island" (18). With the decline of the Pacific War, Tahitians again visited Sydney, and a Club night in June 1945 was attended by a group of "Tahitian matelots" who later accompanied club members to a concert at a military hospital where they danced together (*PIM*, June: 49).

The activities of the Polynesian Club declined in the mid-late 1940s, with a reduction in the number of Polynesians travelling through and/or re-locating to Sydney. But while key Norfolk Islander performers such as Cora Young departed in the mid-late 1940s (in her case relocating to the USA with her new husband, US lieutenant Albert Kleiner), others continued to reside in Sydney and/or return there on a regular basis, performing Polynesian-style music and dancing at both private and public gatherings.

In 1946-47 two young Norfolk Islanders, Jan and Loretta Christian, attended the Polynesian Club and learnt various dances from club members such as Len Moran. Shortly after, the sisters began dancing at commercial venues. In the early 1950s theatrical agent Harry Willis introduced them to singer-guitarist Doug King[33] and the performers formed a trio that played at inner city nightclubs until 1955, when Jan Christian fell ill and was unable to continue. Unlike the glitzier style of hula popularised in Sydney by Australian dancers such as Maisie 'Latani' Smith and Mardi 'Latani' O'Donnell in the late 1950s[34] (which drew more inspiration from Hollywood representations of hula[35] than any form of traditional Polynesian dance); the Christian Sisters performed a repertoire of seated, standing and posture dances similar to those performed at the Polynesian Club during the War. King, who also went on to accompany Smith and O'Donnell in the 1950s, explained the difference in the dancers' styles in the following terms:

> The Christian Sisters were more on the authentic side of hula. For them I would sing a lot of the songs in Tahitian, The Papio[36] and all those numbers in their [sic] language ... whereas Maisie and the girls were more commercial ... By commercial I mean numbers like The Little Grass Shack, The Hukilau Song, The Little Brown Gal ... ones that people had heard and knew. (quoted in Bambrick and Miller, 1994: 76)

Following the Christian Sisters' retirement from live performance, Norfolk Island dancers ceased to play a prominent role in Sydney's live entertainment culture. However, as Section III discusses, their talents were well suited to the development of post-War tourism on Norfolk Island itself.

III. Re-establishing Polynesian performance traditions on Norfolk Island

The first performances of newly acquired Polynesian dance styles took place on Norfolk Island towards the end of the War, when returning dancers appeared in RNZAF shows in 1944-45 (of the type discussed in Chapter 8). Several former Polynesian Club dancers also gave occasional performances on the island in the late 1940s and early 1950s. In May 1950, for instance, Ivy Buffett performed at a fund-raising dance for the local Girl Guide troupe held at Rawson Hall. A report published in *NINE* reported that:

> *At 10.15 Miss Ivy Buffett danced the Hawaiian Hula and a Samoan dance. Small, supple and graceful, she put on a wonderful performance. She was assisted by Mr J. Young (Master of Ceremonies for the evening) who joined in the Samoan dance with humour and abandon. Four young men sang an accompaniment to Miss Buffett dancing and they were so popular that they were asked to sing the same songs again later in the evening.* (16.5.50: 5)

The connection between the Sydney Polynesian Club and Norfolk Island was further strengthened in 1948 when Cherie Cameron, an able pianist interested in Polynesian dance and performance traditions who had frequented the Club, moved to Norfolk Island to live. During the 1950s Cameron encouraged young Norfolk Island girls to perform Polynesian dancing and assisted with various concerts. The most significant dancer to emerge in the post-War period was Mavis Hitch, who learnt from her mother, Hagar Christian (a frequent performer in Polynesian Club shows) and Cameron while residing in Sydney in the late 1950s/early 1960s. Hitch began dancing at the Kingfisher Hotel in the mid-1960s, performing slow hulas and the fast, hip-shaking tamure. Her popularity at this venue led to further work in public concerts that helped re-promote Polynesian dancing styles among younger Norfolk Islanders. In 1968 she began teaching Polynesian dancing to local women and organising dance ensembles for community functions and special events. In her performances from the 1960s-early 1980s Hitch principally danced to recordings of Polynesian music. While there were a number of individuals on the island who would play ukulele and guitar at social occasions, Hitch recalls that, "we had no one on the island who could play the proper dance rhythms I needed for the dances I did back then" (interview, 1999).

During the 1950s and 1960s a number of Norfolk Islanders visited Sydney (on short, medium or long-term bases) to work, study or simply experience metropolitan life. They frequently associated with Norfolk Islanders already resident in the city, forging a connection to the established community and its social and cultural traditions. One such visitor was George 'Steggles' Le Cren. Le Cren learnt to dance, play the ukulele and sing a number of popular Polynesian and hapa haole Hawaiian songs with fellow Norfolk Islanders while on extended visits in the late 1950s and early-mid 1960s. During his time in Sydney he originated a song that, after undergoing various modifications, became one of the best-known contemporary Norfolk Island compositions. In classic folk song mode, the song has been extended and modified in various stages to the present, well-known version. Le Cren's regular collaborator Aline Snell also contributed to the development of the song[37].

Commonly referred to as *The Coconut song*, Le Cren describes its origin as a reaction against the over-valourisation of Tahiti:

> *There were these two Australians I used to see in Sydney who had been*

there and were always going on about Tahiti. Tahiti this, Tahiti that...
Well, I got so fed up that I wrote the song about Norfolk being just as
good – saying the only thing we haven't got is the coconuts. It caught
on. (interview, 2000)

In its present form, the song's verses list a number of the attributes of
Norfolk Island before returning to a chorus of:

We've gut a palm tree
We've gut a pine
We've gut wahines[38]
And never you mine
We've gut everything Tahiti gut
We only nor gut a coconut[39]

During his return visits to Norfolk Island in the 1960s Le Cren became
one of the few male islanders to regularly appear as a dancer, performing
with Mavis Hitch at venues such as the Kingfisher hotel.

From the late 1960s on
Hitch became the most prominent public face of Norfolk
Polynesian-style dancing (increasingly simply referred to as
'hula' on the island[40]) and also
appeared as a featured performer in one of the most significant performance events of
the post-War era, the Pageant
of Norfolk Island, staged in
1967. The Pageant was an ambitious project that set out to
document the history of Norfolk Island, beginning with the
Bounty's visit to Tahiti, then
cutting to the convict era on
Norfolk Island before representing the Pitcairn settler arrival in 1856, the development
of local whaling and tourism
and a finale that featured a
choral performance, to affirm
the community's strong Christian orientation. An (unattributed) article in the *Norfolk*
Islander (NI) newspaper quoted
John Ryves as identifying the
Pageant as an enterprise that
would attempt to establish certain performance practices as

Figure 8: Le Cren and Hitch dancing c 1970. distinctly local ones:

it was hoped to create, by this presentation, music and dancing which would form part of the culture of the island. This performance could well become an annual event. Scotty [David Neagle] also suggested that this group of choirs, dancers, musicians and supporters would be made available for any of the public functions which are to be held through the year... It is hoped that at least two and possibly three performances would be staged of the Pageant during Bounty week. (NI 27.1.67: 17)

The opening sentence is instructive in that it presents the initiative as proactive and interventionist and indicates the strategic advantages of establishing a group of performers and performance items as "part of the culture of the island". Tourism is explicitly identified as a target for the initiative in a subsequent passage:

The Norfolk Island Tourist Bureau is being approached to see that plenty of publicity is given by agents in Australia and New Zealand prior to the event. Mr Eric Jupp has been asked about the possibility of a television coverage. (ibid)

The Pageant was a collaborative community event with various styles and performers involved. Musical director for the overall presentation was Australian composer/arranger/conductor Eric Jupp (whose work is discussed in Chapter 10). In explicit acknowledgment of the continuing influence of Frank Lloyd's 1935 Hollywood account of the mutiny, Jupp compiled much of the incidental music for the Pageant from Herbert Stothart's original film score[41]. The Pageant included several dance items, including a dramatic ballet choreographed by June Ryves relating the story of Barney Duffy[42] and a Polynesian dance sequence set on Tahiti.

The Tahitian sequence enacted the encounters between Tahitian female dancers and the *Bounty* crew that had been represented in the 1930s' films

Figure 9: Tahitian sequence from The Pageant.
(Rear l–r: George 'Steggles Le Cren, Ricky Quintal, Archie Bigg, Eileen Snell, Marina Sellers; middle l–r: Lorraine Battye, Elaine Buffett, Mori Madalyn and two unidentified dancers; front: Mavis Hitch [as featured dancer].)

In the Wake of The Bounty and *The Mutiny on the Bounty* and was choreographed by Cameron and Ivy Buffett.

Rehearsals for the Tahiti sequence of the Pageant extended into a social activity where various aspects of the preparation were accompanied by impromptu performances and conviviality. As an item in *NI* reported:

> *Cherie is teaching 14 people to make the "leis" for the big Pageant and they all congregated at Karl and Mavis' last Monday evening. They had a great time getting paper cut and sewn and the edges serrated. Ricky, Karl and Steggles took along their guitars and while the girls were being taught the art of "lei" making, the boys played Tahitian songs and everyone sung themselves hoarse. It was a most joyous night, according to Cherie, and there are hundreds of "leis" to be made for sale at the Pageant.* (19.5.67: 6)

While the Pageant only received sparse media coverage off the island, it was significant as a representation of Norfolk Island to its own population, inserting Norfolk Islanders' performance of Polynesian dance and music styles alongside the long-established choral tradition as publicly recognised forms of local performance culture. During the 1970s Polynesian music and dance performance became accepted as a standard element in various public events on the island[43]. As a result, by 1980 the 'Norfolk Living' column in *NIN* could confidently assert that:

> *Tahitian dancing, a historical part of Norfolk Islanders' heritage is very much alive on Norfolk Island. There are over 30 descendants of the Tahitian women on Pitcairn Island who have learned this exuberant art form from Mavis Hitch.* (May 1980: 40)

Reflecting the local interest in Polynesian culture (and the growing affluence of some local entrepreneurs as a result of the rise in the tourist industry) Norfolk Islanders also began to engage with the performance cultures of the immediate region. This manifested itself in various ways. In 1975, for instance, Norfolk Airlines trialed twice weekly flights to Noumea (New Caledonia), promoting their service with reference to Noumea's "colourful Polynesian spectaculars – the famous tamure for one: provocative, sensual and typical of the Pacific"[44]. There was also a revival of interest in Maori culture, stimulated, in no small part, by the number of New Zealanders who had moved to Norfolk Island in the post-War period. This interest was evident in a report on the visit of the Tiritea Maori troupe[45] in 1977 published in *NIN*:

> *Crowds of people flocked to the Airport last week to welcome a Maori troupe arriving from New Zealand. The only time that I have ever seen such a crowd of people and cars at the airport was when Governor-General Kerr and his wife arrived.* (February 1977: 38)

The visit was sponsored by the Norfolk Island Lions Club and the troupe performed two concerts at Rawson Hall. Their show included songs and speeches of welcome in Maori language, short sketches, hakas and action songs, performed by female dancers, that the writer described as "most gracefully presented, the voices of the men and women harmonising beautifully" (ibid). Audience participation was required as "Maori ladies came down into the audience and each of them found a man to take on stage to learn how to Haka" (ibid). Male members of the audience responded positively, most taking off their shirts, with the writer commenting that, "soon there were half-naked men prancing around the stage of Rawson Hall" (ibid) The report concluded with the assessment that:

> In all, the show was beautifully relaxed and informal, really as if we (the audience) shared with them. There were some very moving sequences, but the most moving, I think, for Norfolk Islanders, was the presentation of "Ship of Fame". It made me feel all goosey. It was sung first in English, then in the Maori fashion with actions. A most beautiful finale to the evening and a wonderful gesture on the part of the group. (ibid)

The incorporation of a hymn traditionally regarded as a Norfolk Island anthem into a Polynesian cultural show, in which it was also translated into Maori language, provided a further element of Polynesian identification for its Norfolk Island audience.

In 1980 a local Maori song and dance concert group was formed named Te Wa Kaainga ('Home away from Home'). This comprised (in the main) New Zealanders working on Norfolk on short-term visas and a number of Norfolk residents with New Zealand connections. Founder member Rosie Saint grew up in Auckland in a Cook Islander/New Zealand family, playing guitar and ukulele at school and learning Cook Island and Maori dancing with friends and family. For a short period she went to school in Taneatua in the Bay of Islands (where, she recalls, "you went to school for the music as much as to study!" [interview 2004]). Saint arrived on Norfolk Island in 1966 and soon began playing ukulele at parties and participating in the social music scene. Eunice Vercoe, who grew up in a Maori family in Otorohanga, in which singing and music were prominent, arrived in the late 1960s and also became a regular social performer and co-founder of Te Wa Kaainga.

The troupe performed a mixture of Maori and English language songs and developed a song and dance repertoire that mixed different regional Maori traditions. As member Jeanine Brown has recalled:

> Our dance choreography evolved from our practice meetings, we would put different moves together from different tribes and we'd also have different pronunciations of [Maori] words, so we'd sit and talk and decide how to say things – and those talks were great themselves. (interview 2004)

Brown recalls Te Wa Kaainga as both "a chance for us to get together and share our culture and be creative" and an opportunity to present Maori culture to the Norfolk Island community:

> We wanted to put on good shows with the proper materials – which were difficult to get on Norfolk … we would be painting yards of material with texter because we didn't have the money for the proper material. Once we borrowed piu pius from my son's school in New Zealand, but it was difficult to get all the elements right. (ibid)

The troupe began to dissolve in the early 1980s, when several key performers moved off island. Despite this, there was some continuation of their performance styles in the form of the Polynesian culture nights organised by Te Wa Kaainga co-founder Rob Roparti at the South Pacific Hotel in the mid-1980s, mainly targeted at tourist audiences.

Along with Te Wa Kaainga and Roparti's troupe, hula dancers such as Hitch were establishing a marketable image for Norfolk in the 1970s and 1980s as a relaxed, sensuous 'doorstep Polynesia' for Australian travellers that had a greater degree of authenticity (via the *Bounty*/Pitcairn connection) than other similarly marketed Australian tourist destinations of the period (such as the Whitsunday Islands[46]). The establishment of Polynesian-style dancing (and other crafts practices[47]) as forms of Norfolk Island culture reflected an increasing consciousness and assertion of a Polynesian-Pacific identity for Pitcairn descended Norfolk Islanders and, thence – by association – local culture in general[48].

Such cultural developments provided a complement and 'backdrop' to political assertions of autonomy and difference in this period, most notably with the establishment of the Society of Pitcairn Descendants (SPD)[49]. The organisation was founded in 1977, largely in response to the recommendations of Australian Government's enquiry into the constitutional status of the island. Popularly referred to as 'The Nimmo Report', after its chair, Sir John Nimmo, the 1976 report recommended the removal of Norfolk Island's status as an external territory and its annexation by Australia. While some Norfolk Island residents welcomed the proposal, the SPD responded to this threat by appealing to international bodies for recognition of their distinct status and their right to self-determination. In 1977 prominent Pacific politician Peter Tali Coleman, governor of American Samoa, acknowledged them as "fellow Polynesians" and expressed his support for a referendum on autonomy for the island. In 1978 the United Nations Association of Australia also supported calls for a referendum on the issue. Due, at least in part, to such support, the Australian Government reversed its position in 1979 and passed The Norfolk Island Act, which allowed for the introduction of an elected Norfolk Island Legislative Assembly. The establishment of this body led to an official invitation to (then) Norfolk Island Chief Minister David Buffett to attend a heads of Pacific Island governments meeting at the East-West Center at the University of Hawai'i (sponsored by the South Pacific Commission and South Pacific Forum).

Further recognition of Norfolk Island's distinct culture and society arose in 1982 when Norfolk Island gained admission (in its own right) to the quadrennial Festivals of Pacific Arts. The Festivals were initiated in 1971, with the endorsement of the South Pacific Commission[50], and the first was held in Suva in 1972, with the express aim to:

– *Fight against the disappearance of traditional arts in most Pacific countries*
– *Protect them from being submerged by other cultural influences*
– *Start a process of preservation and development of the various local art forms*
(http://www.festival-pacific-arts.org/hisuk.htm)

As such, the Festivals' aims were in accord with the emerging Pitcairn-descended Norfolk Islander movement and positioned the re-established

Polynesian performing arts traditions (detailed in this chapter) in a strategic role as signs of 'membership' of the Polynesian-Pacific community. The 4th Festival, held in Tahiti in 1985, was attended by a six-person Norfolk Islander delegation including Hitch. Direct exposure to various styles of Polynesian dancing led her to distinguish between Norfolk dancing and Tahitian dancing in the following terms:

> We don't dance like the Tahitians do, which isn't surprising since they grow up seeing people dancing and picking it up themselves, rather than learning each bit in a class, so they have it more 'naturally'[51]. That isn't how we grew up so it's different. But we also have our own way, because dancing – a different kind of dancing – has always been something we have done on Norfolk. So there's probably a bit of that in there as well which makes a difference.

> Before some of us went to places like Tahiti, we hadn't really seen the real Polynesian dances anywhere, except in things like Charles Chauvel's film In the Wake of The Bounty, which had some good scenes of Tahitian girls doing a fast dance – a line-up of girls wearing the rauti leaf dress – which gave us an idea of how the traditional Polynesian dancers would have done them.[52] (interview 1999)

Further exposure to various styles of Pacific dancing at the 5th festival in Townsville in 1988, attended by a four member delegation, stimulated Hitch to work with a group of dancers and musicians to present an ensemble performance of music and dance at the 6th Festival in 1992 at Rarotonga. A fifteen-member delegation attended, eleven of who performed a music and dance set. The musicians comprised Don Christian-Reynolds and George 'Toofie' Christian (guitars and vocals), Archie Bigg and Maree Christian-Reynolds (ukuleles and vocals) and Matthew Bigg (drums). The dancers comprised Hitch, her daughter Karlene Christian, Susie Bigg, Erica Reynolds, Pauline Reynolds and Yvonne French. As Don Christian-Reynolds has identified, the ensemble's costumes were carefully chosen to reflect their historical identity:

> We entered under our own banner, which made a strong point about our culture. We tried to dress like the Pitcairners would have done as they came off the Morayshire, a mixture of the Tahitian and British styles. The Norfolk hats went down very well there, it was something very distinctive about Norfolk Island culture. (interview 1999)

The dance material performed by the troupe included a seated hula to The Coconut song and standing hula routines to two Christian-Reynolds' songs, Maes tintoela and Norfolk es auwas hoem (discussed in Chapter 11).

Karlene Christian started dancing as a child, in the early 1970s. By the late 1970s she was a regular performer at various local venues and during the 1980s she began to take an increasing interest in choreography. In 1991, she produced the first integrated Norfolk Island performance material by choreographing dances for a group of songs written and recorded by Eileen Snell and George 'Steggles' Le Cren – Norfolk Island Blues, Mauatua[53], My beautiful Island home and The Coconut song. The tracks Christian performed to were recorded live on Norfolk Island and, although rhythmically loose in parts, provided her with both an original local version of Polynesian music styles to perform to and easily recognisable lyrical themes to illustrate in movement. By virtue of the local origins and referentiality of both the dances and songs these compositions and their routines can be seen to have marked the beginning of an integrated indigenous repertoire. As Christian describes:

When I choreograph the songs it isn't just a case of 'this action fits these words' it's something more inside, more creative. You have to 'feel' what it's about, feel what you are trying to do. For the Maimitti *dance [performed to* Mauatua] *the outfits, particularly the hats, aren't just something the girls wear while they do their dance, they are traditional hats and the dresses are our traditional dresses which we wear on* Bounty [Anniversary] *Day. So the dance has these Norfolk things together with the Polynesian hand movements, which speak a language, a particular dance language. What I did was put these together and make something our own.* (interview 1999)

Christian performed routines to Le Cren and Snell's songs at island fund raising shows and at commercial venues such as the South Pacific Hotel. In the mid-1990s Christian (and her mother) also began teaching dancing at Norfolk Island Middle School and in 1996 took a group of school dancers to Orange (in New South Wales) to perform at the youth-orientated 'Artorama' festival. This was followed in 1997 by a higher profile event when she took a troupe of girls to the 14th Annual 'Schools Spectacular' performance event held at the Sydney Entertainment Centre. The dancers performed *The Coconut*

Figure 10: Karlene Christian dancing (wearing traditional Norfolk hat and adapted style of traditional dress) at South Pacific hotel c1990.

Figure 11: Karlene Christian dancing in Tahitian style costume at Rawson Hall (mid-1990s).

song to an audience of 15,000 per night and were featured in TV coverage of the event. As a result of such enterprises, Hitch and Christian's contributions to Norfolk Island culture were officially recognised through Australia Day Awards in 1996. Although she largely retired from public performance in the late 1990s, one of Hitch's more poignant appearances was at the funeral of George 'Steggles' Le Cren in 2003 when, to the music of *The Coconut song*, she danced around his coffin in an appropriately festive send-off to a generational colleague.

One of the best representations of the dance styles performed by young dancers influenced by Karlene Christian's choreography in the 1990s is included in the souvenir video for Norfolk Island's 1997 Multicultural Festival. This dance, to a performance of Snell's *Mauatua*, is performed by teenage dancer Coby Matthews in traditional Norfolk Island costume (also see Figure 12) and shows the emphasis on delicate upper bodily movements accompanying 'narrative songs' which predominated over the more vigorous hip movements (and general physicality) associated with the tamure (and also the traditional forms of dance revived in Hawai'i in the 1980s and 1990s). In this regard, as a modified form of Polynesian performance, Matthews' early 21st century Norfolk Island hula echoes similar modifications of Tahitian dances to those witnessed by Captain Beechey on Pitcairn Island in 1825 (discussed in Chapter 2). Understood as a form of *localisation*, such modification of source styles might therefore be suggested as the enduring tradition of Polynesian-derived dancing on Pitcairn and Norfolk islands.

Figure 12: George 'Toofie' Christian performing Norfolk's hula with Coby Matthews dancing (1999).

The local tradition of Polynesian style dance continues to the present, being regularly performed in weekly tourist-orientated shows at island hotels. During 1998–2001 singer-songwriter George 'Toofie' Christian and singer Susan Pedel held a residency at the Colonial hotel where they were accompanied by various young dancers (such as Matthews). These performances, and George 'Toofie' Christian's exposure to other Polynesian dancers at the Festival of Pacific Arts in Rarotonga in 1992, lead him to write *Norfolk's hula*, a song reflecting on Norfolk Island's Polynesian dance tradition. Set to a slow, dignified rhythm with an undulating melody line, the lyrics are poignant, appreciative and protective, and provide a fitting summary of the issues explored in this chapter and the status accorded to Polynesian dance in contemporary Norfolk Island culture:

Dem tek et from Tahiti
Tu Pitcairn lornga dem
When religion teck o'er
Dems darns fade waye with time

Hula harn, hula hips from Norfolk Iel
Si how graceful sa darns et in acklan style

Teck acklan sullun lorng taim
Before darns et again
Now we gut et back
We nor gwen lors et

[translation]

They took it with them from Tahiti
To Pitcairn
But when religiousity increased
The dances ceased to be performed

Hula hands, hula hips from Norfolk Island
See how gracefully it's danced in our own style

It took us [ie Norfolk Islanders] a long time
Before it was danced again
[But] now we've got it back
We're not going to lose it

While the first generations of performers to establish and popularise Polynesian-style dance traditions on Norfolk Island may have receded from public appearances in the late 1990s and early 2000s, a significant re-affirmation and re-invigoration of Polynesian dance traditions took place in 2003. This occurred when the island's Multicultural Arts Society included a series of workshops by a Tahitian dance instructor, Hepiua Le Hartel, as part of their annual festival. Le Hartel is a member of a family whose female members are deeply involved in Tahitian culture (with her mother teaching costume design at the Conservatorium of Tahitian Culture in Pape'ete). Le Hartel was assisted by Joell Marie, the French-born director of entertainment at Le Meridien Hotel in Bora Bora, who sang and played keyboards, guitar and Tahitian drums. While the invitation to Le Hartel to run work-

Figure 13: Norfolk musicians performing at the 8th Festival of Pacific Arts in Noumea in 2000
(L-r: Wes Steven, Don Christian-Reynolds, Wesley Cooper, Ashley Gilmore).

shops on Norfolk was a personal one, it reflects the impact Tahitian dancing has had on delegations attending the Festivals of Pacific Arts and the manner in which Tahitian styles and standards of presentation have come to be regarded as paradigms of Polynesian dancing in general.

Le Hartel's workshops were attended by sixty children and adults (including singers Don Christian-Reynolds, Kath King and Alison Ryves) and culminated in a public performance. Discussion with several of those who attended (and also with others who saw the final show), suggest that the classes connected with local perceptions of Polynesian heritage in a manner that one attendee likened to an "epiphany" (pc 2004). The project was so successful that Le Hartel was invited back again in April 2004. A further outcome of her involvement with the local community was her choreography of a solo dance routine to Don Christian-Reynolds's song *Norfolk es auwas hoem* (discussed in Chapter 11). This was subsequently learnt by the composer's daughter Mikiela and danced by her at the opening ceremony of the 9th Festival of Pacific Arts in Palau in July 2004[54].

The popularity of Tahitian dance presentations at successive Festivals of Pacific Arts has caused concern amongst some observers[55]. Their anxiety is that the Festivals – established to celebrate and perpetuate cultural *difference* – might be seen as facilitating a *Tahitianisation* of Polynesian (and broader Pacific) dance practices, homogenising them to a Tahitian 'norm'. While further research needs to be undertaken to ascertain whether any such phenomenon *is* occurring, it was possible to detect a shift in dancing styles on Norfolk Island shortly after Le Hartel's workshops. Attending an island cultural night at the South Pacific hotel in November 2004, for instance, I witnessed a trio of female dancers (Kath King, Tania Grube and Mikiela Christian-Reynolds) showing a more muscular physicality and angularity of gesture in their performance than has hitherto been usual in Norfolk dancing. At time of writing it is too early to speculate on the medium-long term impact of Le Hartel's involvement with local culture. In time, the principal significance of the workshops might be seen to reside in the strong emotional identification and appreciation of those participating and/or in the *re*-revival of local Polynesian dance traditions. Either way, the workshops' success represents an early 21st Century re-affirmation of Norfolk's historical links to Tahitian culture. If Le Hartel's work also facilitates a shift in style away from the island's distinct, localised form of hula towards a more contemporary, Tahitian-modeled standard; this will mark another phase in the history of a cultural practice that retains a powerful significance for its performers and local audiences.

Notes

1. *If* scenes were shot on Norfolk Island, as publicised, it is surprising that I could not uncover any written account or local memory of a film crew visiting in this period. In a small island community that received few visitors at this time, visiting film makers and screen celebrities would surely have been recalled and remembered. The lack of any such memory suggests that location filming on Norfolk may not have eventuated, despite publicity claims for the film.

2. *Photoplay Magazine*, September 2, 1916, described the film as:

   Easily the best Australian historical photoplay produced here and one that should prove of interest to every Australian, in the way in which 'The Mutiny on the Bounty' ... may be summed up. Congratulations are due all round and we have no doubt, with proper projection and with no-one to shout the story in our unwilling ears, that the public opinion will be in favour of the picture produced by Mr Longford. (quoted in: http://www.screensound.gov.au/Expertise.nsf/Sub+Pages/Longford+Lyell+Lecture1 - accessed in 2003)

3. Prior to appearing in Chauvel's film, Flynn had been captaining ships off the coast of Papua New Guinea. He had, apparently, not countenanced a career as an actor until he was approached to play the role of Christian. He went on to become a major Hollywood star in the 1930s-1940s, appearing in many swashbuckling roles.

4. Jane Moulin Freeman has identified that:

   Protestant missionaries deprecated the worship of [the traditional god] *Oro; legislation restricted dancing, and even forbade it. Penalties for dancers and audiences did not stop surreptitious dancing, which included nighttime performances in valleys, far removed from missionaries and administrators.* (1998: 875)

5. In Chauvel's account he refers to Taro by the nickname 'Lulu', here I follow Susan Chauvel Carlsson (2000) by referring to him by his other local name.

6. The image of young, garlanded, semi-clad women is so widely promulgated in contemporary advertising brochures for Pacific island locations as diverse as Hawai'i, Tahiti, Fiji, Vanuatu etc. that it appears virtually obligatory.

7. This is clearly historically anomalous in that the guitar and ukulele were not introduced into Tahitian (or Hawaiian) music until the 1800s. The term *hapa haole* refers to the post-contact genre of westernised Hawaiian style music that flourished in the 1930s and 1940s.

8. Indeed the music seems compatible with that which Chauvel reported as experiencing at Pape'ete's Theatre du Moderne, which he described as:

   a unique house of entertainment, adapted from a large copra shed, with a native orchestra perched on a wall playing jazz tunes upon windy concertinas, banjos and mouth organs, the combined sound of which is only a little weirder than that which comes from Ah Foo's chop-suey shop a little further down the street. (1933: 55)

9. Sourced from a series of disks of musical themes for film released by Brunswick

Records in the 1920s (conducted by Ernest Rapee). (Thanks to John Whiteoak and Chris Long for this identification.)

10. Composed by Earl Wittemore and Felice Lula some time in the early 1920s. (Thanks to John Whiteoak for this information, pc 2003.)

11. The censors also required minor cuts to scenes of floggings on board the *Bounty*.

12. The *ote'a* is a fast dance usually performed to syncopated percussion accompaniment.

13. In the scene some dancers, particularly those at the rear, are clearly less familiar with the routine they are expected to perform than those at the front.

14. Moulin Freeman notes that this style of dance was traditionally known as the *'ori tahiti*, but became known as the *tamure* after a "popular Tahitian song [that] repeatedly employed this word" came to be associated with the movements (1998: 874).

15. See for instance, Chauvel's speculation about sailors "trysting with dusky maidens in this Garden of Eden" (1934: 34).

16. During research on Norfolk Island I was unable to uncover specific documentation as to the precise date(s) when the film was screened (due to the minimal public records of the early 1930s). However, the venue was almost certainly Rawson Hall, which hosted the first synch-sound film screening on Norfolk Island in July 1933 (*NIN* 2.8.33: 6-7).

17. See Section II below.

18. It wasn't until the 1980s that the Norfolk and Pitcairn communities recommenced regular contacts.

19. For an account and discussion of the lives and literary output of Nordhoff and Hall see Briand (1966).

20. Including one on Thursday Island in 1933 (referred to in *PIM* April 1933: 22).

21. Rabone was a Sydney-based historian who also visited Lord Howe Island in the 1930s.

22. *Men against the Sea* (1933), concerned Bligh and his crew's hazardous voyage after the mutiny, and *Pitcairn's Island* (1934), concerned the establishment of the community on Pitcairn. Neither of the books emulated the success of their predecessor and neither was actually made into a film.

23. Also known as Maimitti. Christian also gave his Tahitian partner the European name of Isabella.

24. As my phrasing suggests, this is a speculative comment. Given the lack of surviving Norfolk Island records from this period, and my inability to find Islanders of a sufficient age who can recall this period in any detail, I have had to interpret the material against its historical context.

25. 1933 Norfolk Island census figures quoted in Hoare (1996: 29).

26. I have received conflicting information as to this date, 1941 and 1942 have also been cited, possibly suggesting that the Norfolk Island Friendship Club continued on an occasional, less formal basis for some time.

27. Tipene relocated from Ngapuhi in Aotearoa/New Zealand in the late 1920s. The description "chieftainess" was commonly used in press reports of Polynesian Club events in *PIM*.

28. Initially known as the Pacific Islands Club (PIC). An advertisement for the PIC carried in *PIM* throughout 1937 stated that the Club had been formed "to study the history, traditions, economics, and political development of the Pacific Islands".

29. Also a Tongan dance.

30. John McCoy (*PIM* March 1939: 20), Miss Everett (*PIM* June 1939: 51), Don Adams, Eustace Adams, Henry Adams, Selwyn Buffett, Charles Evans and Henry Nicholson (*PIM* May 1943: 4); Mrs Charles Fysh, Mrs Mapletoft, Freddie Quintal "and other NI soldiers" (*PIM*, September 1943: 33); Mr and Mrs Peter Buffett (*PIM* September 1944:

12); and Fred Snell, Herbert Snell, David Hooker and Mrs K Burgess (*PIM* June 1945: 49).

31. Since Norfolk Island's population at the outbreak of the War was around 1100, a significant proportion of Norfolk Islanders became familiar with the kind of social occasion and dance and music performances that were staged at the Polynesian Club in this period.

32. While this claim is conjectural, it may well have been (at least) one of the first times such a large-scale *formal* kava drinking ceremony was staged in Sydney, given the limited number of Polynesians resident there prior to the 1930s.

33. Anglo-Indian performer Doug King learnt Hawaiian music in Bombay prior to relocating to Sydney in the late 1940s. He recorded albums under a number of pseudonyms (such as 'Ko Lutani of the Cocos Islands' in the 1970s), backed a number of well-known Sydney-based hula dancers in the 1950s and 1960s (including Maisie 'Latani' Smith and Mardi 'Latani' O'Donnell) and continued to perform publicly until the late 1990s. (See Bambrick and Miller [1994] for further discussion).

34. See Bambrick and Miller (1994: 72-84).

35. Such as Hollywood actress Jane Russell's performances in the film *The Revolt of Mamie Stover* (1956).

36. A gentle, Tahitian-language song about pretty girls riding on a merry-go-round at a fair popularised in the 1955 Hollywood film *Mister Roberts*.

37. Don Christian-Reynolds later contributed to rhythmic modifications of the version recorded for use by Karlene Christian in her 1990s dance act (interview 1999).

38. Beautiful women (of Polynesian descent).

39. The song had a partial predecessor in a humorous verse attributed to 'Veritas' that was published on page three of *NIWN* on July 29th 1932. Entitled 'A Coconut Lament', it detailed the rejection of a consignment of coconuts brought to the island on the *Morinda* on the grounds that they could introduce a blight to other crops. The 3rd and 4th lines of verse five declare, "We do not grow the tree that bears/The precious coconut".

40. Collapsing a variety of Polynesian forms into one category.

41. A score that, in turn, quoted extensively from popular British songs of the 1700s and 1800s (including *Rule Britannia* and sea shanties such as *Blow the man down*).

42. A popular story from the convict era concerning an escaped prisoner who hid in a tree for an extended period to escape capture and who cursed his captors when discovered.

43. In 1977, for instance, a fund raising concert for the Seventh Day Adventist Church's annual Christmas party included an ensemble led by Alec Nobbs, called the Sin-garettes, "a group of young guitar and ukulele players who sang a bracket of Hawaiian songs" along with various other performers. (*NIN*, July 1977: 38)

44. Brochure note and copy for an advertisement that appeared in 1975 in the *Norfolk Islander*.

45. A group of young New Zealanders studying Maori culture at Massey University at Palmerston North.

46. See Hayward (2001: 73-87, 101-103 and 153-165) for a detailed analysis of the Polynesianisation of Whitsunday tourism in the 1950s–1970s.

47. Such as reed weaving and fabric design.

48. Despite Pitcairn-descended Islanders only representing 40 per cent of the population by this period (the remaining 60 per cent being Australian and New Zealand nationals, in roughly equal numbers).

49. The society was initially named 'The Committee for Democratic Self-Government for Norfolk Island', then 'The Society of Descendants of Pitcairn Settlers', before opting for the current name. A statement of the SPD's objectives is presented in the

(unpaginated) rear inside cover of their 'political history' of Norfolk Island (Unat-tributed, 1996).

50.

An organisation established in 1947 by the colonial powers in the Pacific to "encourage and strengthen international co-operation in promoting the economic and social welfare and advancement of the peoples of non-self-governing territories in the South Pacific". (http://www.festival-pacific-arts.org/hisuk.htm)

51.   In fact, the revival of traditional Tahitian dancing as a public form has similarities to the Norfolk revival in that the public presentation of Tahitian dancing dates from the 1950s when troupes such as Heiva and Te Maeva re-established traditional styles of dancing as a legitimate cultural activity.

52.   As noted in Section I above, the sequences in Chauvel's film were already a mediated form of traditional dance and their example for Norfolk Island dancers, therefore, a further mediation of traditional styles.

53.   Formerly referred to as *Friendship* or *Mai Mitti*.

54.   See Christian-Reynolds (2004) for a detailed discussion of the Norfolk delegation's attendance at the 9th Festival.

55.   Particularly amongst ethnomusicologists and ethnochoreologists attending.

Chapter Eight

GARRISON DAYS
Norfolk Island during the Pacific stage of World War Two

At the time of the outbreak of World War Two in 1939 there were no military facilities or personnel on Norfolk Island. As in the First World War, a significant number of Norfolk Islanders served in various capacities in the Australian military; one hundred and thirty enlisting for service in the European and Pacific theatres. Japan's entry into the War and, particularly, the thrust of Japanese expansion south-east through Papua New Guinea and The Solomon Islands towards Vanuatu and New Caledonia, brought Norfolk close to the theatre of Pacific conflict and placed it on a strategic north-south air route between Auckland and Noumea. As conflict in the Melanesian region intensified in 1942, the US military investigated the possibility of constructing a runway on the island, judging the area immediately to the east of Headstone Point as the only suitable site and then requested construction of such a facility from the Australian Government. This task was assigned to the New South Wales Department of Main Roads and was initiated in October 1942 with equipment freighted by sea from the USA. One of the first steps was the clearing of the historic Pine Avenue to make way for the runway site, a move unpopular with many islanders[1]. In September 1942 an advance party of the New Zealand Army arrived to garrison the new airbase and the first flight, a New Zealand plane, touched down on the runway on Christmas Day.

Together with the arrival of the construction crews and New Zealand military personnel, the island's balance of population was also altered by the departure of the main body of enlisted Norfolk Islanders in 1941 and 1942 and the departure a number of families who relocated to continental Australia for the duration of the war (and longer, in some cases). Both migrations caused a severe shortage of labour and professional skills on the island. Norfolk Island World War Two historian Gil Hitch has calculated

112

that due to these movements the Island's population dropped to around 700 in September 1942, and then rapidly rose to just over two thousand with the arrival of 1500 New Zealand troops by the end of October (Hitch, 1992: 35). In late 1942 a number of new roads had been constructed, existing ones upgraded and new facilities, such as a radio and radar station, were established. By 1943 the airstrip was in regular use – and Norfolk Island's previous isolation was thereby significantly breached. With Allied successes in 1944 and eventual victory in 1945 service personnel gradually withdrew from the island. (Although the RNZAF continued to administer the airport facility until 1948, when control of the airfield was re-allocated to the Australian Department of Civil Aviation[2].)

During the period 1942-45 New Zealand (and other allied) servicemen constituted the majority of the island's population and created their own institutions and social and cultural events and practices. In this manner, their temporary presence recalled that of the earlier Melanesian Mission but with one significant difference, the service personnel had a far greater degree of interaction with the remnant local population than the Mission's students and staff had. Indeed, the influx of Allied servicemen into the island during the war years had a significant effect on those Norfolk Islanders who remained, many of whom were women. With specific regard to music culture, public functions, such as dances and concerts, introduced new performers and material to Norfolk Islanders.

Concerts and dances were particularly common from mid-1943-1945, as the local sense of threat diminished and a resolution to the conflict seemed in sight. The military band, conducted by Lieutenant Ramsay, performed at several dances at this time. Some of these were held to entertain members of the garrison, with Norfolk Islanders – particularly women – encouraged to attend and prizes were often awarded for best waltz or quickstep pairs (these invariably comprising a male serviceman and female islander). Atten- dances at these were significant, five hundred people attending an Air Force Ball held in September 1943, for instance. Other occasions were held for the benefit of the local population, such as the 'Welcome Home' dance organised in August 1943 for islanders returning from active service.

In a similar manner to the distinction between 'old time' and 'jazz' dance bands on the island in the 1930s (discussed in Chapter 6), there were traditional ensembles, such as the military band, and 'hotter' swing influ- enced outfits. The principal example of the latter was an ensemble formed in 1944, initially known as the RZNAF Station Dance Band and re-named The Gremlins in 1945. The ensemble was a voluntary enterprise whose membership fluctuated according to movement of members on postings but comprised a basic line-up of trombone, trumpet, cornet, saxophone, key- board, guitar and drums, playing a repertoire of popular dance styles of the period (of the style typified by the Glen Miller Band). The ensemble was led by New Zealand tenor saxophone player/arranger Ernie Read in 1944, and then by trombonist/arranger Wilbur Lynam, a US military liaison officer stationed on the island, in 1945[3]. The dances featuring the swing-influenced ensembles were, on occasion, 'livened up' by inebriates who had imbibed the home brewed rough alcohol known as 'soop'. Some indication of the nature and effects of this drink can be ascertained by the definition of the term offered in an article in the RNZAF occasional newsletter *Duffy's Gen* – "a mixture of water, methylated spirits, boot polish (black preferable) and Silvo[4]"(v1 n8 [nd]: 19). The item described soop's effects with references to phenomena such as "the 'paheka-Maori'[5] who performed a wild haka in the middle of the dance floor" (ibid).

More sedate concerts were also staged at various locations, attracting audiences of locals and servicemen, with at least some locals contributing as performers. A concert held in October 1943, for instance was described as follows:

> *A very good attendance of residents and servicemen enjoyed a splendid programme by the "N" Force Band (under the baton of Liet A.S. Ramsay) at the Rawson Hall on Monday evening. Lieut E.W Boyle, who compered the show and acted as stage manager, proved a wonderful community-sing leader and had the hall ringing and swinging with him in both old and new favourites. The Band opened with the rousing march "Sussex by the Sea". Sgt. Clif Martin and Pte R. Swallow played a sweet cornet duet "Panorama" and obliged with an encore. Mrs Francis Buffett sang a charming bracket of soprano solos, "White Dove" and "Trees", both of which were well received. Cliff Martin was heard to advantage in his cornet solo "I hear you calling me" and responded to an enthusiastic encore. Two tenor solos were well sung by P/O R. A. Levy – "The world is mine" and "Bird songs at eventide". Sgt. Burnett gave a delightful rendition of "Country Gardens". Recitations after the fashion of Cyril Fletcher were given by S/Sgt R. P. Foster, while Bdr A.M. Carter rendered "White Christmas" and "Maria Elena" in his usual pleasing fashion. Pte. J. J. Fraser was excellent on the euphonium in "Drake goes West" and encore. The Band concluded the excellent show with a bright bracket. (NIW 22.10.43: 5)*

Other entertainments were organised by ad hoc groups of service personnel such as the 'Moa Cushoo'[6] concert party, which staged an event in Bailey's Paddock at Burnt Pine in November 1943. This was advertised as "Haere Ra Show: – Sketches, Songs, Dances, Patter – Ladies Real and Synthetic – Magicians in legerdemain up to date"[7]. The "synthetic" ladies referred to were servicemen in drag. The announcement for a similar event in December 1944, a drag show featuring impersonations of Mae West, Betty Grable, Ana Sheridan and Hedy Lamar, light-heartedly declared:

> *See all there is to be seen ... Personnel are advised that this show is definitely UNSUITABLE for children under the age of 35, and for married persons. (Duffy's Gen 22.12.44: 3)*

Norfolk Island singer Susan Pedel, who was resident on the island at the time, provides some sense of these occasions with her recollection that these concerts were:

> *Variety events, very influenced by Hollywood musicals. They had colorful Carmen Miranda style things, dancing, singing all kinds of costumes. Nothing too serious ... a lot of fun for the servicemen. (interview 1999)*

While I have been unable to ascertain the identities of the "real" ladies involved, several Norfolk Islander women who learnt Polynesian style dancing in Sydney during the 1930s and early 1940s (discussed in Chapter 7) appear to have danced at public concerts during the final years of the War. Given the lack of such performances on the island over the previous ninety years, this entertainment was a significant as the first stage in a broader cultural revival.

Following the official cessation of hostilities in the Pacific in August 1945, the RNZAF presence on Norfolk Island was slowly reduced. One task the dwindling garrison turned itself to in the immediate post-War period was the completion of a new Rawson Hall on Taylor's Road. This was officially opened in January 1946 with a well-attended variety concert. As Gil Hitch has summarised:

> The transition to peacetime living was gradual. At the end of June [1946] RNZAF personnel numbered 60 and at the aerodrome the routine was much the same as at the war's end ... personnel entertained themselves with fortnightly dances at the Church Army Hut and rugby games. (1992: 93-94)

The final RNZAF contingent departed in July 1948, handing over the airstrip to civilian administration as many Norfolk islanders returned from Australia and New Zealand to rebuild the social and economic life of their island.

* * *

One enduring perception on the island concerns the popular New Zealand ballad *Blue Smoke*. The song is usually attributed to Maori performer Ruru Karaitiana, who is thought to have written the song onboard a troop ship off the coast of East Africa in 1940 and who recorded the number in 1949 (backed by musicians from Jimmy Carter's Auckland-based Hawaiian band). Individuals such as 'Foxy' McCoy recall that the song was popularised on Norfolk Island in the war years through frequent performances by a New Zealand serviceman who claimed (or was otherwise identified) as having written the song just after leaving Auckland on the ship *Wahinui* (interview 1999). While Karaitiana's authorship of the song does not seem to have been subsequently contested (and Norfolk claims are therefore highly contentious), the song's sentiments are apposite for such an interpretation and explain its popularity during the period, not the least with New Zealand service personnel stationed away from their loved ones. The lyrics describe the melancholy of departure, the first verse describing how:

> Blue smoke goes drifting by into the deep blue sky
> And when I think of home I sadly sigh
> Oh I can see you there with loving tears in your eyes
> As we fondly said our last goodbyes
> And as I sailed away with a longing to stay
> I promised I'd be true and to love only you

While it is difficult to find any specific evidence that the performance practices of the (predominantly) New Zealand garrison influenced subsequent Norfolk Island culture, their activities constitute a discrete – if brief – interval in the island's history. The only clear contribution to present-day local music was a singular one that only manifested itself during the research of this book and associated recording projects. In late 2000, George 'Toofie' Christian, (whose work is discussed in Chapter 11), was approached at the RSL club[8] by an older islander, Fletcher Christian, who had heard that he was assembling material for his debut CD recording. Fletcher informed Christian that he recalled a humorous song about Norfolk Island written by a member of the New Zealand garrison, and offered to sing it for him. Christian wrote the words down, memorised the vocal melody and later added a chordal accompaniment and included an arrangement of the song on his 2001 CD *Pilli Lornga N.I.*

The song (at least in the version remembered by Fletcher Christian over fifty years after its original performances) gives a humorous account of the fair and moderate practices of a fictitious institution referred to as the Norfolk (Island) Rangers (an equestrian police force evoking the Canadian Mounties), which appears to have been inspired by the common use of horses as a form of transport on the island at the time. The words, as recalled by Fletcher Christian, comprise:

We are the Norfolk Rangers
We're riding all day long
You'll always find us on the trail
Of those who turned out wrong
So watch you boys and girlies
And don't commit a crime
Or you'll find the NIRs[9]
Will help you serve some time

chorus

Yes, help you serve some time
And in the end you'll find
It's better not to do a crime
Than serve it at Burnt Pine

We never treat our victims
With the slightest of contempt
We always give them plenty of beer
And help them pay their rent
We never give them bully beef
Dried peas or lima beans
We always give them mutton chops
With salad and ice cream

Repeat chorus

Along with its general humorous construction of the 'Norfolk (Island) Rangers' the humour of the second verse revolves around a contrast of the plight of prisoners of the NIRs, who are fed mutton chops, salad and ice cream (and plenty of beer) and (implicitly) garrison troops, for whom bully beef, dried peas and lima beans (and limited supplies of beer) were staple elements of their diet. The song lyrics are similar in style to a number of poems by NZ serviceman W.L. Bremner published in *Duffy's Gen* in the period

1943–45, such as the verses 'NJ (Norfolk Joe)' (22.12.44: 6) or 'Home's the caper' (19.1.45: 6). Even more apposite for the subject of this book was a poem entitled 'Dreams and Realities – about an airman sitting under a tree daydreaming' (1.8.1945: 8), an extract from which describes how:

> He dreamed of his harem in distant Turkey
> And his concubines numbering fifty
> Then he thought of the Ball down at Rawson Hall
> And the dancing girls so nifty ...

> He gracefully glided across the floor
> And Paul Whiteman played all night long
> But his fancies were lyin', cos Somerville-Ryan[10]
> Had just played the Prisoner's Song[11]

Interpreting the undulating melody of the *Norfolk Rangers'* verses and pitch rise of the chorus as similar in style to hillbilly music of the type becoming popular in New Zealand in the 1930s, George 'Toofie' Christian and arranger Denis Crowdy recorded their 2001 version as an uptempo country song accompanied by bass guitar and brushed drums. While this is obviously a modern interpretation of the song, the self-accompanied version of the composition sung by 'Toofie' Christian in solo performances is melodically close to the version recalled by Fletcher Christian and provides one linkage between the RNZAF garrison years and contemporary Norfolk Island culture.

Notes

1. The construction of the runway, and local opposition to it, is the subject of a chapter of James Michener's (fictionalised) account of his service in the US military, *Tales of the South Pacific* (1947) – material for this chapter appears to have been collected during his brief visit to Norfolk Island in November 1945 as part of his work on the US War History project.
2. See Hitch (1992) for a detailed discussion of military facilities and military personnel stationed on the island during World War Two.
3. Information on the RNZAF dance band is principally taken from an unattributed informational item (entitled 'The Gremlins') published in *Duffy's Gen* n4, 19.1.45: 2.
4. A metal polish.
5. 'Pakeha' is the Maori term for white/European New Zealanders, the term "pakeha Maori" suggests a white New Zealander imitating aspects of what was regarded as Maori behaviour.
6. The latter term may be a version of the Norfolk Island language term *kushu*, meaning 'good', 'well' or 'fine'.
7. Text of advertisement in the RNZAF newsletter *Nformation* v2n6 27.11.43: 4.
8. RSL – Returned Soldiers League – a social club (see the discussion of the construction and early operation of Norfolk's RSL in Chapter 10).
9. NIRs presumably being an abbreviation for Norfolk Island Rangers.
10. I have been unable to uncover any information about the individual referred to, who was – presumably – a musician.
11. *The Prisoner's song* was a variation of a 19th Century North American 'folk' ballad that was popularised in Australia and New Zealand by Vernon Dalhart's 1924 recorded version.

Chapter Nine

THE MELODIOUS SONGS OF THE BLEST
Locally associated hymns and their role in Norfolk Island culture

Despite the upheavals of World War Two, some families and, particularly, older islanders appear to have weathered the War years and the arrival of various modernisations without altering their traditional ways of life. In addition to the continuing popularity of church services, this was most evident in traditions of domestic singing to harmonium accompaniment. A vivid portrait of this was provided by the (anonymous) writer of the 'dars Norfolk' column in *NIN* in 1976, reminiscing about one such individual, Gilbert Bailey, who lived to the age of ninety four. The writer reported that in his later years Bailey spent his days walking, rejoicing and playing his harmonium. In a description that suggests that Bailey's instrument may have been one of the originals obtained from whalers' wives, the article noted that:

> *His harmonium gave him his greatest happiness of all. It looked as though it would collapse in one heap of rubble, with its legs splayed out and the hinges on the keyboard cover broken. The ivory keys were orange, they were so old. The stool he sat on was rickety ... When Gil played his harmonium the whole world came alive. His hands were ancient but had no trouble finding the keys, even though they shook on their way down to the keyboard. They found perfect harmonies, and his voice, although a little raspy at 94, bellowed out words to the world's most beautiful hymns – The Pitcairn hymns – hymns of gratitude and praise, of hope and love. The Pitcairn anthem was one ...*
>
> *Music, music – perfect chords and perfect fingering. It was a treat to hear him. He always made me happy. That old man, in an old home,*

badly in need of repair, on an island that was once the scene for the worst convict settlement in the world, in a room full of wood chips and tin dishes – always brought me a great sense of peace. (NIN March 1976: 38)

New Zealander Marie Lewis has a similar recollection of Bailey and his wife at this time, recalling that when she first visited them:

We were immediately ushered into the parlor where he stood and played a hymn as a thanksgiving for our safe arrival ... This was followed when we left with another hymn of thanks to farewell us. This was a common practice among the islanders at the time, a regular important bit of how you went about daily living. (interview 1999)

I. Core Repertoire

As the above comments suggest, the tradition of domestic hymn singing that established itself in the mid-1850s carried on through to the post-War era. Since the early days of settlement, islanders had sung a variety of hymns. These were dependent on family traditions and whether they worshipped in the Anglican or Methodist (and, later Seventh Day Adventist or Roman Catholic) churches and what the specific tastes of the clergy and/or choirmasters at these churches were. Despite variations in affiliation, a core repertoire of locally-popular and locally-associated hymns developed during the 20th Century. This corpus was represented in print in the 1970s and 1980s through the publication of four local hymnbooks:

- Greenaways Press's *Hymns of Norfolk Island* (1971)

- The Seventh Day Adventist Church's *Hymns of Norfolk and Pitcairn Islands* (1976)

- The Uniting Church's *Hymns of Norfolk Island* (1987); and

- The Church of England's *Pitcairn Hymns and Norfolk Favourites* (198?)

Along with particular hymns associated with specific congregations (and/or the particular preferences of the unidentified compilers), all four compilations include the following eight hymns: *Ahava, Bethlehem, Gethsemane, Oakleigh, The Pitcairn anthem, The beautiful stream, The ship of fame* and *Unto us a child is born*. While the short 1971 collection omits them (for reasons unknown), two further hymns are (now) also widely recognised as integral to local repertoire, *In the sweet by and by* and *Let the lower lights be burning*.

While the inclusion of *The beautiful stream* and *Unto us a child is born* in all four collections attests to their popularity in the 1970s and 1980s, these two hymns are not now commonly regarded as especially expressive of local cultural identity. The core locally-associated repertoire over the last two decades thereby comprises:

- *The Pitcairn anthem* and *Gethsemane* – the Nobbs/Driver compositions discussed in Chapter 3 whose authorship is inextricably entwined in Norfolk Islanders' Pitcairn heritage.

- Gustav Quintal's early 20th Century *Oakleigh* (also discussed

119

in Chapter 5) – which has been less commonly performed over recent decades.

• *Let the lower lights be burning, In the sweet by and by, The ship of fame* and *Ahava*.

Given the close association between visiting US whalers (and particularly captains' wives) and the island community (discussed in Chapter 3), and the introduction of Methodism, it is perhaps unsurprising that the latter four hymns originate from the United States. Three of them, *Let the lower lights be burning, In the sweet by and by* and *The ship of fame* also share nautical imagery and themes of overcoming adversity through belief and righteousness that have clear appeal to an island community, let alone one that was involved in the perilous enterprise of whaling in the late 19th and early 20th Centuries[1].

Let the lower lights be burning was written by US singer, songwriter and song leader Philip Bliss in 1871 after hearing the Evangelist preacher D.L. Moody incorporate a tale about a shipwreck in Cleveland Harbor into a sermon which concluded, "the Master will take care of the great lighthouse, let us keep the lower lights burning"[2]. Norfolk Island folklore relates an incident during the late 19th Century when a local whaling boat was pulled far out to sea by a harpooned whale and had to try and find its way back to the island in the dark. In order to keep their spirits up (and seek divine assistance), the crew sang *Let the lower lights be burning* as they rowed. Meanwhile, islanders, realising the boatmen's plight, congregated on the shore at Cascade Bay and lit lanterns for the boat to steer towards. At the same time that the crew saw the lanterns those waiting on the shore heard the strains of the hymn drifting across the waters and knew the crew were safe[3]. This directly evokes the hymn's chorus:

Let the lower lights be burning
Send a gleam across the wave
Some poor faint struggling seaman
You may rescue, you may save

Whatever the basis for this local story, the hymn appears to have become associated with such folkloric memories and was adopted into continuing local repertoire.

The second hymn to have become popular at this time is *In the sweet by and by*, which was written in the USA by composer J.P Webster and writer J.S Bennett in the mid-1860s. The song's lyrics posit an afterlife of bliss ("a land that is fairer than day") awaiting the righteous on a "beautiful shore". The celebration of a place of peace and sanctity has obvious resonances with the Pitcairners newly arrived at Norfolk Island:

We shall sing on that beautiful shore
The melodious songs of the blest
And our spirits shall sorrow no more
Not a sigh for the blessing of rest

and it is perhaps not too fanciful to suggest that the song may have also expressed the longing of Norfolk Islanders to be reunited with their Pitcairn relatives, albeit in the hereafter, in the final lines of the chorus:

120

In the sweet by and by
We shall meet on that beautiful shore

The third hymn that appears to date from the mid-late 1800s, *The ship of fame*, is – if anything – even more central to local song culture. The authorship of *The ship of fame* has remained an unresolved issue on Norfolk. During research on the island in 1999-2001 the usual attribution suggested to me was that it had been introduced to the island in the late 19th Century, possibly from visiting ships' crews or religious activists. Contrarily, a small number of informants believed that it was another George Hunn Nobbs/Driver Christian composition. A recording of *The ship of fame* made on the island in 1956 (discussed below) commences with an introduction, by an unknown announcer, that states:

> *The hymn* The ship of fame *was composed on Norfolk Island when the whaling industry was first started about 1870 and is now the most popular hymn on the island, and especially with visitors.*

The claim that it was composed *on* the island is an interesting one, in that none of the hymnbooks published on Norfolk over the last two decades credit the hymn as locally composed and Driver Christian and Nobbs – who would be the most obvious candidates as composers – are not cited in any printed source as its originators. The hymn's lyrics are written in a distinctly different, more modern and colloquial manner than Nobbs's work and the tune is more joyous than Nobbs's and Christian and Nobbs's other melodies, suggesting that they were not involved in its composition. Like *Let the lower lights be burning*, the song's maritime-themed lyrics – and chorus repeated after each verse – give the composition a clear local appeal. They comprise, in full:

What ship is this you're sailing in
This wondrous ship of fame?
The ship is called 'The Church of God'
And Christ, the captain's name

chorus

Come join our happy crew
We're bound for Canaan's shore
The captain says, "There's room for you
And room for millions more"

What wages do you get on board
The ship that you commend?
We've love and joy and peace and grace
And glory in the end

And what's the crew that sails with you
On board this ship so grand?
The saints of God, all washed in blood
And under Christ's command

Do you not fear the stormy seas
Your barque may overwhelm?

You need not fear, the Lord is here
And Christ is at the helm

Heave out your boat and come onboard
They say there's plenty room
The captain says, "You're welcome now
Make no delay but come"

Then hoist the sails and catch the breeze
And soon the journey's o'er
The ship will land you safe at last
On Canaan's happy shore

Aside from its metaphors of the ship ("of fame") being the church, and Christ being "at the helm", the history of ships transporting the mutineers to Pitcairn and the Pitcairners to Norfolk Island (either or both of which might be analogised as "Canaan's shore") offer a strong point of local identification for the song.

While my own research has failed to unearth any reference to the specific hymn and its lyrics outside of Norfolk Island, Christian music researcher Robin Ryan has identified it as belonging to a genre of US "gospel ship hymns" popular in the early-mid 1800s that have similar lyrics and themes (pc 2004). Amongst these, variants of the hymn *The old ship of Zion* have clear affinities, many of them casting Christ as a "captain" calling to believers to join him onboard and travel to Zion. The version of the hymn published in White and King's 1860 collection *The Sacred Harp*, attributed to Thomas W. Carter (1844), has a particular similarity, with its opening lines:

What ship is this that will take us all home?
Oh, glory hallelujah

and its reference that:

She landed all who are gone before
Oh, glory hallelujah
And yet she's able to land still more
Oh, glory hallelujah

While this identification does not solve the specific issue of authorship of the Norfolk hymn, it identifies the likely context and tradition from which the song emerged.

The other locally associated hymn that continues to be sung on the island in church services is *Ahava*. In an international context the hymn is relatively obscure. Written by American composer Abraham Wood (1752–1804) it is usually referred to by its first line "How beauteous are their feet". It is unclear how and when it entered Norfolk repertoire, how it obtained the word "ahava" as its title and how it attained the status of being a core local hymn. 'Ahava' is an Old Testament reference, a river in Babylon where Ezra gathered a group of jews to accompany him to Jerusalem. On the banks of this river he sought priests to travel with the party, fasted to ensure that God gave him a direct route and then travelled without incident to Jerusalem. The hymn's title, like the lyrics of other locally associated hymns, offers

THE MELODIOUS SONGS OF THE BLEST

allegorical references to the Pitcairners' travel to Norfolk. But the hymn's lyrics only refer to the final part of the Old Testament episode, the arrival at Jerusalem, expressed most clearly in verse 5 of the song:

The watchmen join their voice
And tuneful notes employ
Jerusalem breaks forth in songs
And deserts learn the joy

While we have a fairly clear idea of when these hymns were written, the years in which they entered local repertoire and the period(s) in which they rose to prominence are far harder to ascertain. They are, for instance not singled out for mention by early visitors in the 1850s-1870s, raising questions as to how often and where they were performed at this time and, similarly, are not referred to in late 19th Century accounts. The scant nature of written records of the period 1900-1930 also exacerbates this uncertainty.

II. Musical Style and Recorded Hymns

Despite the concluding point of the above section, there is evidence that a body of locally associated hymns were held to be important to local identity in the 1930s. Reports from the period also suggest that their performance was perceived to be a conscious assertion of traditional Norfolk identity. As discussed in Chapter 7, a presentation on Pitcairn and Norfolk history by Harold Rabone in December 1934 was reported to have included:

vocal and instrumental items supplied by artistes of Pitcairn descent.
Miss Rossiter supplied the accompaniments for these items and also for
the community singing which was a pleasant feature of the evening. Mr
Hugo Quintal gave an item to his own accompaniment which was very
greatly appreciated. The old Pitcairn Hymn "The Ship of Fame" was sung
with great enthusiasm by the audience, the solo being supplied by Mr.
Carty Christian. (NIT 12.12.34: 1)

Carty Christian, who possessed a strong baritone voice, and could also sing bass parts, if required, was a key figure in the performance of the locally associated hymn repertoire from the late 1920s through to the 1950s. At some time in the pre-War period it became customary for Norfolk Islanders of Pitcairn descent to be buried at Kingston with a graveyard ceremony that included singing of *The Pitcairn anthem*, usually led off by Carty Christian. Interpreting the scant historical record of island hymn repertoire in the immediate pre-War period, it seems likely that the local hymns, which were associated with a communal singing practice, were not featured on anything but an occasional basis in Anglican services, which had a strong emphasis on conducted choir singing, but may have been performed on occasion in the Methodist church, which had a greater community orientation in its worship. A report of a Mother's Day service held in the Methodist hall in early May 1934, for instance, reported that:

Mr Carty Christian and the male Choir assisted by organ and orchestra
rendered appropriate selections. The community singing was a marked
feature at this service. (NIT 9.5.34)

In the post-War era, Carty Christian continued as the island's leading male hymn singer. Kik Quintal, one of the island's prominent hymn singers from the late 1950s-late 1990s (who is generally considered to have been Carty's successor) recalls that Christian had a deep love of hymn singing in both sacred and secular contexts:

> Carty Christian had a launch, they used to go fishing, especially in the summer months, they'd go early ... just outside the reef ... they used to sing out there ... Alex Wilson, the administrator at the time [in 1950-52] used to have these musical evenings at Government house and Carty and they used to sing for them, About 5 or 6 blokes, and they'd sound terrific, all harmonising – on hymns like Awake, my soul[4]. (interview 1999)

In 1956, the centenary of Norfolk Island's Pitcairn settlement, community singing of patriotic songs and locally associated hymns played a prominent part in the celebrations and, seemingly in response to this, the Australian Broadcasting Corporation recorded Carty Christian and a small group of other male singers singing three hymns in a room at Government House at Kingston. A letter written by the Administrator, Hugh Boyd Norman, to Charles Moses, General Manager of the Australian Broadcasting Corporation, on November 21st, gives some insight to the recording sessions:

> Frankly, I was surprised at the excellence of the recording. Though I thought it would be good, I did not for one moment imagine it would be as good as it has turned out. If we had had prior warning and the group of men been rehearsed, it would have been a remarkable piece of harmonizing. That group we got together at half-an-hour's notice and without even any preliminary practice made that recording. We are ordering one hundred for sale on the Island as a start.

The recording included versions of The Pitcairn anthem, Gethsemane and The ship of fame. The Pitcairn anthem opens with Carty Christian intoning the words "And then shall the King" solo, with other voices coming in, somewhat unevenly, on the next phrase "say unto them" until all join in on "on his right hand". The most immediately striking aspect of the hymn is its slow pace. Gethsemane, sung in an ensemble version and described by Ryan as "somewhat free metred" (pc 2004) is similarly slow. The ship of fame is a livelier sounding song, by virtue of its slightly faster tempo and its setting in the key of G major. Carty sings the six verses solo, with the choir providing the chorus. Ryan describes this rendition as "typical sea shanty style, very simple", distinguished by Christian's "pleasant timbre and fervent sounding vibrato" (ibid). The recording – which represents the usual style of social performance of the piece – eschews dramatic use of the call and response structure of each verse, which could be realised through use of different voices in the question and answer passages – eg verse 1:

> What ship is this you're sailing in
> This wondrous ship of fame?
> The ship is called 'The Church of God'
> And Christ's the captain's name

Radio New Zealand also made a recording of Norfolk hymn singing in

1948. While I have been unable to ascertain the recording venue or performers, the recordings are of a (mixed male and female voice) church choir, apparently recorded in situ. The three songs featured in the recording were *The Pitcairn anthem*, *Gethsemane* and *Ahava*. The presence of the former two on both records allows us to gain some sense of the common style of singing then prevalent (at least on these hymns).

In the Radio NZ recordings, *The Pitcairn anthem* is sung by the ensemble choir throughout, omitting the solo vocal introduction of Carty's version (which has now become common), and is similar in tempo to the 1956 rendition. *Gethsemane* is slower than the 1956 version and *Ahava* is similarly paced, to the extent that pronounced vibrato/pitch wobble is detectable on some sustained notes. While *Gethsemane* is an earnest reflective song, *Ahava's* funereal pace is more surprising given that its lyrics concern (and frequently refer to) "joy". In terms of its arrangement, the most distinctive aspect is its use of male-only vocal lines in lines 5-6 of the first two verses (although the lyrical rationale for this is far from clear).

Ryan has identified that there is "a real consistency" in the performance style of the mid-20th Century recordings discussed above, one characterised by "dragging tempii, fairly restricted melodic range and repetition of material" (ibid). She also adds that the slow tempos might be taken to suggest that the singers appear to be "savouring the harmonies as they sing", which she takes to be indicative of a "people who really just love to sing" (ibid). This latter comment is one born out by various visitors to the Norfolk community during its first century and provides one explanation for the persistence of the slow tempos that appear to have been transported from Pitcairn. With regard to their pace, Ryan has identified that the tempo is slower than the Maori or Samoan hymn-singing patterns that spread through the western Pacific in the 1800s and early 1900s and were adopted and localised in Pacific communities (such as the Torres Strait Islands and Vanuatu) and also slower than mainland Australian hymn singing of the period (pc 2004).

Any association between mid-20th Century Norfolk hymn performance styles and Polynesian-derived Pitcairn practices is one that must have had a singular resilience to survive a century of school vocal education and the tastes and modifications affected by Australian and New Zealander choirmasters and accompanists. Kik Quintal has recalled, for instance, that "several people have tried to change our ways of singing over the years" and given the example of Gordon Bennett North, a pianist who used to work with ABC Radio in the 1930s and 1940s before retiring to Norfolk Island in the late 1940s, where he began working with island choirs (*prior* to the recordings described above):

> Most of the Pitcairn songs were just played and sung off the cuff [ie from memory] ... Some of the old music was a bit tattered and torn, and he had a look at it and said that some of the notes were wrong ... They didn't go from 'there to there' or some sort of thing ... So he changed them a bit. (interview 1999)

While the two 1950s recordings provide a sense of what mid-20th Century hymn singing styles were, it is unclear what precise changes in tempos occurred between the 1950s and 1990s, aside from observations that they have grown faster over the last fifty years. One of the few references I was able to uncover was provided by regular Anglican organist in the 1990s, Tim Lloyd, who informed me that several of her predecessors (who were not so informed about local traditions) had attempted to raise the tempo of hymns, often with mixed results. According to local lore, on more than one occasion the organist persisted with a faster tempo than the choir, with neither party conceding, creating an unusual polyphony[5].

During the 1960s-1990s the tradition of singing *The Pitcairn anthem* and other locally associated hymns at funerals continued, with George 'Kik' Quintal as hymn leader. The particular experience of attending such funerals, down in historic Kingston, in the dramatic graveyard, close to the shore, where both convicts and generations of Pitcairn descendents are buried, is generally agreed to be a profound one. Numerous individuals interviewed for this book commented that hearing the hymns sung in the open air, in the wind, with the noise of the waves, was particularly poignant. Quintal himself has commented, "you think of a lot of things down there ... sometimes the singing is a bit hard, a bit of a struggle" (interview 1999).

While some tape recordings were made of Quintal singing to organist Daisy Buffett's accompaniment (on hymns such as *Open the gates of the Temple* and *The sun is dying in the West*) during the early 1970s, the only publicly available recordings of his performances are those featured on the 1993 *Pitcairners Church All Saints Kingston Norfolk Island Commemorative Cassette*. This cassette included a range of standard Anglican hymns alongside original compositions by island resident Anne Swift, who also provided organ accompaniment. Quintal appears as featured soloist on two hymns, *I come to the garden* and *There is a land of pure delight*. The only locally associated hymn to appear is *The Pitcairn anthem*, present in a version accompanied by Swift's organ part, led off by a solo male voice and performed at a slow pace, as per local convention.

The cassette is the only recorded legacy of Anne Swift, who relocated to Norfolk Island from England in 1969. Swift, a devout Christian, was a regular organist for the Methodist (and on occasion Anglican) churches in the 1970s and 1980s. In 1983 she wrote and self-published a collection of Biblical songs and psalms set to original music entitled *Let The Island Praise Him*, the introductory note to which states that the collection was "written in the simplest form, for widest possible use" in her "sincere desire and prayer that Jesus Christ might be honoured and glorified" (i). She also wrote a theatrical presentation entitled 'The Story of Creation in Song' (1984), which was staged in 1984 at Rawson Hall, and 'Father Abraham: A Musical Play' (1985). The cassette includes versions of her hymn *Dear father on high* (with words by Beth Quintal), performed by the Chapel Choir, and *Gabrielle's message*, performed by a choir credited as the "All Saints' Singing Group". Despite their inclusion on the cassette, Swift's hymns are now infrequently performed on the island.

In 1991 the Anglican St Barnabus Chapel Choir, accompanied by Tim Lloyd and under the direction of choir leader Julie South, recorded an album under the title *Popular Hymns of Norfolk and Pitcairn*. This album featured the seven core locally associated hymns discussed above and fourteen others. The performance and arrangement of the hymns is closer to modern Anglican hymn singing than the 1950s' recordings. With regards to the locally associated repertoire, the album retained the convention of opening the *The Pitcairn anthem* with a solo male vocal line. However, the version of *The ship of fame* differs from the 1956 versions by using male voices followed by female voices to distinguish the question/answer parts of verses 2 and 4 and female parts answered by male in verse 3[6].

Another cassette album released early in the 1990s under the auspices of the Uniting Church provided a more comprehensive linkage of the sacred, ceremonial and secular performance of hymns on the island. Entitled *Pitcairn and Norfolk Songs of Praise*, the album comprised eighteen hymns, including the seven Norfolk standards. Unlike the St Barnabus recording, the Uniting Church album features material in a variety of styles. Some of the hymns (such as *Jesus stands amongst us* and *Sun of my soul*) are performed in typical Methodist style to an organ accompaniment. The choir is less conducted than the St Barnabus recording and has a looser, more varied approach to vocal harmonisation[7]. The locally-associated hymns are mainly performed in slow tempo versions with a loose communal choral style, the version of *Oakleigh* being notable for a gentler, rolling rendition that is more appropriate to its lyrical theme than more austere previously recorded versions. The version of *The ship of fame* offers a particularly significant connection of the sacred and the social by virtue of being set to a piano part and having a pronounced rhythmic swing that indicates why it has remained a popular sing-along standard at island parties and gatherings.

The Uniting Church album also differs by including solo, duet and small ensemble vocal versions of non-traditional hymns, performed to guitar and/or keyboard accompaniment. The Pitcairn Singers contribute a version of the hymn *Cleanse me* in a folk-gospel style to strummed acoustic guitar accompaniment. The hymn – also known as *Search me, O God* (after its first line) – is a regionally appropriate one, its lyrics being written by Northern Irish evangelist J. Edwin Orr while visiting New Zealand in 1936 (and it is often performed to a modified version of the melody of the Maori/New Zealand sentimental standard *Now is the hour*[8]). The Pitcairn Singers formed in the early 1990s and included, at various times, Clare Edwards, Cynthia Deadman, Marie Beadman, Lorraine Beadman, Kenny Christian and George 'Toofie' Christian. Their main repertoire was locally associated hymns and they also provided occasional live accompaniment for hula performances. Two other songs have strong country/gospel associations, Leo McCoy and Cynthia Deadman perform the Adelaide Pollard/George Stebbins' hymn *Have thine own way Lord* (which was recorded and popularised by US country singer Jim Reeves in 1962); and Susan Pedel sings the Marijohn Wilkins and Kris Kristopherson song *One day at a time*, which was a major hit for US Christian country singer Cristy Lane in 1979. Along with these contributions, the album also features a version of a contemporary Norfolk language song, *The Right whale*, performed by its composer George 'Toofie' Christian (whose songwriting is discussed in Chapter 11).

In addition to the recordings discussed above (and the Eric Jupp arrange-

Figure 14: Pitcairn Singers (mid-1990s)
(l–r: Marie Beadman, George 'Toofie' Christian, Ken Christian, Clare Edwards,
Lorraine Beadman, Cynthia Deadman).

ments discussed in Chapter 10), Norfolk Island's two most prominent
singer-songwriters of the 1980s and 1990s, Don Christian-Reynolds and
Susan Pedel, also recorded versions of locally associated hymns.

Christian-Reynolds featured five hymns on his 1986 cassette album
Norfook es ouwus hoo-em. The versions of *Gethsemane*, *The Pitcairn anthem*
and *Oakleigh* approximate the standard island style of these compositions
with two vocal parts (Christian-Reynolds and Sharon Sandstrom) accompanied by Sandstrom's piano. Reflecting their common social performance,
The ship of fame and *In the sweet by and by* are performed less gravely than
the previously discussed recorded versions. *The ship of Fame* has a subdued
(and low-mixed) guitar accompaniment supporting its lilting delivery, while
In the sweet by and by is performed in an uptempo 1960s folk-style version
with a prominent rhythm guitar part.

Susan Pedel also featured versions of two traditional hymns on her debut
release, *Susan Sings* (1997), accompanied by Christian- Reynolds on guitar.
Her version of *The Pitcairn anthem* is performed at a traditionally slow pace,
to chordal guitar accompaniment and organ washes. By contrast, her
version of *Let the lower lights be burning* is based on a subtle, slow-medium
paced hula groove, provided by Christian-Reynolds's rhythm guitar part,
that gives the song a distinctly different feel to the more standard choral
versions of the song discussed above.

Reflecting her religious convictions and local pride Pedel went on to record a seven track themed CD, entitled *Orl Ucklun*, in 2000. This featured *The ship of fame* and *In the sweet by and by* together with five other hymns. Pedel was accompanied by three backing vocalists (Clare Edwards, Marie Beadman and Michael Nobbs) and a band humorously credited as 'Wiggies Widgetts' which the CD notes identify as comprising Ken Nobbs (piano), Alex Nobbs (organ), Roy Nobbs (mouth organ), Les Nobbs (button accordion), Michael Nobbs (guitar) and Wiggy Knapton (tea-chest bass). Pedel supplies lead vocals on all the tracks, complemented with vocal harmony parts low in the mix and a harmonica part that often mimics the vocal lines. The band supply a strong rhythmic emphasis to the tracks with strummed guitar, piano and t-chest bass giving the songs a 1960s' country/gospel feel with organ parts providing the most obvious association with traditional religious performance of the songs. The CD's live feel is explained by its production context, being recorded in one day, Pedel relating that:

> *it was rather rushed, and the musicians weren't used to what is required when you make a proper recording, but I wanted to record all the old hymns and it was the only real way to do it here.* (interview 1999)

The 1956 recordings of Norfolk hymn singing led by Carty Christian finally emerged on CD in 2003 as tracks incorporated and excerpted in Rick Robertson's Cyclorama soundtrack (discussed in Chapter 10) and also featured as separate tracks on the CD. Robertson's inclusion of the hymns reflects his recollection of hearing them in his youth:

> *As a kid I remember Kik* [Quintal] *leading off the singing with "Then shall the king say unto them on his right hand" and everyone coming in on "Come ye blessed of my father" and it was so powerful – it was overwhelming. I'll always remember it.* (interview 2004)

These remarks, and those cited elsewhere in this chapter, underline the continuing affective power these hymns have on Norfolk Islanders' sense of their culture and identity.

III. Culture, Character and Hymnody

My research on Norfolk Island revealed a strong local perception that the hymn singing of previous generations represented a particularly rich, evocative and emotive expression of island spirituality and community identity that was rapidly disappearing – or at least, *paling* – in the face of growing modernisation, Australianisation and/or irreligiousity. In one sense this perception represents the broader nostalgia of sections of the Norfolk community for a past recalled as simpler and more communal, a romantic imagination of selective aspects of Norfolk's history coloured by perceptions of the present. In another, it represents an accurate perception of the manner in which hymn singing has shifted from being a local, collective endeavour to an activity that takes place in very specific and organised worship contexts.

A set of common perceptions emerged from my research, several of which complement, overlap and/or seek to explain each other:

1. That there are diminished opportunities for communal hymn singing.

2. That the nature of singing in (particularly) Anglican services was distinctly different from traditional community hymn singing (particularly of the core locally-associated repertoire discussed in this chapter).

3. That young islanders (in particular) didn't seem to value and enjoy the experience of communal singing as much as their elders and predecessors.

4. That – with the marked exception of Kik Quintal – current singers lacked the distinct vocal character and skills of revered earlier singers.

5. That current singers were loosing, or had lost, the ability to perform 'natural' four part harmonising

The majority of these perceptions are accurate reflections of changes in socio-cultural aspects of island life in the latter part of the 20th Century. Communal hymn singing has become increasingly compartmentalised into slots, such as performances in dedicated sessions after Sunday services at the Uniting Church or down at Kingston graveyard on Anniversary Day and at funerals. (And even the latter practice is experiencing a decline as community attendance at funerals has tended to dwindle since the early 1990s.) Underlying the general decline is a factor of time.

Prior to the arrival of television and the prominence of tourism as a facilitated all-year round industry, Norfolk Islanders had more disposable time and a greater community orientation. As various chapters of this book demonstrate, social music making was an important part of social and cultural life, giving generations of islanders the opportunity to grow up within a hymn-singing culture which presented frequent opportunities to hear, participate in and learn the nuances of hymn singing. The supposedly 'natural' ability of previous generations of island singers to four part harmonise was, of course, exactly the opposite. Rather it was the result of being brought up within a community in which such skills were present and valued, and from which they were acquired by processes of informal experimentation and acquisition (in the family home, on visits, in concerts, communal events and services). In response to my providing them with recordings of early Norfolk hymn singing for comment, Christian music scholars Mark Evans and Robin Ryan both identified a sense of engagement and absorption in ensemble singing by the vocalists – a sense of mutual listening and interactive performance that produced compelling and emotionally convincing versions of the material. Evans has asserted that these aspects explain the slow tempos:

The tempos found in earlier recordings complement and reflect an attention to detail on the part of the singers and a desire to make the vocal nuances as precise and as precious as possible. (pc 2004)

While the shrinkage of the broader social music context serves to explain the decline in individual investment in skills acquisition and nuance of performance and interpretation, there are contemporary contexts in which traditional singing is maintained (albeit in modified ensemble contexts), such as the work of the Pitcairn Singers and the material performed by Norfolk Island troupes at the Festivals of Pacific Arts. While not community events as such, they represent a clear attempt to continue the local tradition within an organised framework. Providing a bridge from the subject of this chapter to that of the following, one of the clearest indications that the community singing tradition and ability to provide impromptu harmonisation is still present on Norfolk Island was made apparent to me in a secular context.

In May 1999 Australian singer-songwriter Graeme Connors visited to perform at the 6th annual Country Music Festival. During his visit he found that one of his compositions, a song entitled *Pacifica* from his 1991 album *Tropicali*, was popular on the island and had, indeed, been the theme song for Norfolk Island's 1996 multicultural festival. Along with its bouncy Pacific 'strum-along' ukulele-style groove (actually performed live and on record on mandolin), the song's lyrical celebration of Pacific life and identity was typified in its chorus:

> *Whoo-o-oh Pacifica*
> *The gentle heart yearns for thee*
> *Whoo-o-oh Pacifica*
> *Home is the sailor, home from sea*

Key to local identification was the song's first verse, which refers to local community history and heritage:

> *Captain Bligh sailed by in 1789*
> *Between Viti and Vanua Levu*
> *Too blinded by his rage*
> *To see the beauty of those golden shores*
> *Blinded by his rage*
> *To find a hangman's noose in Dutch Timor*

In his live solo concert at the festival Connors delayed performing the song to the conclusion of his act and then attempted to organise the audience into sections to sing along with the chorus. The crowd rose to the opportunity to an extent that surprised Connors. Sitting in the audience, singing along somewhat tentatively, I found myself immersed in a mesh of improvised, overlapping four part harmonisation that grew with intensity and joy with each repetition of the chorus and which transformed the concert into a moment of communal music making that moved the audience to a rapid and emotional high. In this context the deafening applause at the conclusion seemed as much an act of self-affirmation as a response to the song performed on stage and evoked and re-inscribed the deep-seated traditions of local singing and community identity discussed in this chapter.

Notes

1. It is therefore far from coincidental that *Let the lower lights be burning* is also regarded as locally significant on Lord Howe Island, an association that seems to have developed independently of Norfolk Island. See Hayward (2002: 15) for further discussion.

2. Quoted on http://hymnsys.com/sotc312.htm (accessed 30.4.01).

3. This story was related to me by various informants (and with various minor embellishments that I have not included here).

4. An English 18th Century hymn (of devotion) that has not been a prominent local hymn in recent years.

5. This is not to imply that such experiences are unique to Norfolk Island, similar divergences of choir/congregation and accompaniment have been a regular phenomenon in Christian services (due to factors such as limited musical competence, intransigence etc.)

6. Mark Evans has identified that this conforms to broader developments in Anglican worship in which women have become more prominent (challenging male leadership in singing and other areas) and in which four part harmonising is no longer a skill that choir or worship leaders can assume that singers possess. (pc 2004).

7. *Beautiful stream* has a variation in that it features solo verses by Charlie Adams joined by the choir on the choruses.

8. See Hayward (2001: 66 and 2002: 24) for discussion.

Chapter Ten

MODERNITY AND DIVERSIFICATION
Popular music in post-War Norfolk Island

The introduction of regular air services heralded a period of major change on Norfolk Island. Increasingly easier and more frequent contact with major cities in Australia and New Zealand allowed many aspects of Norfolk Island culture to take on a modern and international flavour, as the island caught up with a series of outside developments and fashions. These, in turn, were variously localised and assimilated by islanders and became elements in the creation of new versions of Norfolk Islander heritage and identity.

I. The immediate post-War period

Old time dances resumed in the post-War period. Members of the Bailey family regularly played at dances and concerts and Harvey 'Brookey' Christian still attempted to ensure that propriety was maintained at all times. Other popular dance pianists included Bob Dewey (who moved to Norfolk in the mid-1930s and established a guesthouse in Kingston) and Steve 'Wacko' Menzies. Menzies was one of a number of Norfolk Island men who served with the Australian military during the War. The experience of life off-island and the trauma of conflict led to a sense of communal bonding amongst those who returned, many of whom collaborated in the construction of an RSL (Returned Soldiers League) clubhouse and socialised there in the late 1940s and 1950s[1]. Accordionist Richard 'Ukoo' Douran recalls the self-taught Menzies as a talented "vamper" – "he couldn't play off the music but you'd sing him or whistle him a tune and he would be off, working it all out" (interview 1999). Such a skill was a useful accomplishment at the RSL, where singing around the piano was a regular form of entertainment. David Buffett has characterised Menzies as "the natural leader" on such occasions, "with his strong voice, his repertoire of songs, and self accompa-

133

niment" (pc 2005). The RSL repertoire comprised popular songs of the period together with what Buffett describes as "some such 'soldier' songs" that "were not designed for tender ears" (ibid). Menzies was also a regular performer at domestic social occasions and dances and Buffett recalls that Menzies was particularly enthusiastic about the latter:

> Steve's dance music would compel you to get up and dance. The swing and the harmony 'lifted you' to join in. Steve was also a very good dancer and there was a harmony of both skills when he performed. (ibid)

The first local band of the post-War period was the Cascade Onions, an eight-piece ensemble featuring three harmonicas, two guitars, two ukeleles and a bass. Commencing in 1946, the group played for tourists at venues such as the Hillcrest guesthouse and at occasional public dances before breaking up in 1948, when the various members left to work overseas. Harmonica player Dan Yager recalls the Cascade Onions as "the only band there was around at the time" and recollects that their repertoire included popular tunes such as *Missouri waltz* and *12th Street rag* (interview, 2005).

Along with dances, the pre-war Variety tradition also continued and received a boost in 1950 when Thelma Horner, a New Zealander, set up a new Musical and Dramatic Society that staged a series of plays and concerts over the following decade. Horner had performed as a juvenile in theatre in Christchurch (New Zealand) before studying at the Sydney Conservatorium of Music and subsequently appeared on Australian radio and the New Zealand stage before re-locating to Norfolk Island in 1949. She introduced an ambitious policy and program choice, as manifested in a concert she organised in April 1950, whose program is reproduced here in full[2] to give some idea of the diversity of items offered:

- Ballet: *The Butterfly and roses* – Madam Grand (piano), Francis Bright and the Quintal Sisters (dancers)
- Song: *Habanera* (from Bizet's *Carmen*) – Thelma Horner
- 'Tour': Island Songs in Costume[3] – Marina Adams and Irma McCoy
- 'High Jinks with the Bell Boys and Housemaid' – Francis Bright and Yvonne Quintal
- Song: *Chin-Chin-Chinaman* (from the musical *Geisha*) – John Carr
- Ballet Dance – Francis Bright
- Recitation: Easter Poem and Phone Conversations – Mrs Hawley
- Character Song: *Jewel in Asia* (from the musical *Geisha*) – John Carr
- Sketch: 'Ignorance is Bliss' – John Carr, Thelma Horner, Irma McCoy and Johnny Young
- Duet: *Wanting you* – John Carr and Thelma Horner
- Chorus (led by Marina Adams, John Carr and John Young): *Come to the Fair*

- Hungarian Ballet (with tambourine) – Francis Bright, Thelma Horner and Yvonne Quintal

- Song: *I wonder if love is a dream* – Thelma Horner

In the same year another notable variety concert was held to raise money to support the public hospital. Billed as a 'Minstrel Show', the first half included items such as a performance of *Ave Maria* by Tom Bailey and Gordon Bennett-North that "brought back memories to the listeners" (*NINE* 24.3.50: 1). The second half comprised a blackface "Nigger Minstrels" set, which featured renditions of 'negro spirituals' by prominent island singers such as Carty Christian and Charlie Pat Adams. An anonymous reviewer characterised the event as a financial and cultural success:

> *Last Wednesday night at the Norfolk Theatre found a packed house to witness one of the most enjoyable evening's entertainment experienced on Norfolk Island.* (ibid)

While blackface minstrelsy declined in popularity, variety shows continued throughout the 1950s and 1960s and overseas artists began to feature on special bills. One problem that such shows experienced was a lack of amplification. The appearance of this as a problem reflects shifts in audience expectations of the clarity and volume of sound at concerts and dances (cued, in substantial part, by their familiarisation with gramophone playback volumes and sound quality). The Musical and Dramatic Society responded to public and press criticism by allocating one hundred and fifty pounds for the installation of a public address system at Rawson Hall, comprising one microphone and six speakers.

One ensemble that did not appear to have amplification problems was the brass band that operated in 1950-51. The revival of brass banding on the island was attempted by William Green, who visited the island for a year in 1950 in the employment of the Australian Department of Works and Housing. Green, former bandmaster of the Toowomba Brass Band, received the support of the Administrator and access to the stock of brass instruments he held[4], and organised a public meeting to promote the idea. An ensemble was established, mostly comprising relative novices to their instruments, which began rehearsing in July. An (unattributed) item in *NINE*'s 'About You' column reported that:

> *Screeching and weird noises were heard by the residents of Ferny Lane last Thursday night. Being pay day at the W & H camp, some thought a celebration was in progress. However another report, said to be authentic, states that the Brass Band Boys were tuning up for their first rehearsal. It is pleasing that a new band is in the process of organisation and its members deserve every encouragement.* (28.7.50: 3)

Despite the final note of support offered by the newspaper, the absence of press reports on subsequent performances suggests that the initiative, like its 1930s' predecessor, failed to establish itself as a continuing enterprise.

While performances of classical music in both public concerts and family recitals waned in the 1960s and 1970s, this style was featured prominently on the island's radio station, VL2NI (which began regular broadcasting in the early 1960s[5]), particularly during Michael Moran's term as manager in

135

1971-73[6]. Moran instituted a Sunday evening 'Fine Music' slot, which regular offered lengthy retrospectives of individual composers and attracted a small but loyal and passionate audience. Classical music was also presented in various semi-public events, where programmes of classical music were played on the gramophone to attentive audiences, such as those evenings run by Tom and Dorothy Elliot at their Watermill Valley property. Apart from occasional visiting artists and concerts by school students, devotees of traditional western art music had to principally rely on radio broadcasts and their own CD collections during the 1980s and 1990s.

While popular styles have come to dominate the island's live music culture, light classical music continues to be presented at themed performance evenings (targeted primarily at older tourists) offered by hotels such as the South Pacific. Piano teacher Joan Rawlinson[7] has established herself as a featured performer at such events and recorded a CD of piano standards in 2002, entitled *Norfolk Memories*, to cater for after-show demand for recorded product. The CD includes Bach preludes along with versions of popular songs such as *Danny Boy* and *Moon River* and Hollywood screen tunes such as the theme from *The Godfather*. Guitarist Don Christian-Reynolds and violinist Eric Craig have also mined a similar musical area, securing regular employment at the Colonial Hotel restaurant's 'Italian' theme evenings. As discussed below (and in Chapter 11), Christian-Reynolds has been an active contributor to various aspects of local music culture since the 1970s. Craig pursued a career as a secondary school music educator in Auckland before retiring to Norfolk Island in 1988 with his Norfolk Islander wife Moyna. During his residence in New Zealand he co-founded the Manukau Youth Orchestra, which had the distinction of being the first orchestra to perform on Norfolk Island in 1977. In 1989 he established a Norfolk Island school orchestra, initially using many instruments on loan from New Zealand, that made its offshore debut in Auckland in 1991. During the 1990s the orchestra accompanied various local school productions (including 'Grease' and 'The Wizard of Oz'), often in collaboration with other adult musicians. Craig and Christian-Reynolds's debut CD, *Unplugged*[8], was released in late 2004 and comprises instrumental versions of light classical and popular pieces, many (although not all) with an Italian or Mediterranean theme. Their CD and live set features popular Italian songs such as *Funiculi Funicula* (Denza) and *O Sole Mio* (Di Capua) alongside more diverse items such as Eric Coates's composition *Sleepy Seas* and the Duke Ellington and Juan Tizol jazz standard *Caravan*.

II. Popular music in the 1950s-1960s

In the early-mid 1950s a number of new arrivals contributed to the expansion and diversification of local music culture. One such individual was Franklin Boyer, a US ex-serviceman who had seen duty in the Pacific during World War Two and who returned to Norfolk Island to reside. His principal instrument was piano (although he was also competent on the saxophone). He played in various contexts and ensembles and was notable for performing arrangements of traditional Pitcairn hymns in his repertoire[9]. During the 1950s he also performed at social events with another new musical arrival, pianist Tim Lloyd, a Sydneysider, who first visited the island in 1949 and returned to live in 1953[10]. Boyer also wrote what appears to have been the first regularly performed song about Norfolk Island, a composition entitled *Take me back to Norfolk Island*. Written around 1952, the composition conforms to a genre of 'exotic' place songs popular in Australasia (typified by compositions by Townsville composer John Ashe such as *I lost my heart on Hayman Island*, *Magnetic Island* and *Sunset on Orpheus Island*[11]); which, in turn, appear to have been inspired by resort songs celebrating (and often commissioned by) Honolulu's resort industry in the 1930s (such as *In the Royal Hawaiian Hotel* [1935]). As its title and refrain suggest, Boyer's song also draws on the overlapping genre of "take me back..." nostalgic songs that were particularly popular in the pre-War era[12]. *Take me back to Norfolk Island* was regularly performed at the Paradise hotel in Kingston from the mid-1950s on, usually sung by vocalist Susan Pedel and accompanied by hotel owner Jim Hamilton on piano. The sheet music for the song was also available for sale at the venue in a souvenir edition (published in 1958) and Pedel eventually recorded the composition in 1997 on her cassette album *Susan Sings*.

Take me back to Norfolk Island is a slow-medium tempo ballad, often found in postwar dance band repertoire, with a chordal progression that easily implies a country/hula feel (given appropriate lyrical cues). Pedel's 1997 recorded version uses (and complements) the lyrical and melodic theme of the composition as a showcase for aspects of her individual vocal character. The main vocal techniques deployed in her recording comprise a frequent movement of pitch and volume up into individual notes, starting quietly just underneath the target pitch and rising in volume to it, and a controlled use of vibrato on particular words or phrases for emphasis[13].

Figure 15: The Paradise hotel (c1960).

137

This allows her to convey a rich melancholic nostalgia in lines such as:

Old acquaintances will meet you
Such a smiling, happy throng

and facilitates dramatic emphases on lyrically significant phrases such as the second line of the following couplet, emphasising the first word and stretching the last:

Take me back to dear old Norfolk Island
That's where I belong

These techniques – and the overall delivery – distinguish performances of the song from much of the vernacular island repertoire detailed in the following chapter and made the composition Pedel's signature song for several decades.

Many post-War tourists shared the same kind of 'exotic-Pacific' vision of Norfolk Island that Boyer conveyed[14]. One frequent visitor in the late 1950s, New Zealander Vera Lewis, wrote lyrics that expressed her enjoyment of the island set to the tune of a foxtrot that she had heard on the radio[15]. On her next visit to Norfolk she recalls that "I played it and [local musician] Alec Nash got the tune off on his accordion and when we went to a ball they played it" (*NIN* 26.3.80-21.4.80: 37). The opening verse comprised the following lines:

Oh haven't you been to Norfolk Island?
The paradise in the Southern Sea
Haven't you seen the stately pine trees?
That fascinate your memory

This perception of Norfolk Island was also shared by another 1960s' visitor, Eric Jupp. Best known in Australia for writing the music for the popular 1960s' Australian children's TV series *Skippy*, Jupp and his orchestra also fronted the ABC Television music series *The Magic of Music*, which was broadcast in between 1961 and 1975[16] (and which produced twenty two spin-off albums, an eight album *Readers Digest* boxed set and two subsequent CD compilations). Jupp was a frequent visitor to Norfolk Island in the 1960s and became interested in local history. In 1966 he became actively involved with the group of people who staged the 1967 Pageant of Norfolk Island (discussed in Chapter 7). As advance publicity for the event emphasised, Jupp and members of the organising committee were attempting to create an enduring cultural representation of the island that would convey its history to visitors and reaffirm it for islanders. While the 1967 pageant attracted interest and attention, it was not subsequently re-staged. Various factors were involved here. First, the event was ambitious and time-consuming to mount; second, Jupp's music did not appeal to younger islanders, who had become caught up in the pop and rock boom of the 1960s; and third, the high profile input of Jupp and Australian performers distanced the pageant from the culture it professed to represent. In this regard, the Tahitian sequence (also discussed in Chapter 7) was perhaps the most successful, in local terms, serving as an enclave of local culture in an otherwise highly mediated production.

Jupp facilitated the contribution of Australian singers and performers and arranged the show's score, drawing on Herbert Stothart's music for Lloyd's 1935 film *Mutiny on the Bounty* (which, in turn, had quoted extensively from popular British songs of the 1700s and 1800s – including *Rule Britannia* and sea shanties such as *Blow the man down*). Jupp also modified the music of a song written by pianist Rose Arthur with lyrics by choreographer June Ryves entitled *The ballad of Barney Duffy*. The song relates a story from the convict era that has been retained in local folklore, the escape and subsequent capture of a convict named Barney Duffy[17]. Its lyrics proclaim how:

> *Hidden away in the heart of a tree*
> *Seven years of liberty*
> *There he was safe*
> *There he was free*

[chorus] *Barney Duffy*

Jupp visited and lived on the island intermittently in the late 1960s and 1970s, and gave occasional performances at the Rawson Hall, accompanying his wife Shirley Macdonald on piano, and also jammed informally with musicians such as trombonist Kenny Gordon at the Paradise hotel.

At the suggestion of local hotelier Joyce Dyer, Jupp initially sought to record a version of Boyer's *Take me back to Norfolk Island*. Frustrated by Boyer's delay in approving this, Jupp wrote a new song entitled *Beautiful Norfolk Island*, which he recorded and released in 1973 as the title song of a four-track 7inch vinyl EP (together with versions of *The ballad of Barney Duffy* and arrangements of *The ship of fame* and *The Pitcairn anthem* sung by his regular collaborators Macdonald and Neil Williams). The EP was released in a souvenir, colour gatefold sleeve edition complete with cover photos of the coast and inland of Norfolk Island, an eight page illustrated booklet

Figure 16: l–r: George Golla, Eric Jupp, Shirley Macdonald and Kenny Gordon at the Paradise (1969).

139

describing the island's history and a transcription of the lyrics to the title
track:

Beautiful Norfolk Island
Jewel of the sea
Green and ever peaceful
Rich in history
Under the mantle of Heaven
It will always be
Beautiful Norfolk Island
Paradise to me

In the late 1970s these four tracks were repackaged, together with added
tracks (*Amazing grace, Jesu joy of man's desiring, The stranger of Galilee* and
Ave Maria) from Shirley Macdonald's vinyl album *How Great Thou Art* (1973)
– a collection of sacred songs (recorded in Sydney but with a sleeve design
of Macdonald in front of St Barnabus Chapel). Like the preceding EP, this
album was also released under the title *Beautiful Norfolk Island* and has
continued to be available in island shops (and advertised in the *Norfolk
Islander* newspaper) for the last thirty years, most recently in CD format.
Particularly prior to the release of local choral and singer-songwriter albums
in the 1990s and 2000s, Jupp's album served as a standard musical
memento of a visit to the island and has thereby represented the island to
outsiders over several decades – despite the indifference of many locals to
its original music and representation of the Pitcairn hymns.

Musically, Jupp's EP/album has little connection with prior Norfolk
Island culture. The title track has some tenuous association by virtue of
being in waltz time, strummed on an acoustic guitar and featuring slow
sliding vocal lines that (very faintly) evoke a Polynesian choral feel. *Barney
Duffy* is included as a melodramatic number, declaimed by Neil Williams in
a style – and with a chorus vocal arrangement – that recalls the delivery of
songs in classic Broadway musicals such as *Oklahoma*. *The ship of fame* is
recorded as a duet between Shirley McDonald and Neil Williams (with
backing chorus). The vocals are accompanied by a strummed chordal guitar
part that gives it a brisker pace than usual in Norfolk Island performances
and its arrangement also features flute embellishments. *The Pitcairn anthem*
is closer in pace and feel to its traditional island style, although it is recorded
in a light operatic arrangement that lacks the slurring and lilt of island
community performances.

A very different impression of Norfolk life was recorded in song by
another 1960s' visitor, Harry Robertson. Robertson was a Scottish sailor
and singer-songwriter who emigrated to Australia in 1952 and initially
found work with the Tangalooma Whaling Company in Moreton Bay (near
Brisbane). In 1956 he spent a season whaling at Norfolk Island during the
final years of the fishery. He later recalled his experiences in a song entitled
Norfolk Whalers that was included on his 1971 theme-album *Whale Chasing
Men: Songs of Whaling in Ice and Sun* (and in its accompanying songbook).
The album attracted considerable publicity in Australia and Robertson went
on to record further songs and wrote material for various ABC TV produc-
tions. His songs are typically set to basic three chord guitar accompaniments

and make prominent use of his earthy, strongly-accented declamatory vocals and detailed descriptive lyrics.

In his album notes for *Whale Chasing Men* Robertson describes how he was struck by "the number of people who lined the cliff tops, some 300 feet high at Cascade Bay" to watch the arrival of the whaling boat he sailed on to Norfolk. The sleeve notes tie this initial experience to his later discovery of the history of local whaling "one night while in conversation with one of the older inhabitants". These experiences led him to compose his song about the local whalers. The lyrics bracket four verses of description of small boat whaling practice with verses describing the anxious anticipation of the whaler's families, Verse 1 stating:

High on the cliffs of Norfolk's green isle
Women and children are waiting the while
Far down below the whale boatmen row
As after the humpback the Norfolk men go

And the final verse concluding:

The joy on friends' faces, what pleasure to see
Their loved ones return with the prize of the sea

Along with its topical inscription in Robertson's song, Norfolk Island also had another connection with the Australian folk revival in the form of a visit by folklorist and performer Alex Hood in 1975. Hood appeared at Rawson Hall and at the island school, presenting and discussing aspects of Australian folklore, explaining how didjeridus are made and performing his version of a traditional Aboriginal brolga dance[18]. Hood's promotion of aspects of Australian folklore and the sudden popularity of bush bands (ensembles mixing aspects of Australian bush ballads, Anglo-Irish music and rock instrumentation) in the late 1970s and early 1980s brought the forms considerable prominence in continental Australia[19]. Due, in no small part, to the style's assertive Australianness, bush band music failed to catch on with Pitcairn-descended local performers and largely bypassed the island until the mid-1980s when three Australian school teachers working on the island on short term contracts formed an acoustic ensemble named the Norfolk Whalers[20].

The band, comprising Wayne Courtney, Brian Mercer and Stuart Sullivan, on guitars, vocals and lagerphone (percussion stick), played at local hotels, mainly catering for the tourist market, and were notable for producing one of the first locally released cassette albums, entitled *Norfolk Island*, in 1986. The album comprised sixteen tracks, twelve of which were standards from the Australian bush band repertoire (including *Click go the shears*, *Bound for South Australia* and *The Ryebuck shearer*) and four originals. Three of the four original songs – Mercer's *The Hell of the Pacific* and *The Bounty saga* and Courtney's *Barney Duffy* – refer to the period prior to the Pitcairn settlement of Norfolk. *Barney Duffy's* lyrics present a summary of Duffy's life in a similar vein to that of Ryves and Jupp's earlier song (discussed above), set to a mid tempo acoustic guitar and percussion accompaniment and simple melodic line. *The Bounty saga* is a jaunty mid-tempo song, suggestive of a shanty, which summarises the events of the mutiny and its aftermath in a straightforward and simple fashion. *Hell in the Pacific* is a mid-tempo song describing the harshness of life during the convict settlement days from the point of a view of a prisoner cautioning the "lads of Sydney town" not to embark on a life of crime and risk ending up on the island.

Despite the band's popularity with visitors and its production of the cassette album, it has largely disappeared from the cultural memory of the island, or, at least, of island musicians[21]. One of the reasons for this excision appears to have been the ensemble's choice of name and theme song, asserting themselves (even by implication, rather than necessary intention) as a Norfolk Island ensemble representing a Norfolk Island history. The cover of their cassette crystallises this with a shot of the trio at Emily Bay and the prominent wording 'The Norfolk Whalers – Norfolk Island'. The ensemble's theme song elaborates this further. Performed at slow-mid tempo pace to strummed guitars, its lyrics, sung by Courtney with Mercer adding harmonies on the chorus, are delivered from the point of view of a local whaler in verses such as:

> *With* our *hands on the oars*
> *And* our *feet upon a brace*
> *We pull with all our might*
> *For a whale is tough*
> *And he'll not give up*
> *Without a bloody hard fight*

This aspect is further underlined in the lyrical phrase "For the Norfolk Whalers are *we*" (my emphases). As Chapter 11 discusses, this kind of assumption of local identity and expression by an Australian band playing a distinctly Australian style of music was distinctly ill-timed in terms of the political sensibilities emerging on Norfolk Island in the mid-1980s and while no opprobrium appears to have accrued to the individual band members, who continue to have personal connections to the island community, their brief career forms only the faintest footnote to local memories of the decade.

III. Dance music

The late 1950s and early 1960s were a transitional period when old time dances continued at the same time as pop and rock and roll music began to be imported to the island on discs and radio. One of the ensembles that operated on the cusp of the transition was Wacko's Wonders[22]. Somewhat confusingly for outsiders, the band was named after (previously discussed) island pianist Steve 'Wacko' Menzies, who only guested with them occasionally[23]. Accordionist Richard 'Ukoo' Douran founded and led the band. He taught himself to play by ear after having some lessons from Harvey 'Brookey' Christian in the mid-1950s and formed Wacko's Wonders in response to a shortage of island musicians:

> *After Harvey Christian died there was no one left to play ... so I asked Mett 'Bubba' Nobbs if she would play along with me, with me as accordion player. Her brother Tiwi was a good saxophone player and so we got together and played a couple of times but decided that we might*

need a slap bass for our sound. There wasn't one on the island but we thought that we might get Charlie Bailey's old cello and use that. Well, I asked but no luck there. We didn't have the money to buy one so I made one out of a tea-chest, with a broom handle up as the neck and a stick up the top to tighten the string. That worked fine, it just made a deep bass, a kind of 'throb'! We had a couple of blokes that played it ... I started on a little twelve bass accordion, twelve keys on the left. Then I switched to a 58 but I thought I was too good for it or something ... and I switched to a 120! It was real heavy to hold all night! (interview 1999)

The band used to play at the Paradise every Friday night, providing background music for the first part of the evening and then dance music after dinner. Douran recalls that the band weren't paid to play there but instead "we'd get a carton of beer – and Tiwi only drank rum – so that made

Figure 17: Richard 'Ukoo' Douran (date unknown).

more for us!" (ibid). Wacko's Wonders also played various functions at Rawson Hall:

> We used to play the regular old time dance numbers, the waltzes, foxtrots, barn dances, they were all the go. The main dance was the barn dance because everyone changed partners, so you could dance with everyone ... We took over from Brookey ... He was pretty strict ... But we weren't like that, we just kept going whatever! When we played our first dance at Rawson Hall they wouldn't let us stop. We were going until four in the morning when we were supposed to knock off at twelve. (ibid)

Pianist Alec Nobbs joined the band in 1961 but they broke up in 1962 when they were the only musicians left after the others dropped out. Wacko's Wonders were succeeded as the regular Paradise band by ensembles featuring musicians such as pianist Ken Nobbs, guitarist Les Macrae and drummer Daniel Yager that performed more modern material.

The era of regular band accompaniment to old time dances had come to an end and this traditional social entertainment was increasingly confined to special events. By the mid-1960s even the traditional institution of the Bounty Ball, held on Anniversary Day, was being modified by new fashions and behaviour, as a reviewer for the *Norfolk Islander* noted:

> And now on to the Dance ...
>
> One of the best Anniversary Balls Norfolk has seen for many years. The hall was really packed and apart from the ladies dressed in their period costumes there were many very lovely evening gowns and short dance frocks.
>
> Music was supplied by Clive Weir, Geoff Ryan and the two Smith boys, Ken and Alec Nobbs and Mr Jack Bailey. The evening was compered very ably by Greg Quintal who, with other assistants, are to be congratulated on the successful 110th Anniversary Celebration.
>
> The highlight of the evening was the demonstration of "Mod" dancing given by members of the visiting University Architectural team. In the modern vernacular they really appeared to be "way out" – minus shoes, socks, stockings, arms and bodies twitching and gyrating. (NI 10.6.66: 2)

Such "way out" "mod" behaviour was also increasingly popular with young islanders and, as the following section outlines, the latter part of the decade saw significant changes in live music and youth culture.

IV. Roaring Days – The live music scene in the 1960s and 1970s

Writing in 1975, a contributor to the *Norfolk Island News* recalled summer holidays in the late 1960s, when young Norfolk Islanders would return from study or employment in Australia and New Zealand, in the following terms:

> What carefree days they were – lazing at the beach, barbecuing down

Kingston at night ... It was terrific sitting around a fire with everyone joining in the singing ... What would happen now if a group of youngsters "piled up" in the middle of Burnt Pine with their guitars? Cars that passed were stopped, keys taken and the occupants urged to join in the fun. Today's police would have a fit. ('Twist' – NIN 3.11.75: 18)

This brief account gives some insight into a pattern of social behaviour that developed on Norfolk Island in the late 1960s and early-mid 1970s. Such activity represented an irreverent and occasionally anarchic reaction against traditional social attitudes and morés that took its cue from the Sixties 'counter-culture' that spread from North America and Western Europe to the southwest Pacific. As in other parts of the West, such rebellious behaviour accompanied and interacted with significant developments in popular music. On Norfolk Island, this period saw a significant flowering of musical activity and the establishment of a generation that went on to form the core of a succession of island ensembles that performed until the early 2000s.

During the 1960s and early 1970s there was a gradual loosening of liquor laws in response to tourists' desires to purchase alcohol easily at their hotels. While the motive behind relaxations in legislation may have been the development of tourist trade, some hoteliers also saw the possibility of securing extra local patronage. The management of island hotels such as the Paradise at Kingston and the Kingfisher Airtel at Anson Bay, for instance, managed to secure a special licence to serve alcohol to all-comers. This succeeded in attracting a large number of patrons but also led to tensions over the different behavioural expectations of guests and locals and occasional incidents arising from this.[24] Problems of this kind led the Kingfisher management to publicly threaten to restrict service to residents and dinner patrons – if "a small minority of locals" continued to "disrupt" the evenings "by acts of vandalism" (*NI* 1.4.66: 13). In the event this threat was not carried out and, despite continued problems, the hotel developed as a popular venue for tourists and locals alike. There were also tensions between tourists and local patrons when it came to musical tastes.

The Paradise continued as one of the main centres for live music throughout the 1960s. In 1966 a new pop orientated band started at the venue, initially featuring George Smith on keyboards, his brother Dennis on drums, Jeff Ryan on bass and guitarist Clive Weir. Through a series of line-up changes George Smith continued as the pivotal member. As he has emphasised, "who was in it changed a bit as time went on but we played the same kind of things – same songs, in some cases" (interview 1999). Significant additions to the band in the late 1960s included Dave 'Ace' Rodgers on lead guitar, George 'Toofie' Christian on rhythm guitar and Ivens 'Toon' Buffett on vocals. After Dennis Smith's departure, first Robert Wotherspoon and then Allan Macrae played drums. The band found itself effectively catering for two audiences. As George Smith has recalled, the owner, Eric Semple established this by stating:

"I don't care what you do after ten o'clock but you play for my guests when you first start." So we used to play a few waltzes and a bit of

country music and as the night went on he just let us play what we wanted and get loud ... and more raucous ... and that was the rules and when the other pubs started having entertainment that was the same thing, you always played for the guests 'til 10 o'clock. (interview 1999)

A 'shift' pattern developed whereby most tourists would tend to retire to bed around 10pm just as locals began to arrive. The band's repertoire – for their later, more "raucous" set – featured a variety of contemporary material including Beatles and Creedence Clearwater Revival songs. According to a variety of musicians and former patrons interviewed for this research, the "more raucous" music that would start up often matched the behaviour of those in attendance, with advanced inebriation and fights being less than infrequent occurrences. In venues such as the Paradise, music and social interaction also continued on many occasions after the bar had closed and the formal entertainment had concluded, as various local performers sang and played together.

Debates about licencing came to a head in March 1967 when the issue of granting public bar licences on the island was discussed at a public meeting at Kingston council chambers. The anti lobby, led by the Anglican Reverend Phillip Kitchin, gained the support of the meeting and the situation stalled around an awkward compromise whereby hotels could gain licences to serve all-comers but bars catering more specifically for locals were prohibited. There were also anomalies to this legislation in that there was no minimum age for consumption. This attracted adverse comment from many visitors and was also a concern for local parents. An article published in the *Auckland Evening Post* by a New Zealand visitor stated:

Figure 18: Allan 'Perry' Macrae, George 'Toofie' Christian and George Smith (1969).

Figure 19: On stage l-r: Kenny Gordon, Don Christian–
Reynolds, George Smith (obscured) and David Rodgers
+ Alan Dyer (front) (c1971).

Everyone frequents the bars for the four licensed hotels on the island. Up until last month there was no age restriction for drinking – they hadn't thought of imposing one and it was rather staggering to have a drink with an attractive girl one night and then see her cycling to school the next morning. Lads and girls as young as 14 lined up at the bars and the publicans had no recourse but to serve them. (reproduced in *NIN* 22.9.75: 23)

While alcohol was a staple aspect of youth culture, locally-grown and imported marijuana was also consumed from the mid-1960s on and stories about local marijuana smoking even surfaced in the *Sydney Morning Herald* (in April 1976), leading the *Norfolk Island News* to go into defensive mode and run a corrective story which identified that "'pot' is smoked reasonably regularly by two small groups on the island, and by a very small sprinkling of adult individuals" adding that the "drug problem appears ... to be less than in almost any mainland city" (*NIN* May 1976: 7). While the latter is debatable, it appears that harder drugs were less prominent on the island than on the mainland.

147

In 1967 the Kingfisher began promoting itself as an all-week entertainment venue, with the following advertisement appearing in the *Norfolk Islander* (v2n28 10.3.67: 16):

WHAT'S ON AT THE KINGFISHER

Friday Night

Open Night – Cocktail Hour 6-7 p.m. with Warwick Davey at the piano. After Dinner - Jazz dancing to midnight to the Music of the "Mutineers"

Saturday Night

Open Night – Cocktail Hour 6-7 p.m. with Warwick Davey at the piano. After dinner modern and jazz dancing

Sunday Night

$1.50 dinner – followed by Film

Monday Night

Housie – Proceeds to Sunshine Club

Tuesday Night

Open night – Go-Go Dancing

Wednesday Night

Open night – Dancing to the "Mutineers" WEEKLY TALENT QUEST – Vocal or Instrumentalist - Weekly prize 1 Bottle of Champagne Finals to be held during "Bounty Week" First Prize $50.00 2nd Prize $25.00

Thursday Night

Open night – Dancing 7.30 p.m. – midnight by the swimming pool (weather permitting) to the music of the "Mutineers"

"The Mutineers" was one of the names the management gave to musicians employed at the venue. Rather than rely on local performers, the Kingfisher experimented with bringing in overseas musicians in the late 1960s. The high cost of this – in terms of airfares – meant that the management had to adopt some sharp employment practices. According to George 'Toofie' Christian:

They used to get in Australian and New Zealand musicians to work. But they'd also expect them to work in the bar and do other duties, which'd often surprise them and they'd either leave before their six month contracts were up ... Or – if they didn't – they'd be sacked because otherwise they'd have to be given permanent jobs. (interview 1999)

In contrast to the Paradise, which had poor acoustics and a stage close to the bar (leading bar staff to constantly complain about the volume of the band), the Kingfisher had a longer hall, with the bar at the opposite end from the stage, and was considered as a good venue for performers. Its prominence was short-lived however, since it closed down after a severe fire in 1970, leaving the Paradise, South Pacific, Norfolk and Castaway hotels as the main live music venues. During the 1970s South Pacific manager Alan Dyer became an enthusiastic employer of local musicians, frequently acting as a compere at performances, singing standards such as *Alexander's ragtime band* and *Rock around the clock* and performing comedy turns and humorous dance routines.

One significant addition to the island's pool of musicians was Don Christian-Reynolds[25], who relocated to Norfolk in 1970 after teaching guitar, ukulele, bass and mandolin in Sydney, running a music shop and performing with a pop band entitled The Stardusters. Soon after his arrival he formed a trio named Lantana with bassist David Rodgers and drummer Max Hobbins. After two periods off the island, in 1969 and 1973, George Smith returned to regular performing in the mid-1970s, appearing at the South Pacific, Paradise and the Hotel Norfolk, and formed Sneaky with his brother Dennis and bassist Phil Billman. Another new band formed at this time was Albatross, a quintet comprising drummer Raymond 'Smudgie' Cooper, guitarists Kim Davies and Billy Nobbs, singer Lorraine Hayde and bassist Gary 'Tayte' Svendson. Sneaky continued until 1979 when the Smith brothers departed temporarily for Australia. In a short item that identified the camaraderie of local performers and their link to the social sphere of the island, *NIN* carried an item on Sneaky's final ('Blast Off') gig that reported:

> *music for young and old played at different times during the evening by all the musicians who had played during the past year ... It was also*

Figure 20: Don Christian Reynolds and John 'Puggy' Meyer (c1973).

an opportunity for the new Freeway group to introduce their type of music. (March–April 1979: 36)

Freeway comprised Billman, guitarists Kim Davies and Max Wright and drummer Wayne Irvine and had a rockier orientation than their predecessors.

In 1980 Smith returned from Australia and, together with Cooper, Davies and Hayde, formed a band named Mutinee. Hayde left in 1981 and was temporarily replaced by Alan Macrae before Shane McCoy joined as lead singer. This line-up went on to perform throughout the decade. Their sets included hard rock material, covering tracks by bands such as The Angels, Police songs and a variety of Sixties material, such as Ben E. King's *Stand by me*, since, as McCoy has emphasised, "here as a band you've gotta be middle of the road, you've gotta be able to play for seniors and [do] new rock songs" (interview 1999). The band also featured two more locally orientated compositions. The first of these was a version of the Beatles' *You're going to lose that girl* in Norfolk language, "a spoof song... people recognised the song but not the words!" (ibid). The second was a (Standard English) original entitled *Narrow minds*, which McCoy refers to as:

> a 'stick it up yers' [song] ... I aimed it at a couple of people ... It was about going to a party and you walk in and every eye's on you ... I slapped [it] down and said "Here fellows, this is what we're gonna do, this is about how it goes, let's add to it", so we did ... we put in like a heavy rock beat to it.[26] (ibid)

Along with Mutinee a number of other bands attempted to explore harder rock sounds in the 1980s-1990s. Cooper also performed in another 1980s band, Eze Rock, featuring guitarists Pete Ilyk and Max Wright and bassist Brian Dews. Other notable local musicians included guitarist Lee Hamilton-Irvine, who performed in bands such as Kardoo in the early 1980s and led a punk rock group named Poxtrots in 1985-86. Irvine recalls that despite writing a number of original songs the punk band only performed occasionally, "usually in the intervals of other band gigs", since it "wasn't the kind of music any of the places wanted to have then" (or after, it appears) (interview 1999). Another active island rock musician was Wayne Pendleton, who performed with Hamilton-Irvine in The Calici Brothers[27], an ensemble that appeared regularly in the mid-late 1990s. The latter's repertoire was eclectic and featured early British 'progressive pop' hits (such as T. Rex's *Get it on* [1971] and Jethro Tull's *Locomotive breath* [1969]) alongside more contemporary material. Performance opportunities for these bands were however more limited than their predecessors due to a reduction in live venues from the late 1980s on, which Kim Davies has explained in the following terms:

> From the late 1980s on the live music scene started dropping out and bookings started drying up – hotels did other kinds of entertainment. Television hit the island and the kinds of visitors coming changed. The tourists we had used to be a mix of ages, there were a lot of young ones once and they'd want to come and hear live music, to dance, on holiday.

They are mostly older now ... they want the dinner-type evenings, singalongs and stuff. (interview 1999)

As a result, a younger generation of gigging rock musicians has not emerged into the island's live music culture and – as discussed in the following sections – young players wishing to perform anything aside from country material have been unable to get significant public exposure.

V. Country music 1980-present

Although Mutinee set out playing a mix of middle of the road and heavier rock material, as the decade progressed the band began to feature more country music in their sets since, as McCoy has identified:

What we found was that no matter who came here if we reverted to country – modern country – they enjoyed it a lot more than what we were trying to pull in with the younger crowd. That's how we headed into country rock, with me being more [into] country than the rest of them, that's the way we went. (interview 1999)

McCoy's personal engagement with country music reflected a local interest that had persisted since the 1930s. Shane McCoy's uncle, 'Foxy' McCoy, has recalled that:

Country music was popular in the 1930s – there were stacks of records on the island in the 1930s, everyone had those old spring-loaded wind-up players – singers such as Wilf Carter, Tex Morton, [British yodeller] Harry Torrani (who sang Swiss Sweetheart Yodel) and Hank Snow ... During the war – and after – we would get together with guitars, ukuleles, squeezeboxes and have sing-songs at people's houses. Or if there was a radio program on featuring Tex Morton, or someone else we all really liked, we would listen and sing afterwards. Radio 2KY [from Sydney] was popular – we'd have the old radios with big valves and aerials stretching up to the top of the pine trees, right up high, to get a good reception. (interview 1999)

While there were small social gatherings of aficionados that included impromptu music making, there were no regular country music perform-ances on the island in the 1960s and 1970s. However, country remained popular on radio and disk and continuing interest led to the formation of the Country Music Club in the early 1980s, a loose performing troupe that included, at various times, Archie Bigg (harmonica and vocals), Clive Chap-man (steel guitar), Shane McCoy (guitar) and Cynthia Deadman and June Ryves (vocals). The band used to perform at the Bowling Club bar and an (unreleased) live recording from 1981 features ensemble 'sing-along' vocals, chordal guitar accompaniment, lap steel introductions and breaks and harmonica lines. The material featured on the recording comprises a selec-tion of songs from the early years of hillbilly and honky-tonk country (such as The Shelton Brothers' *Just because*, Gene Sullivan's *When my blue moon turns to gold again* and Hank Williams's *Cold, cold heart*) and three (uniden-tified) mid-tempo lap steel led instrumentals. In the early 1980s their performances sustained country music as a live form on the island and set the seed for the expansion of the genre in the 1990s.

Interest in country music also provided a popular social song in the form of a lyrical revision of Merle Haggard's 1969 hit *Okie from Muskogee* that is sometimes referred to as *The dreamfish song*[28], in reference to the hallucinogenic, nightmare-inducing effects of eating the naenwe fish[29]. While I have not managed to obtain a full text of the lyrics (and while the revisor[s] remain unknown) the first two lines of Haggard's original:

We don't smoke marijuana in Muskogee
We don't take our trips on LSD

were commonly substituted by:

We don't smoke marijuana on Norfolk Island
We take our trips on hoem naenwe

The latter half of the song's opening chorus line, "I'm proud to be an Okie from Muskogee" was also substituted with "a Norfolk Islander". A Norfolk language version of this song was also performed on occasion in the early 1970s (which I have also been unable to access).

The continuing interest in country music was exploited in 1993 through the establishment of an annual country music festival, initially conceived by Kathy Le Cren and subsequently organised and developed by prominent island businesswoman Gayleen Snell. Snell developed the festival as an off-season, late autumn tourist attraction. With the support of Air New Zealand, she established the Norfolk Island Country Music Association Inc. (NICMA) and recruited an organising committee, with Kim Davies as president, Jackie Pye as secretary and New Zealand country singer Tracey-Maree Houia as initial co-ordinator. The first festival was held in May 1994 and has been held each year since. In her 'Welcome from the Patron' preface in the 1995 festival program, Snell emphasised the local connection:

Country music's origins evolved in small country communities such as Norfolk Island, so it seems fitting for this community to see its continuance and play host to this year's festival.

The programs of the festivals have enshrined this local connection by featuring local artists alongside the Australian and New Zealand acts, who feature in respective national showcase nights, a 'hoedown' evening and the 'Trans Tasman Entertainer of the Year' Awards night. Informal adjuncts to the main festival have also provided valuable points of connection for local performers. As Davies has characterised:

At the festival all the musos get together, hang out and play whatever they want, in jams or do other things that they haven't been contracted for ... They don't worry about what their contract or agent might say because they are over here and it's kind of 'Norfolk Rules' – or 'no rules' – just play with who you want. (interview 1999)

The Nightriders

Mutinee disbanded in 1989 but the inauguration of the annual country music festival prompted members of the band to re-group. Their previous country music repertoire was now something that had a fashionable focus and allowed the band to develop a new identity as The Nightriders. The initial line up of Smith, McCoy, Davies and Cooper was augmented with the addition of singer/guitarist Alan Maisey in 1997 and bassist Phil Billman in 1999. At various times performers such as Wayne Pendleton have also played with the band (at the time of their second Tamworth visit) and singer Kim Friend has guested on various occasions, often singing a version of Jackey Ralph Quintal's poem 'The day they caught the bull' to the band's accompaniment.

Since their inception, the Nightriders' sound has been typified by a tight rhythm section, strong lead and harmony vocals and Smith's distinctive Hammond organ sound. The Nightriders performed at the first Norfolk Island country music festival in 1994 and received sufficiently favourable responses to continue their new direction. Appearing in 1995 they became acquainted with visiting Australian outfit the Dead Ringer Band, whose leader, Bill Chambers, was impressed with their performances and offered to arrange them a slot at the 1996 Tamworth country music festival, Australia's premier country music event. Smith recalls that, "I don't think we took them very seriously at first but they arranged it for us" (interview 1999). Their performance at the event came as something of a shock to a band whose previous biggest gig had been to an audience of 400–500 at the first Norfolk Island country music festival. McCoy has related:

[It was] the first time I had ever gone there to the festival. I'd forgotten what a crowd was like. We played at the Bicentennial Park in front of 12,000 people and if I was a bar of chocolate I would have melted into that bloody stage, or walked out ... And me being the lead singer up front ... (interview 1999)

The band's performance was evidently well received since they were invited back in the following year. Cooper has emphasised that:

People over here might not have realised how much work we did to get the band up to scratch for Tamworth, we stepped up another level that I didn't know we had. You don't go down as well over there as we did without being good, there's so much competition ... We were also pretty unique, no one else had that Hammond organ in country then, that made us distinct. Even so, when we played at the muso's club in Tamworth we were pretty nervous but Shane killed 'em all with that Hank Williams stuff, no one was playing that then (though they do more now). Kasey Chambers joined us on stage a few times too, she'd sung at Up Country when she had been on Norfolk and it was great working with her, although we had no idea of how big she was going to become after. (interview 2004)

Despite these two high profile performances, and other invitations to play in Sydney, Brisbane and New Zealand, the Nightriders have stayed a local part-time band due to their family and professional commitments (with Smith being chief minister in the island assembly in the late 1990s). McCoy also emphasises the band's continuance as due to the enjoyment that members get from it rather than a desire to be stars (in any context).

The Nightriders' repertoire has consisted almost entirely of covers by various US country and country rock acts, such as The Eagles and Willie Nelson. Although they have not released any recordings they recorded six

153

Norfolk Island

NIGHT RIDERS

Country Rock Band

Shane McCoy & Alan Maisey ~ Rhythm & Main Vocals
Kim Davies ~ Lead Guitar
George Smith ~ Bass & Keyboards
Smudgie Cooper ~ Drums

★**APPEARING**★

*Figure 21: Nightriders poster (1999)
(L-r rear: Alan Maisey, Raymond 'Smudgie' Cooper,
Kim Davies, George Smith + Shane McCoy [seated]).*

tracks (in an eight hour session) in 1998 that they deemed unreleasable due to their sound quality. These tracks comprised covers of Hank Williams' *Cold, cold heart*, Arthur 'Big Boy' Cruddup's *That's allright mama* (memorably covered by Elvis Presley in 1954) and Dwight Yoakam's *Pocket of a clown* together with three originals, a version of the old Mutinee number *Narrow minds* and two numbers contributed by New Zealand singer-guitarist Alan Maisey, *Norfolk* and *The stranger* (the latter co-written with his then-wife Emma). The lyrics of *Norfolk* attempt to bridge the rural roots of country music and Norfolk's isolated Pacific island location through the analogy featured in the song's chorus – of Norfolk being (effectively) "a little country town – in the middle of the sea". The song formed part of the band's live set in the late 1990s, sung by Maisey, with his usual high-set vocals, to a brisk, mid-tempo country-rock arrangement. The song's imagination of Norfolk Island spans its European discovery in 1774 ("James Cook claimed this paradise for the modern world"), the penal era of the early-mid 1800s ("We've had convicts from old Blighty"), the Pitcairn settlement ("Descendents of the mutineers") and the present:

*Those awful cruel days have well and truly gone
From this ocean mountain peak
But there are still a few for whom this past lives on
They come and go each week*

before concluding:

*We'll play our music now
And sing our songs for you*

154

So that you can see
This old-time whaling
Isolated country town
Has the Pitcairn legacy

In this manner, the song recalls Gayleen Snell's festival program characterisation (quoted above) and offers one possible identity for present day Norfolk Island, one significantly different to that of the hybrid Polynesian/Pacific identity discussed in Chapters 7 and 11.

The Dead Ringer Band/Kasey Chambers

Similar connections between isolated rural towns and the island were made by Australian country rock outfit The Dead Ringer Band (DRB) in the mid-late 1990s. The DRB had a more sustained relationship with the island than simply visiting to perform and championing the Nightriders at Tamworth. During the band's first visit in 1995 they met and became friends with members of the Menghetti family (their initial contact being celebrated in song in *This flower* on singer Kasey Chambers' debut solo album *The Captain* [1999]). Bassist Diane Chambers later commented that:

> *We really, really felt instantly at home on that little island and with the people who were to become our lifelong friends. Maybe it was because we too are easy-going simple, home-grown folk, whose values are more focused on quality of life and friendship. Whatever it is, Norfolk seemed to take us into their hearts, and we took them into our hearts.* (quoted in Lomax III, 2001: 128)

Inspired by their experiences on the island in 1995 and return visits in 1996, at which time Kasey Chambers began a relationship with Kurt Menghetti (celebrated on the title track of her debut album), the band decided to record their fourth album, *Living in the Circle*, on Norfolk, setting up a temporary studio in a house on a quiet road near Headstone. Bill Chambers described it as:

> *Just a beautiful old building, made out of Norfolk Island pine. It had lots of different rooms, it had a nice bit of carpet on the floor, it had wood everywhere, it just looked like a perfect studio.* (ibid: 151)

The album was released in 1997 with a front, rear and CD surface design sampled from Norfolk Island stone walls and the CD booklet included a reproduction of a painting of the sun setting behind Norfolk pines painted by Kurt Menghetti, together with a prominent dedication to the Menghetti family. The album provided the band with two substantial Australian country radio hits – the Kasey Chambers' composition *Already gone* and a cover of Maria McKee's *Am I the only one* – and attracted highly favourable reviews in Australia and the United States. The prominent acknowledgement of the island in the CD packaging also created a pride-by-association on Norfolk Island. The mutual appreciation between the two was further enhanced in 1999 when Kasey Chambers' solo album was released and established her as the most prominent and commercially successful Australia country performer of the early 2000s. Along with the two previously mentioned Norfolk associated songs, a third album track, *These pines*,

155

cleverly plays off previous 19th and 20th century US folk and country songs in its reflection on Norfolk pines[30].

Alison Ryves

Along with the Nightriders the other most notable local performer to have been encouraged and facilitated by the local country music scene was Alison Ryves. Born in the United Kingdom, she moved to Canada at the age of ten, then relocated to Philadelphia in the USA four years later, where she became interested in folk and country music:

> When I was fifteen I got a job working in a coffee house music club called the Main Point in Bryn Mawr, the university town outside Philadelphia. This was way back in the days of the folk scene [in the late 1960s/early 1970s] and then the electric phrase. People who played at the club when I worked there included James Taylor, Linda Ronstadt, The Eagles, Jackson Browne, Tim Buckley then Emmylou Harris. There were also lots of old Blues players, they all came through because there was a guy in Philadelphia called Dick Waterman who was the manager of people like Sonny Terry and Brownie McGhee, Muddy Waters and BB King back then, and so they all used to come to the club. I kept working at the Main Point until I was twenty-four, while I was studying for a degree in Visual Arts at university in Philadelphia, so I saw a lot of music! (interview 1999)

After completing her university degree, she returned to Canada, then moved to the UK to study and work as a potter before relocating again, this time to Norfolk Island, in 1980, to work at the Cottage Pottery (at Anson Bay). She subsequently married Steve Ryves, the owner, and has resided on the island since. Despite a long interest in music she did not begin singing in public and recording until the mid-1990s. As she has explained:

> I was very involved in the music scene at Bryn Mawr but never singing in public. I had this bad case of nerves – I froze whenever a microphone was put in front of me! I got so far as being in a group who rehearsed all the time but when I got up on-stage I totally froze and refused to do it! So that was the end of that. I didn't start singing in public until the Country Music Club in Norfolk Island, in 1993, which went OK and I just enjoy the opportunity of singing now. (ibid)

The Country Music Club was a separate entity from the previously discussed 1980s' club. It was based at a disused shop in Burnt Pine that had been loaned by its owner Sherree Irvine and renamed 'Up Country'. It held regular low-key performance and jam nights at which various members of the Nightriders and other local musicians played. The venue closed in 2002 but members of the audience and the performers who played there remember it with considerable affection as a friendly social environment. My own experiences in attending the club in 1999 confirm this as on separate nights I witnessed a range of performances from youngsters making their public debuts (warmly received by those present) through to 'all star' jams by members of Australian and New Zealand acts appearing at the festival.

Inspired by the experience of singing live at the club, Ryves wrote six songs that were produced and arranged by Murray Cook and recorded and mixed by Chris Townsend at B.J.B. Studios in Sydney in January 1998. These were issued as a CD EP entitled *Feels like home*. The CD's packaging emphasises the Norfolk Island theme, with its front-cover shots of Ryves strolling on Kingston's Cemetery Beach. The rear cover image comprises a close-up of a distinctive island woven hat (made by Mavis Hitch) on the sand. The inside of the CD cover contains information about the recording and, on the facing page, a shot of an Anniversary Day procession at Kingston with the words of the second verse of the title track superimposed:

When the people gather for Bounty
They march from the pier down the row
Till they reach the graves of their families
Then they bow their heads in prayer
Oh the island hats look so lovely
A breeze rustles the skirts
When they sing that Anthem of Pitcairn
You hear pride in every note
This is their home, oh their island
They came here by sea
In search of a home
To this beautiful island
Filled with sunshine
And majestic pine trees
And the sound of the seas
And it felt like home
Felt like their home
It felt just like home

This verse is significant for describing a continuing local tradition and its cultural and emotional significance. The photograph of the Anniversary Day procession complements Ryves's lyrics, and the song's restrained vocal delivery and arrangement, with the sense of proud solemnity conveyed by the partly bowed heads and traditional costume. The song itself is notable for the precise nature of its cultural-identificatory address. The song, (and the CD), are entitled *Feels like* home (my emphasis) and the lyrics of the first and third verses bracket the focus of verse two with a more personal/family perspective. The first verse has the song's protagonist looking down at the island from a plane as she returns, declaring that "as the wheels touch down on the tarmac/I know I'm coming home". The final verse returns to this personal connection and links it to the ancestral graves of the Pitcairners described in verse two, describing how:

Now my mother sleeps down-a-town
Where the sea breezes gently call her
And the sun shines down just to warm her
And I know that she is home

Oh I have a tie that binds me
I'm linked from the heart to this land
And I'll live out my days in the sunshine
'Cos I know I've found my home

Despite a pronounced sensitivity to such issues on the part of many Pitcairn descended Norfolk Islanders, her carefully articulated celebration appears to have drawn little (if any) critical response for its statements of local identification. The congruity of her song (and its sentiments) to island culture was inscribed in its public performance at the 1998 Country Music festival, where Ryves sang the song on-stage, backed by the D'Silverados.

Two of the other songs on the CD have lyrics addressed to Norfolk Island. *Valley song* is a straightforward celebration of place, describing both the location of the composer's home and the pine clad island's deep valleys, hills and frequent ocean views, embroidered with piano melodies extending the vocal lines; while *Prelude to Love* concerns a romantic assignation on a beach and features a prominent Fender Rhodes electric piano part, providing a distinct tonal colouring and a soulful, jazzy feel. The EP's other tracks comprise an effectively catchy country-pop song, *One way street of love*, with a prominent piano part (in a style reminiscent of Glen D. Hardin's work

Figure 22: Alison Ryves onstage at the 1999 Norfolk Country Music festival.

with Emmylou Harris's Hot Band in the mid-late 1970s); a simple, but prettily accomplished homage to New Orleans, *Cajun style*, with Ryves's voice complemented by a funky piano line; and a short, Country/Blues acapella track, *The box* (with Sydney musician Andy Travers on high harmonies).

The dominant musical style of the EP derives from the modern country music popularised by performers such as Emmylou Harris and Rosanne Cash in the 1980s and 1980s and more self-consciously traditionalist performers such as Alison Krauss, Gillian Welch and Iris Dement in the 1990s. These styles, and particularly their poppier, country mainstream counterparts, such as Reba MacIntyre, became widely popular in Australia in the 1990s, and spawned their own local interpreters, such as Gina Jeffries. The popularity of these styles on the island has been boosted by the success of the Norfolk Island Country Music festival. Ryves identifies this factor as key to her choice of musical inflection, also claiming wider musical tastes (in Celtic music, for example) but seeing country as the most facilitated and thereby opportune style to work within (at present). This latter factor is significant, since stylistic development is rarely, if ever, unaffected by the contexts of venue policies, local communities of taste and/or availability of musicians to collaborate with. As Ryves emphasises, "singing country music is just about the only way you can perform here at present, the only way you can get a band with you" (interview 1999).

As an active member of the island's Community Arts Association, she attended the Festivals of Pacific Arts in 1992 (in Rarotonga), 1996 (in Western Samoa), 2000 (in Noumea) and 2004 (Palau). In 1992 she joined George 'Toofie' Christian and Don Christian-Reynolds, singing material such as *The Coconut song* as accompaniment to Karlene Christian's dance performances. Although unplanned and unrehearsed, she also performed at the Opening Ceremony for the 1996 Festival, when the organisers required Norfolk Island to contribute, despite their delegation (officially) including only visual artists (Ryves attending in her capacity as an artist and potter). Ryves, who does not play an instrument, and visual artist Sue Pearson, an occasional hula-style dancer, hurriedly worked out a (one-number) routine together, performing a version of George 'Steggles' Le Cren's song *Norfolk Island Blues* (discussed in Chapter 11). In the absence of musicians in their party, Ryves approached the contingent housed next to them, from Rapanui (Easter Island), members of which agreed to quickly rehearse an accompaniment, performed by two mandolin players, a guitarist and a percussion player tapping stones together. As Ryves emphasised, "we didn't have any language in common but the music communicated itself, and it worked out fine" (ibid). The eventual performance proved memorable:

The Opening Ceremony was this elaborate occasion, in front of an audience of some 4000 people. Some islands had dozens of dancers on stage for their turns, really elaborate and impressive ... A bit daunting! Then Sue and I got up with the Easter Island musicians, and we did our little song! As we later found out, the Opening was being televised live in Western Samoa and round the Pacific. So we were there, representing Norfolk Island, with our pale skins, and all these Pacific Islanders [were watching]. *I know quite a few people* [on Norfolk Island] *might not agree with us in that role perhaps, but we were there, as who we were, doing our best and people at the Festival really appreciated it ... and, well, that's all you can say. We* were *the Norfolk Island representatives who were there.* (ibid)

Her experience in this role encapsulates a number of the (complex and problematic) issues concerning identity maintenance, negotiation and expansion in a changing global environment (represented here by the international spaces of cultural festivals and television broadcasting).

Ryves's second release, a CD album of original compositions entitled *Dancing with the storm* (2003), included two tracks (*Sweet Jane* and *Without your love*) recorded in Sydney with Murray Cook and ten tracks recorded at Manuka Studios in Orewa, New Zealand arranged by guitarist Rob Galley and produced by keyboard player Mike McCarthy. *Dancing with the storm* is dedicated to Ryves's sister Sian Quantrill, who died in tragic circumstances on the island in early 2001. Quantrill arrived on Norfolk Island in 1989 after living in Canada where she had worked in college and local radio. She was a volunteer presenter on Radio VL2NI in 1989-90, presenting a show entitled 'Folkways', and again in the mid-1990s, presenting the late afternoon program. During this period she also performed as a vocalist in occasional groups playing at local restaurants and hotels and wrote and recorded demos of five original compositions (none of which obtained release or airplay during her lifetime). *Beachcombing* and *Too close to you* (recorded with local guitarist Wayne Pendleton) and *Burning me inside* (recorded with Murray Cook) set vivid lyrical meditations on emotions, affections and betrayal to Celtic/folk styled vocal melodies and guitar accompaniments. Two further tracks, *Fluid retention* and *Dangerous woman* – both recorded with Cook – have a similar lyrical themes but were, respectively, set to a funky guitar and digital percussion groove and a brooding, atmospheric soundscape with processed vocal interjections and low-mixed sustained keyboard chords. The demos evidence a talent that was unfortunately denied further exposure through her untimely demise.

The lyrics of several of the songs on Ryves's *Dancing with the storm* reflect and, in the case of songs such as *Golden angel*, explicitly address her sister's death and Ryves's sense of loss. *Sweet Jane*, the album's only acapella track, which features Ryves and a harmony vocal by Jeanine Beattie, also evokes her sister through verses that recall shared childhood, young adulthood and middle aged experiences and memories.

Musically, the album has a well-honed, radio-friendly mainstream country/rock production that reflects the musicians' professionalism and depth of experience. Along with those tracks that reflect her family tragedy, the album also includes several other songs that inscribe aspects of Norfolk Island life and history. *Dancing with the storm* draws on Ryves's own experiences, or, more specifically those of her husband Steve, a fisherman, in relating the impact of a storm on island life in its opening and closing verse:

Wind in the east, three days at least
There's a storm blowing on the island

And the boats are high and dry
There'll be no fishing outside
When the waves break so heavy on the reef

and also suggests alternative ways to pass the day:

You can meet me down at Duffy's Whale[31]
Dance with the wind and laugh with the gale
Hand in hand we'll walk along the shore
See the ocean crash, hear it roar

The Turtle's song is an atmospheric ballad performed to an acoustic guitar accompaniment and gentle percussion groove. Its lyrics evoke the spaces of the ocean, the isolation of Norfolk Island and a lulling tranquility: "The turtle's voice is a haunting sigh/ As he sings the moon his lullaby" and also cross-reference Euro-Celtic mythologies, referring to the turtle singing "Of the selkie's fears, the mermaid's tears/ For all those lost beneath the blue". A further composition, *The Fiddler's tune*, accompanied in similar style, evokes Anglo-Celtic ballad traditions. Its twelve verse narrative relates a folkloric tale from Norfolk's penal settlement period concerning a fiddler imprisoned on the island whose embryonic romance with the Governor's daughter is thwarted by her removal to Australia. According to local lore, his ghostly presence and the sound of his fiddle can still be discerned on occasion at the (present day) Administrator's residence. Suitably complemented by fiddle lines (played by Marion Burns[32]), Ryves's lyrical narrative and direct vocal delivery evoke comparison to the styles of Anglo-Celtic balladry that took root in the North American Appalachians and, in turn, provided a formative influence on the development of hillbilly music and its eventual offspring, country.

One track recorded during the New Zealand sessions but not yet released is *Pine Tree*. Accompanied by chordal guitar parts and featuring a lyrical slide guitar solo in the middle eight, the song offers a warm lyrical paean to Norfolk, with lines such as "Norfolk on a sunny day/ Who could ask for more?" and "Live life at a better pace/ That's the Norfolk way". Broadening the theme, the song combines these emphases with lines that suggest the changes and turmoil affecting local life in the early 2000s following the murder of Janelle Patton (and foreshadowing the murder of Ivens 'Toon' Buffett in 2004): "You have a future in your hands/ So care for what you hold". Together with its references to traditional Pitcairn foods and Anniversary Day festivities, and lyrics that incorporate everyday Norfolk language phrases (such as "Hey yorlyi whatawieh"), the song both extends the sensibilities represented in Ryves's earlier composition *Feels like home* and connects to the Norfolk-Pitcairn song tradition discussed in the following chapter.

VI. New Generation Performers – the 1990s and 2000s

Distinct from the group of musicians discussed in previous sections of this chapter, three other, younger island performers – Rick Robertson, Andre Nobbs and Ben Boerboom – have pursued different paths, on and off the island, reflecting different musical sensibilities and goals.

161

Rick Robertson

The most successful professional musician to emerge from (rather than relocate to) Norfolk is also notable for pursuing a stylistic path outside of the standard genres popular on the island, working in jazz and various jazz-funk and jazz-electronica ensembles. Robertson was born in New Zealand, to a Norfolk mother, Janice Davison, and a New Zealand father, Gary Robertson, and relocated to the island in 1969 at the age of nine. Robertson began playing trumpet in a boys' brass band organised by Kenny Gordon that performed at various social events in the early 1970s. He was a self-taught musician, influenced by jazz artists such as Louis Armstrong, Humphrey Littleton and Sarah Vaughan and by contemporary bands such as Santana[33].

Robertson left the island in 1976, finishing school in Auckland and then studying agricultural science at Massey University at Palmerston North, New Zealand. He then spent almost ten years playing and touring with New Zealand bands such as Billy TK, Ardijah, When the Cats Away and the Kenny Pearson Power Band before moving to Australia to study jazz at the Sydney Conservatorium in 1990. In the 1990s he played saxophone with jazz-funk bands such as D.I.G. (Directions in Groove), recording a series of singles, EPs and albums, and also formed an ensemble named Baecastuff (a Norfolk Island word referring to the tobacco bushes that grow as weeds on the island). The ensemble combined 1970s' jazz influences (such as Miles Davis and Ornette Coleman) and newer dance styles (such as 'jungle'/drum and bass) and have (to date) released three CDs, *Big Swell* (1997), *One hand clapping* (1999) and *Out of this World* (2000). The second and third albums include the Robertson compositions *J.E. Road* and *Rocky Point*, inspired by Norfolk Island places. *J.E. Road* comprises an evocative, relaxed jazz-funk groove led by contemplative saxophone lines, while *Rocky Point* has a cooler retro jazz feel, featuring Robertson's sax lines and Philip Slater's trumpet parts[34].

Robertson visited Norfolk regularly in the 1990s and 2000s. In the mid-1990s he performed in a jazz trio with Max Hobbins (drums) and Wayne Pendleton (bass) during holiday breaks and in 2001 he wrote and recorded a song entitled *It's a very lovely day on Norfolk Island* during a visit. The track, a light digital reggae ballad, featuring jaunty synthesised accordion parts and a middle eight saxophone break, proclaims the pleasures of "sitting looking out to sea" and taking it easy. Principally intended for local listeners (and not released in any form to date), the track continues to receive occasional airplay on Radio VL2NI. In the following year he also worked on another project, providing an ambient sound arrangement for a recording of linguist Alice Buffett's poem *Baek t'baisiks* – an eleven verse account of the establishment of the Norfolk-Pitcairn community that was released as a (single track) CD[35].

As discussed in Chapter 9, Robertson has also worked on another significant local project. During visits to the island he has often played saxophone at family occasions, frequently performing versions of traditional island hymns. Impressed by such performances, Marie Bailey commissioned him to produce a musical accompaniment for her Cyclorama tourist attraction (which opened in 2003) that was released on CD (by the Cyclorama) in the same year. Robertson was interested in this project since he had long regarded saxophonist Jan Garbarek's work with Norwegian folk music as inspirational, identifying that he has "always wanted to get that traditional Norfolk sound, that deep feeling, and interpret it" (interview 2004).

The Cyclorama soundtrack comprises a 29 minute long low-dynamic accompaniment to the display's images. Entitled *The Journey – Portsmouth to Norfolk*, the piece uses sampled vocal and string sounds, sound effects and saxophone and flute parts. While Robertson has emphasised that the track is not meant to work as a 'stand-alone' composition (ibid), it is a highly effective mood-piece in its own right, as its succession of sounds suggest vignettes from the voyage of the *Bounty* (including musical references to dancing to the fiddle on board the ship and the festivities that greeted the crew at Tahiti). Two thirds of the way through the piece, following an extract from the 1954 choir recording of *Gethsemane*, the audio composition features a short humorous anecdote of Pitcairn life, recounted in Pitcairn language by (current) Norfolk-resident Pitcairn Islander Trent Christian. Following the 1954 recording of *The Pitcairn anthem*, *The Journey* features a conversation between Trent Christian and his sister Tania, in-role as period Pitcairners discussing the wisdom of a move to Norfolk. This sequence is followed by a string arrangement of *The ship of fame*, to signify *The Morayshire's* voyage. Tania and Trent Christian then converse in the role of Pitcairners arriving at Norfolk (noting the absence of palm trees and the prominence of pines). The 1954 version of *The ship of fame* then features and the piece terminates shortly after.

Andre Nobbs

Unlike Robertson, who established enduring professional roots in Sydney during the 1990s, singer-guitarist Andre Nobbs returned to the island in 2001. Like Robertson, Nobbs's musical career developed overseas. Nobbs began learning guitar while growing up on Norfolk in the 1980s but didn't begin to seriously develop his musical skills until relocating to mid-north coast Queensland in 1996. His live performing career began by accident, after attending a performance by his bass guitar teacher's band, Asphalt, when the singer failed to show and he was asked to deputise:

> I'd never sung in public before but I didn't know anyone there around Gladstone then so I thought "What the Hell?" and got up and did it ... Later that night the band came round to my house and asked me to join them ... So that started it. I said I'd join but only if they paid for me to get vocal tuition. (interview 2004)

Nobbs received tuition from prominent Queensland singing teacher Norma Tanner and began performing with the band, which changed its name to Guroove. At this time he began songwriting and one of his compositions, *Adrenalin Rush* – a fast-paced and lyrically intense rock number, was included in their sets. In 1998 he worked in a group named Fourte with singer Debbie Welsh before joining Eight Ball, a rock band playing covers and working around the Queensland regional circuit. During this period he kept writing songs "as much for my own reasons as to get them played" (ibid). A journalist for the Brisbane weekly magazine *Rave* heard him sing some of these at a social gathering and contacted him later with an invitation to play at a music festival in Brisbane dedicated to originals. At short notice he assembled a band from former members of Guroove and hurriedly rehearsed funk-rock arrangements for a number of his songs. The festival performance was well received and, following work offers, the line-up was named Headspin and went on to tour extensively around Queensland, supporting bands such as Grinspoon, The Whitlams and Frenzal Rhom, and had a residency at the Mercure Hotel at Rockhampton. Press reviews often cited The Red Hot Chili Peppers as a point of comparison for the band. After touring and winning several awards, Headspin began recording material for an intended debut CD but broke up in mid-1999, with Nobbs going on to perform as a solo artist, accepting the support slot on a tour by veteran Australian rocker Jimmy Barnes. His solo material is marked by its intense and often highly personal lyrics and a guitar style based on funky rhythmic accentuation, alternating with arpeggios and regular movement up and down the fretboard, giving his material a feel similar to that of early 2000s' Australian 'roots' musicians such as John Butler.

In 2001 Nobbs re-joined his son Dylan on Norfolk Island and has provided engineering support for visiting Australian and New Zealand performers and set up a recording studio. While he has performed occasionally since returning, in bands, solo and in a duo with Don Christian-Reynolds, his main activity – in addition to earning a living from non-musical employment – has been writing new material, ranging from songs for a concept album, intended to be performed with former members of Headspin, and songs and instrumentals inspired by Norfolk life and its history. While respectful of the island's musical heritage (as represented by the musicians and songwriters discussed above and in Chapter 11), he summarises the problem for young musicians on the island as follows:

> It's not easy to play on the island, if you're younger or if you've got different musical tastes ... There's a group of musicians of a similar age that have made the music that you hear around – and they've done that well – but there isn't much room for anything else live ... and limited venues to play it. I don't think that's healthy and I'd like younger players to come on and play and write originals in different styles or it will all get closed in ... The usual [country-related] island style is one thing but there's other genres too – you've got to keep where music is moving to if you want to get younger musicians involved. (ibid)

Ben Boerboom

Born in New Zealand, Boerboom relocated to Norfolk Island in 1990 with his family and attended Norfolk Island Middle School until Year 10. Developing an interest in heavy metal, particularly the lyrically dark, sonically intense genre known as 'death metal', he taught himself drums (and later guitar). During his school years he began jamming with guitarist John Buffett and went on to form a band named Caktus, with the addition of

Sasha Connolly on bass guitar. While the band rarely performed live – due to the absence of local venues catering for the genre – Boerboom released a seven track CD in 1997 entitled *Endless Mass Depression*. Recorded by Lee Hamilton-Irvine, the CD featured five of his own compositions and two further co-authored ones. Reflecting his personal tastes, the dominant musical style is heavy metal and the lyrics show the influence of the death metal genre, with song titles such as *Matricide*, *Fiend* and *Father Abuse*, reflecting Boerboom's admiration for bands such as Metallica, Slayer and Megadeath.

After releasing the CD, which got some (very limited) airplay on Radio VL2NI, Boerboom continued developing his musical skills, acquired an eight-track recording system and recorded and released a second CD in 1999. Unusually for a rock composer, Boerboom has identified that:

> *I wrote the songs at home, using the eight track, using the drums – I'd drum them out and build them up from that. I was learning as I did it, seeing what I could do, my singing wasn't that good then so I was learning it all.* (interview 2004)

Although credited to Caktus, Boerboom played all instruments, sung and wrote the songs (the only other contributor being Paul Buffett, who received a co-writer credit on the first track, *Dark seasons*). Stylistically similar to its predecessor, the drum and guitar playing were tighter and more integrated than on the first album and the songs (such as *Anencephalic*, *To kill and be happy* and *Misery*) were, if anything, harsher and more lyrically confrontational than its predecessor.

Drawing on his developing rock drum skills, Boerboom teamed up with Lee Hamilton-Irvine (bass) and Simon Brown (guitar) to form a covers-orientated rock band named Alcatraz that performed and occasionally gigged on the island in 2000-2001. The band's output is represented on a CD entitled *Two songs straight* that combines fuzzed guitar and drum-driven hard rock tracks with more melodic 1970s' style rock songs (reflecting the different creative personalities involved). Similarly to Caktus, Alcatraz's opportunities to perform live were limited by their inability to secure gigs at venues catering for the core audience for the style:

> *That's the problem here. You've got the older musos who've been doing their thing for years and they have the places to play. And the tourists, they're mostly older and don't want anything like we'd play. Places like the Brewery play more techno – for that crowd – and that left us out.* (interview 2004)

Disenchanted by this situation and keen to travel and experience the international music scene, Boerboom spent much of 2001-2003 in the United Kingdom, based in Reading, attending rock gigs and festivals and joining a hard rock band named School for the Gifted. The band performed in England and Denmark and Boerboom recorded an album with them entitled *Burning Needle* (2002) before returning to Norfolk Island in late 2003. While working to build up his savings, Boerboom also recorded a third CD under the name Caktus, entitled *Hymns to the Hanged*. This eleven-track release included re-recordings of earlier material (Dark seasons, To kill and be happy) along with new compositions, including his first song with a local theme, *Island prison*:

> *I wasn't interested in writing anything about Norfolk before, like any of that stuff about the island that the others* [older songwriters] *sing, but I had this idea about the old prison* [the penal era settlement] *that I got into. When I was writing it I got the idea of including a bit taken from* The Coconut song *but really twisting it to make it something else:*

We got the dope fiends
We've got the crime
We've got the victims
But never you mind

We got murderers, molesters
Walled up in stone
Decompose in your cell
Til they bury your bones

> *So I asked the Le Cren family and they were ok about it – although lots of others might not be ... Some people have told me that they think the song is about present day Norfolk – "Beauty hides all ugliness/ I don't need this emptiness/ This island is killing me". That wasn't what I had in mind but if they think that and if they want to get angry about it, then maybe nothing's changed here ...* (interview 2004)

Reflecting the sentiments expressed above, Boerboom made it clear in an interview with the author in 2004 that he felt that the island offered him no opportunities to follow his own genre tastes or desired career path and identified a move to Sydney or Brisbane in 2005-2006 as the most promising option for him.

* * *

The careers and perceptions of the three musicians profiled above illustrate the issues faced by musicians whose interests lie outside the mainstream of Norfolk's established music culture. Their responses to these issues are also salient. In terms of local culture, the migration/continued absence of performers with newer (and/or different) musical interests has tended to produce a degree of stylistic atrophy. This, in turn, risks creating a self-sustaining cycle that inhibits the generational refreshment of the pool of island musicians who have served local culture from the 1970s to the present (and of local music culture more generally). While new country music performers, such as Justin and Mardi Pye, are emerging, it is likely that the medium-long term future of popular music performance on Norfolk Island will require significant contributions from returning performers, changes in local performance venue policies and/or the organisation of new types of events and networks by younger music aficionados.

Notes

1. Thanks to David Buffett for supplying me with information on Menzies and the RSL context.
2. This is a re-punctuated and re-formatted version of programme published in *N.I.N.E.* 28.4.50: 4.

3.   I have not been able to identify which 'island' songs these may have been or what the "costume" referred to comprised. This may be a reference to a Polynesian themed item.

4.   Presumably those acquired for the original 1920s brass band.

5.   A local informational broadcasting service was initially established in 1952. A series of agreements with Australian bodies such as ABC Radio and the copyright protection and collection agency APRA led to funding from the Norfolk Island administration for the establishment of the radio station Radio VL2NI. For a historical and institutional analysis of the station in the period 1952-2000 see Coyle (2000).

6.   He presents a thinly fictionalised account of this in one narrative strand of his novel *Point Venus* (1998).

7.   Local singer-songwriter George 'Toofie' Christian has been one of her most regular and dedicated pupils in the early 2000s.

8.   Recorded by the author on a digital minidisk recorder at Craig's house in 2001.

9.   Cited by Tim Lloyd, interview with the author in 1999.

10.   Lloyd learnt piano playing while at school and wished to proceed to further study on the instrument but was persuaded to train as a secretary and start work at the age of fourteen. Her piano playing was further disrupted by the storage of her instrument during World War Two and she only began sustained activity as a keyboard player upon her relocation to the island.

11.   Which were included, together with works by other composers, in a sheet music album entitled *Blue Mist – Musical Settings of Australian and New Zealand Place Names*, published in 1952.

12.   A selection of which are included on Erik Damberg and Ruth Wilson's 2003 CD *Sunset Palms* (including a version of *Take me back to Norfolk Island* modeled on Pedel's).

13.   Thanks to Denis Crowdy for his discussion of this track with me.

14.   Bob Dewey also apparently wrote a song about Norfolk Island that he played on occasion in the 1940s and 1950s. I have not been able to find any reference to its lyrics or melody.

15.   Referred to by her as "something about 'Reproachfully Yours'" (*NIN* 26.3.80 – 21.4.80: 37).

16.   Material recorded for the show, and subsequent album releases, included a number of Jupp's own compositions together with a range of contemporary popular songs; film musical and show tunes and compositions by 20th Century composers as diverse as Duke Ellington, Mikos Theodorakis and Ernesto Lecuona. Jupp worked extensively with vocalists Shirley McDonald and Neil Williams and many of his recorded songs employ a prominent chorus section.

17.   This popular story is the principal incident from convict era history that has been perpetuated in local folklore.

18.   The brolga is a heron-like bird from northern Australia. Aboriginal clans such as the Yolngu include imitative dances in their repertoire.

19.   See Smith (2002) for a discussion of the rise in bush band music in this period.

20.   Apparently less in tribute to Robertson's song than the local whaling tradition it celebrated.

21.   Notably in this regard, no island musician I interviewed or talked to informally about local music history mentioned the band to me and it wasn't until dancer Mavis Hitch told me about them and gave me her copy of their cassette that I became aware of their existence. When I asked my island musician friends about them later, several claimed to have forgotten about them and others identified them as disassociated from local music culture (and therefore not relevant to my research).

22.   Also referred to, at various times, as "Wacker's" or "Whacko's" "Orchestra".

23.   Accordionist Ukoo Douran recalls:

We were called 'Wacko's Wonders' even though Wacko wasn't in the band! ... We painted it on the tea-chest [bass] *– He didn't mind!* [He] *sometimes filled in for us when we weren't playing.* (interview 1999)

24. Two interviewees for this book described problems between newly-wed husbands (often visiting the island on honeymoon trips) and young islander males paying "unwelcome attention" to their wives as being a regular source of friction and, on occasion, fights. Michael Moran provides similar descriptions in his novel *Point Venus* (1998).

25. Who added his maternal surname soon after arriving on the island.

26. McCoy has described the act of song writing as a therapeutic activity, not something that (for him) is about getting finished material to perform:

I came home from a party one night, it took me twenty minutes to write that. It's the only bloody thing I've ever written really ... all the others I've just chucked away ... I get into a mood of writing ... and I might write a page out then ... Because it doesn't bother me ... You get into a mood type of thing [then it's out of your system]. (interview 1999)

27. Named after the calici virus, introduced to kill rabbits in Norfolk Island and Australia in the 1990s.

28. It was also suggested to me that a separate song may also have carried this title but I have been unable to ascertain whether this is correct.

29. The nightmare-inducing effects of the naenwe, caused by a naturally occurring chemical, are well-known on Norfolk Island. I can personally attest to the effect and the vividness of the nightmares that result from consuming it.

30. See Carriage and Hayward (2003) for further analysis of *The Captain* and Kasey Chambers's songwriting.

31. A coastal location near Cemetery Beach.

32. A New Zealander who visited the island on several occasions in the 1990s, playing concerts and giving workshops at the school.

33. Artists he became acquainted with after acquiring a trunk-load of albums that had been brought to the island by saxophone player Pat Lush.

34. Robertson also wrote and performed a composition entitled *Kingston* in 2004, inspired by the arrival of the *Morayshire* with the Pitcairn migrants in 1856 (which has not yet been recorded).

35. The poem (and author's translation) is featured in Buffett (2004: 230-231).

Chapter Eleven

LARNA ACKLAN'S YUNG'UN
Norfolk Island language and heritage in song

This chapter reflects on the role of song in the Norfolk Island community, with particular regard to songwriters working within a Pitcairn-descendant heritage and identity. This chapter's separation of this area from that of other island songwriters with different cultural backgrounds, such as – most prominently – Alison Ryves (whose work is discussed in the previous chapter), should not be understood as an implicit elevation of the work of Pitcairn heritage performers above other local songwriters. Rather, I have separated the two in order to identify the social and political influences behind the creation of the first wave of contemporary Norfolk Island songwriting in the 1980s and the factors influencing the resurgence in local songwriting in the 1990s and 2000s. This chapter, in particular, relates developments in songwriting to the rise of Norfolk Island language as a public medium and discusses the manner in which that language has been preserved and deployed in song. English language compositions by Pitcairn heritage writers are also analysed within the context of local biculturalism and bilinguality. Since many of the most recent wave of songs have been recorded, I also discuss the nature of their arranged and produced form.

> [**Note** – See the description of my approach to Norfolk Island language use, vocabulary and translation that I present in the Introduction to this volume. The transcriptions and translations presented in this chapter are my own and, on occasion, differ from previously published versions.]

I. Early 20th Century songs
When I first began research on Norfolk in 1999, my familiarity with the music history of other oceanic regions (such as the North and South Atlantic) led me to anticipate that there would be a local tradition of vernacular songs acquired from visiting whalers and other mariners that may have persisted into the early 20th Century. I was therefore surprised

169

not to find a single reference to *any* maritime songs being performed in the 1800s or 1900s. The apparent absence of such a repertoire on Norfolk Island suggests that the Pitcairn settlers who arrived in 1856 did not bring any such material with them and did not subsequently acquire it on Norfolk Island[1]. This is curious, since other, similar regional communities, such as, most pertinently, Lord Howe Island, acquired maritime repertoire in this period (see Hayward, 2002: 4-29). Discussions with Norfolk Islanders suggested that the religiousness of the original Pitcairners might have prevented them from adopting secular material from visiting mariners. However, as Chapter 2 detailed, this explanation is questionable, since Pitcairners learnt a variety of dance tunes and steps and at least one popular Victorian parlour ballad (*The sailor boy's early grave*) from early-mid 1800s visitors. Also, as discussed in Chapter 3, similar music and dancing was common in the early days of the Norfolk settlement. A more likely explanation for the lack of vernacular sea-songs is that whaling boats do not appear to have used Pitcairn or Norfolk islands as 'rest and relaxation' stopovers in the same manner that they used Lord Howe Island (for brief visits) or the more populous leisure and re-provisioning base of Honolulu (for longer stays). In Pitcairn's case, this appears to have been due to its small population, the low availability of alcohol, its religiousness and difficulties in landing there. In Norfolk's case, these factors were compounded by the presence of Australian authorities and the moderating influence of the nearby Melanesian Mission (the same factors that made the island such a favoured stopover for whaling captains' wives). Deprived of taverns and/or impromptu alcohol-aided festivities, it appears that visiting whaling crews had little incentive or opportunities to perform and share their song repertoire with the local population.

My second assumption – based on previous research on the music of the Whitsunday archipelago and the Torres Strait – was that there would be a tradition of locally written songs dating back to the early days of Norfolk settlement. I initially attributed my failure to locate and identify these practices as due to inadequate historical records and/or the reluctance of islanders to volunteer information on cultural history to an outsider. In response to my queries as to the reasons for the apparent lack of a local song tradition, several residents again emphasised the religiousness of the initial Pitcairn settlers and early Norfolk community as a factor. In particular, I was offered the explanation that the set of hymns discussed in Chapter 9 had, to a large extent, filled the role that traditional/'folk' songs did elsewhere. I was initially sceptical since I had no previous knowledge of cultures in which (the same) group of hymns were sung in both secular and sacred contexts in this manner. However research appeared to support this claim. One resident (who requested anonymity in print), recalled for me that at public venues, particularly during the 1960s and 1970s:

> When everybody had had a few drinks, if there was no other music playing, someone would start up singing a hymn, sometimes on their own or other people would join in, and afterwards they'd get straight back to whatever they were doing – talking and drinking, and arguing and fighting sometimes too ... And this could happen several times in

an evening with no one batting an eyelid. All quite normal – for here, at least.

Alice Buffett has described impromptu performances of the locally associated hymns in terms of islanders wishing to express a depth of emotional feeling through one of the cultural forms "closest to their hearts" (interview 1999).

But while the locally-adopted hymn repertoire has played a central role in local culture, other material has also been present. In addition to the hymns, a locally originated composition, *The Norfolk ode*, has also been significant as a ceremonial song. The song's lyrics have been attributed to musician and hymn writer Gustav Quintal, who was teacher and headmaster of the island school in the 1890s-early 1910s (and writer of the hymn *Oakleigh*, discussed in Chapters 6 and 9). There seems to be little evidence to support this claim however and more recent opinion tends to favour a temporarily resident Australian schoolteacher in the 1920s or early 1930s as the lyricist. Given that Quintal died in 1919 and that there is no written evidence that the song was performed before the 1930s the latter explanation seems more plausible.

Whatever its authorship, *The Norfolk ode* appears to have been written as a direct local response to the themes and spirit of the opening verse of the Australian anthem *Advance Australia fair* (using closely similar wording in most parts[2]) and, indeed, was sung to the tune of the latter. Its lyrics comprise:

On Norfolk's sunny seagirt isle
We'll raise our voices high
In praise of verdant hill and dale
Beneath a kindly sky
The laughing waves that lapping o'er
Loud in anger roar
We'll join our song in cadence wild
Around our craggy shore
In joyful strains then let us sing
Through waves' tumultuous roar

Our island home is but a speck
On ocean's bosom wide
It's dear to us, since, boys and girls
It is our home and pride
The lofty pines will beckon us
If e'er abroad we roam
And palms and ferns welcome us back
To this our island home
No heartier welcome shall we get
Though all the Earth we roam

Our land is rich with luscious fruit
With fish our waters swarm
Our valleys deep are gay and rich
Our land abounds in nature's gifts

Of beauty rich and rare
Let's bless the giver of good things
Who all this good did plan
And let us thankful be to him
For his great gifts to man
And let us thankful be to him
For his great gifts to man

Advance Australia fair was written by Scottish-born Sydney resident composer Peter Dodds McCormick and first performed in public in 1878. The song was published by Palings and attracted growing attention at a time when federation of the separate Australian states was being proposed. It achieved significant prominence when it was sung by a large choir as part of the inauguration of the Commonwealth of Australia in 1901 and began to enter the repertoire of schools soon after. The song had no official status as an Australian anthem until 1974 when the Australian Government headed by Gough Whitlam accepted it as an alternative national anthem to *God save the Queen*. It then became formally adopted as *the* national anthem in 1984 under the Hawke Government[3]. Given this, there was nothing politically confrontational – let alone subversive – about adapting the song as a blueprint for a local celebration of place and identity in the early 1900s. *God save the Queen* remained Australia's (and thereby Norfolk Island's) national anthem, with *The Norfolk ode* as a local complement. In latter years however, following its elevation in Australia, factors such as the recognition of the song's melody as that of the Australian national anthem has led to a decline in its prominence. This situation led Norfolk Island songwriter Don Christian-Reynolds to propose an alternative musical arrangement in the early 1990s that has not, so far, been commonly adopted on the island. Christian-Reynolds's version retains elements of the melodic contour and chordal structure of McCormick's music but eschews the anthemic declamation of its choruses. A version of the modified composition was featured on Christian-Reynolds's 2004 CD album with Kath King, @ *Norfolk* (discussed below), sung by his daughter Erica to her father's picked guitar accompaniment.

Although I came to recognise that locally associated hymns (and *The Norfolk ode*) formed the core of an enduring local repertoire, I continued to search for evidence of forgotten songs. My impetus here was a hypothesis that if the hymns had come to be regarded as the most important and enduring facet of Norfolk Island song culture might not other songs have been overlooked and/or forgotten for this very reason? This proved a more productive lens to view Norfolk's cultural history through, since, as it transpired, there is evidence of secular Norfolk Island song composition dating back at least as far as the early 20th Century. As I came to realise, the minimal profile of these songs in public cultural consciousness on the island resulted from a perception prevalent (until very recently) that they were little more than curiousities that were only (if at all) of interest to families or individuals related to the original songwriters.

Due to this situation, the identification of such songs proved a protracted process (and, indeed, extended the research period for this volume by several years). One of the most significant early finds in this regard was a composition that fulfilled various of the criteria for having become a 'folk' song over the years since its initial composition – it was known by more than one person, each knew a slightly different version and its authorship was unclear and disputed. Inquiries made by Rick Kleiner to two senior island women, Maude Buffett and Audry Scott, confirmed the song as being sung in the 1930s. Buffett remembers it as being entitled *Ucklun* (now commonly spelt *acklan* – meaning 'ours/us'). While various accounts of its authorship have been suggested to me[4] it seems certain that the song's words were written by George 'Putt' Nobbs, probably in the late 1920s or early 1930s, and express aspects of his own experience of local schooling as an islander for whom Norfolk was his principal language.

The Norfolk terms used in the song differ slightly from standard late 20th Century Norfolk usage and the lyrics and translation of these below are based on a recorded version of the song performed (unaccompanied) by Maude Buffett in 2004 and written versions supplied by Audry Scott and by Nobbs's great granddaughter Rachel Borg. Where the versions differ substantially I have principally used Buffett's as the guide text, made some (individually footnoted) amendments from Borg's version and footnoted Scott's variant. It is, of course, a matter of conjecture how close my collated version is to the original. My translation attempts to convey the sense of lines rather than their literal translation. While it is unclear whether the song was written to a melody or subsequently attached to one, the vocal melody recalled by Buffett in 2004 comprises a simple, primarily descending, stepped pattern that is similar to many children's songs intended to be easily learnt and sung. The lyrics comprise:

> *I wish I'll larna yorlyi*[5]
> *How hard we lekl sullun fine*
> *Fe read en write in good English*
> *En tull et auwas mine*
>
> *We come a school mus every day*
> *Fe try a larn a thing*
> *We read en write en talk en play*
> *En sometime us a'sing*
>
> *An when we all go hoem from school*
> *We nawa try en do*
> *Dem thing auwas teacher tulla us*
> *We nawa talk et too*
>
> *How can we larn ef dars de way*
> *All yorlyi gwen e'do*
> *Cos yorlyi know before I larn*
> *Dar thing I tull es true*
>
> *We bin examine et again*
> *We wussan fuss I b'lew*
> *Cos yorlyi know dem English maen*
> *We naewa ell deceive*

En cos auwas examiners es
Peter, Tom en Jack
Do yorlyi frighten ef
We nor gut any prize fe tek[6]

Now I se done en now I bet
All yorlyi glehd es me
En tull dar thing how wawaha[7]
En semiswaye es yu[8]

[translation]

I want to convey to you all
How hard it is for us children
To read and write in good English
And express ourselves [using it]

We come to school most days
And try and learn something
We read and write and talk and play
And sometimes we sing

And when we all go home from school
We never try and do
The things our teacher told us
And never talk it [ie English] *either*

How can we learn if that's what
All of us do
Because you all know
That what I say is true

We have been examined again
[And] *we were worse than we believed*
Because you know that the English men[9]
[Are someone] *we can't fool*

And because our examiners are
Peter, Tom and Jack
Don't be concerned if
We don't get any prizes

Now I have finished and I'll wager
That you are all glad it's me
[Who has] *stated the case self-importantly*
In the same way that you do

Artfully written as a child's naive and straightforward statement of the disjuncture between the languages of school and home, and the difficulties in achieving English language skills in this situation, the song neatly encapsulates the state of school education on Norfolk Island in the late 1800s and early-mid 1900s. During this period Australian school teachers attempted to assert English as the only permissible and legitimate language, banning the use of Norfolk in schools and punishing those who they caught using it. The song survives as a significant contemporary critique of early

20th Century schooling and expectations of local children. The contemporary recollection of this song, apparently only sung in public on a few occasions, emphasises its special status as an oral commentary on an externally imposed educational system.

II. Post War songs

Beverly Simpson

Aside from George Hunn Nobbs and Driver Christian's hymn writing and the two compositions discussed above, the first Norfolk Islander who is currently recalled as having originated songs is Beverly Simpson[10]. Simpson grew up on Norfolk Island and recalls her Australian father, Frank Downes, who had been blinded at Gallipoli during World War One, as a "very musical" person who used to play the banjo-mandolin and who encouraged her to sing socially. After a brief relocation to Sydney in 1939, during which her father died, Simpson returned to complete her schooling on Norfolk during the War years and then went away to study nursing in Auckland in the early 1950s. Her nostalgia for the island, and a particular young man, led her to compose a song with the following lyrics.

Beneath Norfolk skies
Where love never dies
To you dear, I'll always be true
With pine trees above
And sweet songs of love
I'll always remember you

These cities I'd exchange
For your Norfolk charms
And one precious moment
With me in your arms
And when I return to Norfolk, then
We'll never part again (Because I love you)
We'll never part again (I tell you truly)
We'll never part again

The lines have ascending and descending melodic patterns before moving to the concluding section that includes the bracketed sections as semi-spoken 'asides'. Interviewed in 2004, some fifty-two years after she composed the song, Simpson was unsure as to what extent she had borrowed the melody from a previous composition. Performed at a slow tempo, Simpson sang the song at parties on her return to the island, often backed by friends and family vamping accompaniments on piano or ukulele. As she recalls:

As people got to know it they started adding on the ending. I'd get to
the final "We'll never part again" and someone would add something
like "in your pink pyjamas"! And someone like Stegs [George 'Steggles'
Le Cren] would add something else ... And it would go round and round
until we'd all crack up! (interview 2004)

The song does not appear to have continued in local social repertoire beyond the 1960s and Simpson only recorded it onto tape in 2004, after being contacted by the author and Don Christian-Reynolds, thereby allow-

175

ing for its re-insertion into local performance culture[11]. Simpson's second song was not written until 1999 when, moved by contrasts between sections of the island community and major international calamities, she wrote two verses of a song about unity and harmony (the third being written by Bob Wyndham). The lyrical theme is summarised in the concluding lines of its third verse:

> This is my home, my dream and my shrine
> But other hearts in other lands are beating
> With hopes and dreams that are the same as mine

Set to the melody from the hymn *Be still my soul*, the song has been sung on occasion at the island's Uniting Church.

Peke Evans

Along with Simpson, another islander who originated songs in the post-War period that have not been absorbed into continuing repertoire was Peke Evans. When interviewed by the author in May 1999, his son David 'Bubby' Evans was keen to emphasise that his father "didn't *write* any songs he just sang some", specifying that "when he gets a few [drinks] under his belt he sorta wanta sing and he makes up little songs". Peke Evans performed his songs at parties and after-hours sessions at licensed venues to a small group of friends and family during the 1950s and 1960s. He sang without musical accompaniment and, depending on the occasion, his son, or other companions who knew particular songs, would join in. His compositions appear to have been short in length and reflected on island life and experiences, such as romance and fishing. One of the best remembered of these is a short piece usually referred to as *Cascade Bay*. His son has recalled the lyrics of this as:

> In Cascade Bay
> Where fishes play[12]
> We sail away
> Across the bay
> With eyes of blue
> And place for two
> What is it I can do?
>
> God bless the day
> I never will forget
> Until I'm old and gray
> God bless the day
> In Cascade Bay
> The day you stole
> My heart away

Colleen Crane collected and transcribed a longer version of *Cascade Bay*, complete with melody line, in the early 2000s. At time of writing (early 2005) I had been unable to compare the two versions but Crane's was scheduled for inclusion in a Norfolk Island Girl Guides fund-raising booklet entitled *Norfolk Songs and Poems* intended for publication in late 2005. This booklet, and the inclusion of Evans's material, represents a shift in local perceptions of the value of such oral culture, which otherwise would have been lost to posterity.

Another brief verse – not included in the Guides' publication – which 'Bubby' Evans could recall a fragment of, was more humorous:

This is the girl I brought back from New Zealand with me
This is the girl who solved the mystery
I don't know what she's talking about
Her face is like a watermelon with a slice cut out

George 'Toofie' Christian, who heard Peke Evans perform his verses to friends in locations such as the Paradise hotel, has commented that "they weren't so much proper 'songs' as what he'd say in a certain way, it was his voice and how e'd sing em out in this funny voice that'd get me" (interview 2004).

George 'Steggles' Le Cren and Eileen Snell

The first original composition to become part of an enduring social repertoire on Norfolk Island was Le Cren and Snell's *The Coconut song*. The song has a simple, repetitive melody with a narrow note range and is sung in a paralinguistic (speech-like) manner, usually to a ukulele and/or guitar accompaniment. The song's lyrics are in a mix of Norfolk Island language and SE, and (as discussed in Chapter 7) refer to Norfolk Island within the context of the re-Polynesianisation of local performance culture in the early-mid 20th Century. The song illustrates its general theme of affinity to Polynesian/Tahitian culture with reference to specific individuals, who thereby became commemorated as performers, as in verse 1:

We gut Eileen[13] *singin' a hula tune*
We gut Marina[14] *swayen underneath the moon*

The song was most often performed on the island by Le Cren and his long-time performing partner Eileen Snell. Like Peke Evans's songs, performances of *The Coconut song* were almost always at social occasions – rather than formal concert events – and often involved the two performers leading communal singing of the composition. Performing socially, the duo became associated with a group of songs inspired by Norfolk Island themes and the *Bounty* saga. Together with Le Cren's *Norfolk Island Blues*, their repertoire included several Snell originals, the best known of which are *My beautiful Island home*, *Sunset over Anson Bay*, *Du we loas auwas wieh* and *Mauatua*[15].

When interviewed together in 1999, Snell and local linguist and historian Alice Buffett described the social context of songwriting in the 1960s and 1970s in the following terms:

ES: *We did a few more but we can't tell you about those ones because they're …* [laughter from both] *They're not for the tape recorder!* [more laughs]

AB: *No, this is playing around … see you and Stegs, people get together around and they'll throw in a clause or a sentence or part* [of] *a sentence and laugh and defy anyone else to say anything else. In a small*

177

community you daren't – you know [repeat these things in public] –
with a name or anything like that.

The culture that Buffett is referring to is one in which songwriting
existed as part of a broader oral fabric of jibes, humour, social commentary
and observation. While some compositions, such as *The Coconut song*,
crystallised into a stable text that was repeated over decades, others were
essentially ephemeral. The survival of Le Cren and Snell's songs referred to
above is largely due to the rise in local song and dance culture during the
1980s and 1990s, in response to tourist interest and the cultural politics of
the 1980s described below.

Snell and Le Cren's visibility as cultural figures has been far more limited
than any of the other contemporary songwriters discussed in this chapter
due to their (and particularly Snell's) marked aversion to performing in
public and their reticence to have their work recorded and released. For these
reasons, the duo remain distinctly 'internal' to Norfolk Island culture;
songwriters and performers who are best known to the circle of predominantly Pitcairn-descended Norfolk Islanders who they socialised with over
the past three decades. The only recording of their songs and singing was a
live tape made in 1993 (or 1994[16]) which featured Snell (guitar and vocals),
Le Cren (ukulele and vocals) together with vocalist and ukulele players Rosie
Saint and Jenny Holland. This recording session was organised to provide
versions of the songs for Mavis Hitch and Karlene Christian to use as an
accompaniment for their dance shows. The tape has never been made
available commercially and only a handful of copies exist.

Norfolk Island Blues is a short composition sung to a melody and chord
progression similar to that of Peter DeRose and George Brown's song *Have
you ever been lonely?* (written in 1933 and recorded by various artists,
including Patsy Cline), with lyrics in mixed Norfolk and SE. Snell has
described that the song was written by Le Cren in Sydney to express his
homesickness (pc March 2005). Three four line verses praise the beauty of
Norfolk pines, the island's peacefulness and the pleasures of courting by
moonlight, with the chorus reiterating:

Yu law wun pretty Norfolk gael
She might like yu too
But when yu liiw you gwen gut wun thing
En dars dem Norfolk Island Blues

[translation]

You love a pretty Norfolk girl
She might like you too
But when you leave you're going to get one thing
And that's those Norfolk Island Blues

Snell has written songs in both Norfolk and SE on a variety of topics.
Her most didactic composition is *Du we loas auwas wieh* ('Don't let us lose
our culture'). The song's theme is made explicit in the first verse:

We gwen be wun sad en forgotten race
We slowly lorsen plenty Norfolk wieh

[translation]

We are going to be a sad and forgotten people/race
We are slowly losing much of our Norfolk culture ['ways']

The lyrics continue with the assertion that the solution to this situation is the education of young islanders in local traditions. Verse 2 singles out language as a prime concern:

Talk auwas language all d'time
So ell stick in dems mine
Du it now, d'we wait
Soon gwen be too late
Auwas language es unique
Ef we loas et dars weak
Du we loas auwas wieh

[translation]

Speak our language all the time
So it will stick in their [ie young people's] minds
Do it now, we shouldn't delay
[It's] soon going to be too late
Our language is unique
If we lose it we [and our distinct identity] will be weakened
Don't let us lose our culture

The third and fourth verses describe the traditional function of fishing and the need for community solidarity. The first six lines of the chorus also identify traditional agriculture and cooking as important elements of local tradition:

Plunt a plun en a tayte
Dig a tarla, plunt a yarm
Y'hohli d'pilhai[17] show dem how
Fer make auwas pie
Melk a cow fer get a cream
Dem ell steams dem fish in

[translation]

Plant bananas and kumera [sweet potatoes]
Dig a hole, plant a yam
Show them how to prepare mashed vegetables and fish
[In order to] make our pie
Milk a cow to get some cream
To steam the fish in[18]

Snell has explicitly associated the song with the continuing work of Alice Buffett, describing it as about "what Alice's [1999] book is about" (ibid) and it remains a vivid summary of a number of those aspects of traditional Norfolk culture also explored in the work of George 'Toofie' Christian (discussed below).

Snell's best-known song, originally entitled *Friendship*, sometimes referred to as *Miamiti* but now identified by its writer as *Mauatua*, was consciously written to represent Norfolk culture in a broader context. Snell recalls the origins of the song as follows:

When they were going to the festival of Arts in Vanuatu for the first time they were going to go up there and sing some Pitcairn song and I said 'Well that's not our song – that doesn't come from Norfolk' so I thought 'Right I'm going home to write a song', just out of the blue. And I did. Half an hour ... I got it ... I was amazed. (interview 1999)

The song serves to introduce the culturally mixed history of Norfolk Islanders to an audience and to invite them to visit. The lyrics identify Fletcher Christian and his Tahitian consort Mauatua as founders of the community. Reflecting the ceremonial context, the song opens with a declaration of affinities:

Es guud un f'si all acklan together
Especially all dem from Pitcairn
Cos we es all a brothers en a sisters
Mine said we all kam fram

[translation]

It's good to see all of us together
Especially those from Pitcairn
Because we are all brothers and sisters
Whatever place we come from

Snell's two English language songs, *Sunset over Anson Bay* and *Norfolk Island my beautiful home*, are emotive paeans to the island and Snell's pride at being an islander. *Sunset over Anson Bay* is a lush romantic celebration of the beauty of the sunset ("you'll never see such a beautiful sight like this") and twilight ("that's when the moonbeams play") at Anson Bay. *Norfolk Island my beautiful home* expands the frame of reference to the whole of the island and its history, with a chorus that stresses that "I'm proud to belong *to* you" (my emphasis) – effectively asserting an indigenous pride and identification with a greater social, geographical and historical entity.

The versions of *The Coconut song, Du we loas auwas wiea, Mauatua, Norfolk Island Blues* and *Norfolk Island my beautiful home* recorded in 1993/94[19] are based on similarly paced ukulele and acoustic guitar grooves with loose, impromptu vocal harmonising. The recording now serves as an audio memento of a particular style of social music making that was prominent in the mid-late 20th Century and is now in decline on the island.

SPD Song contest
Along with Snell's continuing work in the 1970s–1990s, Norfolk Island language songwriting received impetus from local cultural and political factors in the 1980s. As discussed in Chapter 7, the autonomy – and related identity – of Norfolk Island was under threat following the recommendation of the Australian Government's Nimmo Report in 1976 that Norfolk Island lose its external territory status and be absorbed into Australia. Many (although not all[20]) of the group of activists galvanised to oppose this subsequently channeled their energies through the Society of Pitcairn Descendants (SPD)[21]. The situation alerted islanders to other kinds of threats to island identity. The early-mid 1980s was a period when the introduction of (English language) Australian television programs and the rise in num-

bers of tourists were perceived to be threatening the continuing use of Norfolk language. The two most notable cultural responses were a Norfolk Island language song contest, held in 1984, and the production of Alice Buffett's pioneering publication *Speak Norfolk Today* (written in collaboration with the Australian linguist Donald Laycock), first published in 1988 and subsequently expanded, revised and republished in 1999.

The song contest was organised by the SPD in conjunction with a George Hunn Nobbs commemorative 'Back to Norfolk Week' and was announced in the *Norfolk Islander* newspaper on June 23rd, with its conditions of entry specifying that the competition was "open to anyone", that "the melody or tune must be of new and original material" and that "the words or lyrics to the song must be written in the Norfolk/Pitcairn language". Entrants to the songwriting competition included Don Reynolds (*Norfook es ouwus hoo-um*) Susan Pedel (*Dar Bounty mutiny*) and temporarily resident Australian Seventh Day Adventist pastor Keith Jackson (*God's blessing to acklan*[22]).

Don Christian-Reynolds

Christian-Reynolds won the SPD competition with *Norfook es ouwus hoo-um* and received a $1000 prize. The song was published in sheet music form by the SPD, with its lyrics written in what Christian-Reynolds regarded as "what seemed to be the best spellings at the time" (interview 1999). For reasons of coherence with other Norfolk language texts discussed in this book, I have transcribed the lyrics of the prize-winning song in the form discussed in my preface to this volume and I henceforth write the song's title as *Norfolk es auwas hoem*. The vocal melody and delivery of the verses resemble *The Coconut song* – and many subsequent local compositions – by having a narrow range melody (mainly within the range G to C) that favours a paralinguistic delivery. Christian-Reynolds's habitually breezy mid-tempo delivery of the verses has a strong Anglo-American 1960s' folk style that suits the scenarios of island life and pleasure that the lyrics present, as in verse 1:

> Hey! Yorlyi cum naawe daun a taun?
> Tek ar buggy daun orn e saen
> Dem warta bin es coolun en sink saf outa sight
> En sullun orn Norfolk cah 'fraid en a night

> [translation]

> Hey everyone, [do you want to] come swimming down at [Kingston] town?[23]
> Take the buggy[24] down onto the sand
> The water is cool and refreshing and [the] sea is calm
> And none of us on Norfolk are afraid of the night

Following this, the chorus provides significant melodic variation by dipping down to B and C notes, suggesting a sense of gravity for the dramatic historical emphasis of its final lines – "En after dar en fifty six/ We sael en daun-a-taun". The chorus's lyrics give a sense of the history that motivates the SPD (and which inspired the song competition), making a clear political statement of ownership in the first two lines:

Norfolk es auwas hoem
Orl acklan law lewen orn auwas oawen

[translation]

Norfolk [Island] is our home
All of us love living here on our own

before the historical summary of the third and fourth:

From Tahiti en dar Bounty *to Pitcairn*
En after dar en fifty six, we sael en daun-a-taun

[translation]

From Tahiti on the *Bounty* to Pitcairn
An after that we sailed in down at [Kingston] town

In its original version, the song included seven verses addressed to topics such as the menu of a traditional island picnic (Verse 2), Anniversary Day celebrations (Verse 3), Kingston history (Verse 4), the island assembly (Verse 5), fishing trips (Verse 6) and, in the final verse, the significance of the *Pitcairn anthem*:

Auwas Pitcairn anthem, sing et daun a taun
Auwas fathers pass et daun lorngtaim
Alwaes bin auwas song, en sing et when sullun se gorn
Orl acklan give auwas law daun a taun

[translation]

We sing our Pitcairn Anthem down at [Kingston] town
Our forefathers passed it down from a long time ago
[It's] always been our song, and [we] sing it when people die
All of us [Norfolk Islanders] show our love down at [Kingston] town

Since winning the song competition, *Norfolk es auwas hoem* has become a staple of both Christian-Reynolds's live sets and the repertoire of island performance troupes. Given its length, it is not surprising that the most regularly performed version of the song is an abbreviated one.

Christian-Reynolds's debut cassette album, entitled (and spelt) *Norfook es ouwus hoo-um* (1986) was recorded at the SDA media centre in the north Sydney suburb of Wahroonga in 1985, with arrangements credited to Christian-Reynolds and his (then) sister-in-law Sharon Sandstrom, who also contributed piano and harmony vocal parts. The cassette featured three versions of the title track[25] and the five locally-associated hymns discussed in Chapter 9 together with versions of Harry Robertson's *Norfolk whalers* (discussed in Chapter 10) and a Standard English version of Jackson's *God's blessing to acklan*, entitled *Home of our dreams*.

Harry Robertson's song *Norfolk whalers* attracted the attention of Christian-Reynolds for both its maritime theme and local relevance. His cover of the song in live shows is similar in style to the original but includes what he regards as a minor but significant modification – "a little change to politicise it a bit" (interview 2000), altering the second line of the original chorus of "Row my love row and bring back to me/The king of the ocean, the prize of the sea" to "The king of the ocean, *from Norfolk's own sea*". The latter reference is a specific response to the Australian Commonwealth's unilateral annexation of a 200 mile territorial area around Norfolk Island as part of Australia's fishing zone in 1979. This move, which gave all financial benefits to the Commonwealth, was regarded on the island as a violation of the spirit of the Australian 'Norfolk Island Act' passed earlier in the year which made provision for the island to "support itself from its own resources".

While thematically and sequentially similar, Christian Reynolds's SE version of Jackson's *Home of our dreams*, sung to Sandstrom's piano accompaniment, reveals the (unrecorded) Norfolk language version as a relatively 'free' translation of Jackson's original, modified to fit the style and rhythm of the language. The song's lyrics offer a relatively straightforward account of the relocation of the Pitcairners to Norfolk and of the charms of the island. Musically, the song has a hymn-like feel although its melodic range encompasses several short high note passages that would make it a difficult choice for easy-performance hymn repertoire[26]. Despite Christian-Reynolds's inclusion of the song on his cassette, neither language version was adopted into local repertoire and the composition was rarely performed in the 1990s and 2000s.

After releasing the *Norfolk es ouwus hoo-um* cassette, Christian-Reynolds wrote a second local language song that he has continued to perform regularly since, *Mais tintoela* ('My sweetheart/lover'). The song is a love ballad with an undulating melody in the verses, rising affirmative melodic lines in the first and second and fourth and fifth lines of the chorus and a concluding descending melody for the summary half-line phrase "Ai law yu" ("I love you'). Christian-Reynolds invariably sings the song to a picked chordal accompaniment on the verses and strumming on the choruses, giving a warm, emotive interpretation of the lyrics and melody (as befits a love song to his wife). The song is particularly notable for its inclusion of several romantic metaphors and allusions present in Norfolk usage. The first of these provides the song's title, *tintoela* being a word with picturesque origins. Its signification of a sweetheart/lover derives from a historic custom:

> *Back in Pitcairn and early Norfolk days, parents and older relatives would keep track of the moral behaviour of young people who they suspected of having premarital relationships by tying a tin billy with spoons in it under the beds. Practical jokes of that kind were often played on the newly-weds and other older people suspected of roaming elsewhere.* (Buffett, 1999: 101)

Two other allusions link maritime phenomena with love. The first is effective but relatively straightforward "Dem ai f'yuan maek mais heart kepsais" ('Your eyes make my heart capsize') but the second, like that of the word *tintoela*, has a more specific local meaning. The concluding verse of the song has its lover-protagonists on a beach talking about the dramatic emotional impact of their first kiss and describes how:

Auwas hearts se kaina pilli
We semes en wan faas boet

The initial line translates relatively easily, "It was as if our hearts were joined together" but the second resists compact translation since it compares the emotional linkage and exhilaration of love to a whaling phenomenon experienced on the island in the late 19th and early 20th centuries. When boats rowed out to catch whales they attempted to secure them by harpooning them. When the first harpoon penetrated the whale the creature often sped off at a rapid pace, trailing the boat precariously behind it while the crew hung on tightly. This phenomenon (known in New England [USA] as a 'Nantucket sleighride') is referred to on Norfolk as a *faas boet* ['fast boat'], apparently derived from the cry the harpooner would make when the harpoon connected. Translated to a love song, the sense of excitement and risk-taking is an effective, locally referential enhancement of the song's descriptive lyrics.

Mais tintoela first appeared in recorded form in 2005, included along with the traditional hymn material and versions of *Norfolk es auwas hoem* featured on his debut cassette on a compilation CD of material recorded by Christian-Reynolds and by singer-songwriter Kath King entitled *Kath & Donald @ Norfolk*.

Figure 23: Susan Pedel and Don Christian-Reynolds performing at a wedding reception at Steel's Point (1983).

Together with his two Norfolk language songs, Christian-Reynolds wrote a third original composition that became a staple of his live repertoire in the 1990s, a SE language song entitled *Sirius and Supply* that related the story of the wreck of the supply ship HMS *Sirius* off Kingston in 1790. Sung and played with gusto, in the style of a sea shanty, the song's chorus relates the moment of wreckage in three and a half declaratory lines, with a softer and more sombre concluding half-line:

Southerly winds without a word took Sirius by surprise
The seas came up, waves were high, the reef began to rise
Cut away the anchor, the halyards, the sheets and tacks let go
Captain yelled 'Abandon ship!'
- Now Sirius lies below

During the 1990s Christian-Reynolds also performed a version of Susan Pedel's *Hili sohng*, one of a series of locally-themed compositions written by her in the 1980s and 1990s, which was also included on *Kath & Donald @ Norfolk*. The short, humorous composition refers to the local tendency to *hili*, spending hours in idleness and putting off work whenever possible, satirising the practice in its lines:

We no want a'work
En we no want t'plieh
'Cos we gut hili dis dieh

[translation]

We don't want to work
We don't want to play (relax)
Because we've got to *hili* (idle) today

Susan Pedel

Pedel was born on Norfolk Island in 1933. Her mother, Keren Buffett, who died when she was eighteen months old, was a well-regarded singer and her foster mother, Esther Quintal (her mother's first cousin), was a popular social pianist. Due to the depressed state of the local economy, her family moved to New Zealand when she was four, relocating to Mercer, then a poor, predominantly Maori-populated suburb of Auckland. Pedel recalls this experience as a formative one:

I was very much influenced by Maori music, which I still love. I started school in New Zealand at the age of five and some of the first things you did at the school then was learn this Maori song called Pokarekare Ana[27] *and learn to dance the Highland Fling! I didn't continue doing the Scottish dancing but I will never ever forget the power and beauty of the Maori music. I think it is the most glorious singing music and it just stayed with me and stuck in my mind.* (interview 1999)

When World War Two broke out Pedel's family returned to Norfolk Island. As discussed in Chapter 8, the New Zealand garrison exerted a significant influence on local culture in this period and Pedel attended concerts staged by air force personnel. The New Zealand influence also spilled over into schooling, with the Maori *Wai ta poi* song being taught in school. Pedel recalls that singing was a strong part of the curriculum in the

1940s with the headmaster, Lyall Rippon, who was a trained singer, teaching sight-reading, vocal projection and part-singing to pupils.

After completing her intermediate school certificate[28] in 1949 she left the island to live and work in Sydney. Although she did not aspire to a career in singing, she entered numerous talent competitions at dances "for the fun of it", several of which she won (singing contemporary popular songs). Cash prizes for the contests she entered were often up to ten pounds, a sizeable amount for the time. During the 1950s she lived on the Central Coast of New South Wales and began singing at clubs, eventually becoming the singer with the resident dance band at the Florida Hotel in Terrigal in the mid-late 1950s[29]. During this period she wrote a ballad about relationship

Figure 24: Susan Pedel at an RSL Club social function (c1985).

tensions entitled *Try again*, which she used to perform with the band (and which she later recorded on her 1997 debut album). Pedel returned to Norfolk Island in 1960, after her marriage broke up, and soon commenced singing at the Paradise, backed by hotel manager Jim Hamilton. At this venue, she often performed the song *Take me back to Norfolk Island*, written by Franklin Boyer (discussed in Chapter 10), which came to be something of a 'signature song' for her.

During the 1960s Pedel was involved in establishing a Musical and Dramatic society, presenting excerpts from musicals such as *South Pacific*, *My Fair Lady* and *Oklahoma*. She also appeared in the Norfolk Island Pageant singing *The ballad of Barney Duffy* (discussed in Chapter 10). Pedel characterises the song as "not easy to sing but very dramatic" and recalls that, "I insisted on singing it in the dark in the stage version to let its atmosphere tell the story, and inspire the audience's imagination" (interview 1999). Australian Broadcasting Corporation documentary maker John Shaw came to Norfolk during the Pageant and shot a sequence of Pedel performing the song under Bloody Bridge (a historic convict location near Kingston) that was subsequently broadcast on ABC TV.

Pedel's public performance activities declined in the 1970s, due to family commitments, but she became active again in the 1980s. One area that she was involved in was school education, writing material to give local children "a sense of island culture and stories with a sense of fun" (ibid). One of the earliest children's songs she wrote was *Hatai maes finger* ('Here is my finger'). As Pedel recalls:

> *I have been going to the island play centre for over 20 years, playing piano and singing. One day, in the mid-1970s, a Maori pre-school teacher from New Zealand visiting, came along and sang and showed the children a Maori action song. Then afterwards she asked them if they would do a Norfolk Island children's song for her (so that she could learn it and take it home with her to show her children) ... But we didn't have one, and I thought that was terrible, we didn't have anything in the island language that the children could do. So I came home and wrote one which referred to the fingers and toes and arms and legs in* [Norfolk] *language. And now the school children all learn* Hatai maes finger *so they have something to start them off with the language and something all the other children can remember too.* (ibid)

Another early song, which she taught in schools in the late 1970s was entitled *Graab'lieg* about the prickly bindi weed. The song arose from Pedel telling schoolchildren how when she grew up on the island children usually didn't wear shoes, and since it was painful to tread on the bindi, they used to have to be careful about where they walked. As she recalls, "the children used to like it and used to do the actions of walking through the grass – it was a fun thing to do with the young ones" (ibid).

Pedel's own compositions mainly draw on the simple, catchy melodic traditions of children's songs and 1960s era folk music but are also distinguished, in her performance of them at least, by her utilisation of vocal techniques such as movement up into the target pitch of a note and use of

187

controlled vibrato along with occasional semi-paralinguistic (speech-like) passages.

From the 1980s through to the early 2000s Pedel frequently performed for tourist groups, often together with guitarists such as Don Christian-Reynolds, George 'Toofie' Christian and Pitcairner Trent Christian, and often with young local hula dancers. These shows would provide audiences with an introduction to the island's culture and, to this end, Pedel's entry into the 1984 song competition, *Dar Bounty mutiny*[30], gave a succinct summary of the events between the *Bounty's* departure to Tahiti and the establishment of the Norfolk Island community. In live performance for tourist groups, the lyrics were often interspersed with translations of Norfolk phrases (such as "Now orl dem nor like Captain Bligh/Cos he too nasey" ['All of them took a dislike to Captain Bligh/Since he was so unpleasant/unreasonable']), giving an introduction to Norfolk language use as well.

Another of Pedel's historical songs, written in the late 1990s, *Dar Bounty shake*, concentrated on one central aspect of the 'foundation myth' of Pitcairn and Norfolk island society, namely that it was the irresistible allure of Tahitian women, particularly their dancing, that prompted the *Bounty* crew to mutiny. Originally intended for Karlene Christian's dance troupe, the song expresses its theme through a short instructional lyric about dancing, prefaced by the declaration:

Come yorlyi do dar Bounty shake
Dars thing cause dar Bounty mutiny

[translation]

Come on everybody, do the *Bounty* shake
It's the thing that caused the *Bounty* mutiny

Pedel taught children to dance to the composition as part of her school education work and Christian-Reynolds and Pedel performed the song live at the 1998 Multicultural Festival opening with three schoolchildren dancing.

Pedel has also written compositions for special occasions, such as her SE title song for the island's 1998 multicultural festival – 'Culture of the oceans' and her multicultural 'anthem' *One world*. Other recent compositions have commemorated everyday aspects of Norfolk Island life. *Farewell to Fredick's Age*[31] was written in 1998 to farewell a particular local landmark, a cliff edge above Cascade Bay that was removed to ensure the stability of the slope above the jetty. The song was performed live on the cliff top at a farewelling ceremony and the first verse of the song summarised the occasion:

Memories are all that's left
Of this glorious island sight
Where each of us has spent some time
Where the stately pine trees swayed
And p'raps some of us have played
We're here to say goodbye to Fredick's Age

Several of Pedel's original songs are featured on the cassette (and now CD) album *Susan Sings*. The album was recorded in 1998 at BJB Studios[32] in Sydney during a brief visit to Sydney for the Carnivale festival, where she performed with Don Christian-Reynolds. The release features *Dar Bounty mutiny* and *One world* along with her earlier song *Try again*, her cover of Boyer's *Take me back to Norfolk Island*, the Victorian parlour ballad *Home sweet home* and versions of *The Pitcairn anthem* and *Let the lower lights be burning* (discussed in Chapter 9). Pedel followed this up in 2001 with her album of hymns *Orl Uclun* (also discussed in Chapter 9).

Archie Bigg

Along with the songwriters discussed above, Archie Bigg played a prominent role in the creative life of the island as a poet during the 1990s. Bigg grew up in Sydney in the immediate post-War period, speaking Norfolk language with his mother Beattie and his aunt Vina and playing ukulele and singing at social gatherings. The music he recalls performing as a youth included hillbilly songs (such as Hank Williams' material), hapa haole songs (such as *In the Royal Hawaiian Hotel*) and various Pacific island language songs. Later, in the early-mid 1960s, he also attended the Polynesian Club in Sydney. During his childhood and youth, his family frequently visited Norfolk Island and, as he recalls:

> *Every holiday that I came home ... you made your own entertainment and we always carried a couple of ukes and a guitar in the car wherever we went. We'd just go down to Kingston or wherever and light up a big fire and we'd sit around and we'd sing for hours, terrific – wonderful fun ...* (interview 1999)

Returning to the island in 1967 he soon became involved in local culture by being invited by Scotty Nagle to be one of the performers in the Tahiti segment of the Pageant. Later, in the 1980s, he was one of the instigators of the Country Music Club (discussed in Chapter 10). While interested in songwriting as an activity, he has felt that his lack of formal training is a drawback ("because I don't read music and write music I haven't actually put any of the poems to music") and his main creative output in the 1990s was poetry. In 1998 local musician Lee Hamilton-Irvine recorded Bigg reciting fifteen of his poems. The recordings were released in cassette and CD format under the title *Morla el Do* ('Tomorrow will do'). Thirteen of the poems are in English and the remaining two ('Da bass side orn Earth' and 'Ent me') are in Norfolk language. The poems cover a range of Norfolk Island topics, (such as the legend of Barney Duffy and the experience of being a tourist bus driver). 'Da bass side orn Earth' ('The best place on Earth') is a celebration of the island's natural landscape that is distinguished from other material on the album by virtue of opening and closing with excerpts from a choral rendition of *In the sweet by and by*[33].

George 'Toofie' Christian

The late 1990s and early 2000s saw the emergence of a significant new local singer songwriter, George 'Toofie' Christian. Christian began songwriting in the mid-1990s after twenty five years of performing in various local pop, rock and country covers bands (discussed in Chapter 10). Initially taught guitar by Les Macrae in the 1970s, he further developed his musical skills by taking piano and music theory courses with local piano educator Joan Rawlinson in the 1990s and 2000s. Christian's first composition was *The*

Right whale, recorded on the *Pitcairn and Norfolk Songs of Praise* CD (discussed in Chapter 9). In 1998 he wrote a second composition on local culture entitled *Norfolk's hula* and followed this in 1999 with two further Norfolk language songs, *N.I. Blues* and *Hoemsick for N.I.* In contrast to his first song, these three compositions were initially private creative works, in that he did not perform them in public until 2001. Christian has discussed his inspiration to write songs as a personal heritage project:

> What I am trying to do when I write a song, and its words, is something which helps remember and keep alive some of the actual things that happen in the island which are getting lost ... things like how I miss hearing the horses cantering up this road, the clay road, as they came up the bridle track. Sometimes it just hits you that that's gone, then I sometimes get up in the night to write it down right away before it fades and goes again.

> I try to put things in my songs that come back to you, like the sound of the whalebird coming in, and you'd know they were going to lay and you could pick the eggs up in October/November ... things like that ... The things you miss when you are away from the island, like hearing the tamey, with its fantastic whistle, and the robin redbreast. When you grow up here and go away you really miss them. (interview 1999)

With regard to music, Christian proffered the following characterisation at our first interview:

> I am trying to get a sound for Norfolk that's distinctive, that's why I like playing around with major 7th chords and things like that. I think that's a way we can get a distinctive sound for our music. I'm trying to get a subtle, different sound, like some of the things Jimmy Buffett does, a little jazzy or bluesy, plus trying to keep a hula swing – that beat – going, that island feel you could dance to, to do a hula-style dance. And not just songs, I'd like to work on doing some instrumentals with a hula feel to them, the half western style we do – not just copy the Cook Islands or Hawaiian styles, they're theirs and ours is different. Musically we are probably closer to Hank Snow, his hula songs, than the Pacific Islanders' hula music, with that strong drums rhythm. (ibid)

This is a sophisticated manifesto of musical intentions and demonstrates an attempt to create a "distinctive" local style through synthesis of elements drawn from western 20th Century music traditions that have, in turn, drawn on non-western forms such as Hawaiian music and various Afro-Caribbean and Latin American styles. As befits a culture such as that of Norfolk Island, premised on syncreticism, it is a music of mergings and localisation.

The references to Jimmy Buffett's work are notable in a regional context. While Buffett currently resides far outside the critical canon of western 'roots' and world musics established by European and North American writers, critics and broadcasters – seen as irredeemably tarnished by his commercialism and blatant tropical hedonism – his work has had an enduring appeal in the Pacific. As I discussed in my study of the music history of the Whitsunday archipelago (2001), his music has been popular with regional singers and audiences[34]. Buffett also has a more direct relevance to Norfolk Island in that Alice Buffett identified him as a descendant of the original English Buffett family and invited him to perform on the island in 1987, where he played a packed-out solo concert at the Rawson Hall. The musical aspects that Christian refers to are the minor chords and inversions that Buffett uses in his arrangements and the assimilation of elements of other (mainly Caribbean) music styles to flavour his country-rock based sound. The second influence Christian cites, Hank Snow, was born in Nova Scotia (on the Atlantic coast of Canada) and first came to prominence as a country singer-songwriter in the late 1940s. While many of Snow's songs were mainstream country in style, he also recorded several songs in other (then) popular idioms, including *hapa haole* Hawaiian/country fusions[35] such as *Bluebird Island* (1952), recorded as a duet with Anita Carter. *Bluebird Island* communicates a (non-specific) island feel through both its music and its lyrical scenario[36]. The track is based around a lazy swing groove and includes Hawaiian-style steel guitar and country fiddle solos in the middle eight. The combination of similar *hapa haole* and country elements is discernible on several of the tracks on Christian's debut CD (as discussed below), where they are also combined with folk styles.

During a conversation with me in May 1999 Christian identified that the lack of opportunity to perform original music on the island, combined with an uncertainty about how new local songs might be received, limited his motivation to write more songs and to try and capitalise on his songwriting ability. Highly impressed by his work and aware of the restrictions of the situation he was in, I offered to fund and organise the production of an album of original songs through the Coral Music label run by Macquarie University's Department of Contemporary Music Studies (DCMS). Christian expressed considerable interest in the proposal and by early 2000 had written eight new songs and learnt and arranged the 1940s' song *The Norfolk Rangers* (discussed in Chapter 8). Following a submission of a demo of this material, recording sessions were undertaken at the DCMS studios in Sydney in January 2001 with the resultant album being launched on Norfolk Island in September 2001. The final CD, entitled *Pilli Lornga N.I.* ('Sticking with/to Norfolk Island'), featured eleven tracks[37] and appeared with a 16 page CD booklet including song lyrics, glossaries of Norfolk terms and photographs.

I acted as executive and assistant producer on the project and DCMS staff Denis Crowdy and David Hackett produced and engineered the recordings. Due to pressure of recording time, Christian sang and Crowdy played rhythm and acoustic lead guitar on all tracks, with a number of other musicians associated with the DCMS performing on bass, percussion, cello and flute and British guitarist Mike Cooper guesting on lap-slide guitar on four songs. Given these contributions, the album might best be thought of as a collaboration between a Norfolk Island singer-songwriter and a team of Australian producer/performers[38]. That said, with the exception of *Sweet Taytes*, all the album tracks were based on the chord sequences, vocal melodies, feels and styles of the original demos, with Cooper's slide guitar parts being the most obvious innovation. As principal arranger, Crowdy

191

Figure 25: George 'Toofie' Christian at DCMS studios (2001).

described his approach as "trying to bring out the feel, that richness, in Toofie's songs and voice" (interview 2001).

The album includes eight songs in Norfolk language and three in SE. Along with his version of the NZ WW2 song *The Norfolk Rangers*, Christian's two SE songs, *Friendship* and *Sentry* describe events from the penal colony period of the early 1800s (prior to the Pitcairners arrival), their language being appropriate to this context. The eight Norfolk compositions include a personal song about matrimonial break up (*N.I. Blues*), a historical incident (*The Right whale*), reflections on Norfolk's past and present (*Sweet taytes, Bridle track, Lewen in harmony* and *Hoemsick for N.I.*) and two songs about the history and appeal of the hula, in general (*Rhythm of the hula*) and with specific regard to Norfolk and Pitcairn history (*Norfolk's hula*).

The Right whale appears in a similar version to that recorded on the *Pitcairn and Norfolk Songs of Praise* CD but with the addition of a cello part (played by Jaime Riffel) and a low-mixed bass part. The musical elements support Christian's clear, slow vocal delivery (which switches to speech pattern on the line "Call'n out 'Fast Boet'". The song's narrative relates a well-known island story of how the fortuitous arrival of a rare right whale[39], and the prompt action of local whalers in catching and killing it, enabled the community to raise enough money to pay for an elderly woman's medical treatment in Australia and to complete construction of their church. The song's first two verses describe the predicament of the island community in the early 20th Century while the latter two describe the practice of small boat whaling, as in verse 4:

Catch'n a whale es wun skilful art
Fer hewh wun harpoon
Straight fer de heart
Call'n out 'Faas Boet'
En orf dem go
For many long hours
Lorng ou-wus dem was in tow

[translation]

Catching a whale is a skilful art
[That involves] throwing a harpoon straight into its heart
Calling out 'fast boat' [to indicate connection to the whale]
And off the boat goes
For many long hours
The boat is towed along [by the whale]

The song's chorus, introduced by a rise in pitch from the verses, re-affirms the divine intervention involved (and reflects Christian's faith as an elder of the Methodist church):

Dems prayers were aunsud
En sent from above
Wun right whale come
Tu daye ieland we love[40]

[translation]

Their prayers were answered
And sent from above
One right whale came
To the island we love

Christian's 1998 composition *Norfolk's hula* is a richly appreciative tribute to the local hula tradition that was reintroduced in the 1930s. As discussed in Chapter 7, the song's opening verses offer a succinct account of its loss and recovery which is intensified by the chorus's description of the personification of the grace of the hula in the dancer's body:

Hula harns, hula hips from Norfolk Iel
Si how graceful sa darns et in acklan style

[translation]

Hula hands, hula hips, from Norfolk Island
See how gracefully they dance in our own style

In order to emphasise the song's reflective address to themes of *appreciation* of hula, rather than hula dancing itself, the recorded version of the song is sung to a subdued (nylon string) picked guitar part in the verses alternated with more accentuated strumming during the choruses. Other instrumental parts comprise cello lines low in the mix and a short, restrained picked (steel string) guitar solo in the middle eight.

Christian's two 1999 songs have more personal aspects. *N.I. Blues* is a slow-medium paced acoustic song, loosely addressed to a former wife, whose 'bluesiness' is explicitly emphasised in its chorus:

Now I gut d'blues
Dem nasey N.I. blues
I gut d'blues
En I gut et fe yu

[translation]

Now I've got the blues
The nasty N.I. blues
I've got the blues
And I've got them because of you

Over four verses the song moves from an account of his ex-wife's departure on a DC4 airplane for Sydney, his resort to alcohol to dull the pain, his emerging sense of self-sufficiency and, finally, his 'cure', inscribed in the final chorus's revision as

I nor gut de blues
Any more fe yu

The album version features prominently-mixed lap steel slide guitar lines performed by Mike Cooper and a brushed drum accompaniment that give the song a 'period' feel appropriate to its historical setting (in the DC4 era). *Hoemsick for N.I.* explores another aspect of personal emotions, the memories and homesickness of young people, such as Christian's own children, who move off-island to study and start their careers. Introduced as inspired by a dream, the song provides a vivid and evocative account of the sounds and sights of Norfolk's natural environment, fancifully represented in verse three through the imagery of:

Orchestra gwen soon strike up
Blackbird es dar conductor
Said tamey en roben ell sing wun duet
Fe d'fantail do wun ballet darns

[translation]

The 'orchestra' is about to strike up
With the blackbird as the conductor
Where the tamey [golden whistler] and robin sing a duet
To accompany the fantail's ballet dance

The material that Christian specifically wrote for his debut album included two songs inspired by his interest in local history and his friendship with local historian Les Brown. *Sentry* relates the odd tale of a group of prisoners who attempted to escape the convict settlement by getting one of their number to impersonate a sheep in order to surprise and overpower a guard. The vocal melody of the verses, sung in a paralinguistic manner, dips into the chorus/refrain "Halt who goes there?" to provide dramatic emphasis and the overall mood of the song (accompanied on the album by chordal and lap steel guitar parts) is one of sorrowful recollection. While the theme of the second SE song, *Friendship*, is equally tragic – concerning the wreck of the schooner *Friendship* in 1835 and the (unnamed) protagonist's failure to reach his destination – the song's feel is more 'up' than the previously discussed tracks due to its brisk paced and syllabically dense chorus:

Destination mission station
At Mangungu near Hokianga
To be with Reverend William White
His brother

This aspect is highlighted on the recorded version through the rhythmic emphasis of a tambourine part and the addition of flute lines on the chorus, giving the song a 'pop-epic' feel (akin to that of Edison Lighthouse's 1970 hit single *Love grows*, which features similarly accentuated choruses).

Christian's second hula-themed song, *Rhythm of the hula*, is a lyrically simple and direct celebration of Polynesian dance and its associated music, inspired by his attendance at the Pacific Arts Festival in Rarotonga in 1992. As the song developed through its demo and studio stages the original guitar accompaniment (which had similarities to the Hank Snow hula style discussed above) was consciously modified by guitarist/arranger Crowdy into a Hawaiian slack-key style rhythm part that was accompanied on the album version by Torres Strait Islander singer Seaman Dan's producer/accompanist Karl Neuenfeldt[41] on ukulele and Cooper's lap-steel lines, giving the song a firm hula accent. In live performances of the song subsequent to the album recording Christian has retained this inflection.

The three remaining songs on *Pilli Lornga N.I.* evidence Christian's affection for and commitment to the island (as inscribed in the album's title). *Lewen in harmony's* verses offer brief inventories of the island's marine life, the singer taking obvious pleasure at enunciating the Norfolk island words, and commentary on how tasty particular types of fish are – as in verse 1:

We gut dar ofei, y'hohli en a nufka too
How gude si cook et orn a barbecue

[translation]

We've got trevally, herring and kingfish too
Which are great to barbecue

These lists and cooking descriptions are contextualised by the song's chorus, which emphasises the need to minimise pollution on the island and in its surrounding waters in order to maintain its natural resources:

Lewen in harmony
Oo'da daye iel of pine tree
Haewa keep et clean
From a plastic en debris

[translation]

Living in harmony
Out here on the isle of pine trees
We have to keep it clean
From plastic and [other] debris

On the album version the short verses are accompanied by strummed guitar parts and bass lines and the chorus (and general theme of harmony) are reinforced by the addition of Christine Carroll's flute part, embellishing the vocal melody and providing a short central solo and coda. *Bridle path* and *Sweet taytes* offer perhaps the album's most concentrated expressions of Norfolk's heritage. The former, directly inspired by Christian's memories of the sound of horse's hooves along a bridle track near his home in his youth, contains words, phrases and anecdotes of mid-20th Century Norfolk life that are relatively impenetrable without either personal knowledge or interpretation. Introduced by Christian's specification that the song involves "Think'n waye Norfolk usa be", the song eschews choruses and offers various recollections of particular horses and horse riding experiences in successive verses, before ending with the reflection:

Dar d'waye Norfolk bin usa be
Now gut a tar seal en car fer family
Sullun des daye would wonder how
Dem would lewe ef haewt' tu gu back tu dar now

[translation]

That's the way that Norfolk used to be
These days there are tar-sealed roads and families have cars
Some of us might wonder how
We would live if we had to go back to the old way of life

Recorded to an appropriately cantering country-rock rhythm, propelled by Klare Kuolga Meere's bass part and Guy Morrow's brisk brush drumming, the song's recollection is given a body and impact that matches Christian's memory of the physical experience of riding and horse care.

Sweet taytes is particularly significant as a reflection and inscription of the island's agricultural heritage. The topic first attracted Christian in 2000. Visiting his home one morning, he mentioned to me that he had an idea for a possible song and then exited the back door only to re-emerge shortly after and place three different kinds of kumera (sweet potatoes) on the kitchen table. Somewhat bemused, I asked for further explanation, and he related to me the manner in which Norfolk Islanders used to grow a variety of types of kumera as a staple crop but had now abandoned most of these, since the commencement of regular food deliveries by ship. Intrigued by this topic I encouraged him to write the song but he expressed reservations. When quizzed, he stated his concern that it might be too specialist a topic and also – in an aside – quipped that neither the Beatles nor the Rolling Stones had written songs about vegetables so he wasn't too sure he should either... Despite these misgivings the song was eventually written and I had the fortunate experience of being at the concert at which he premiered it. The song was well received, particularly by one male member of the audience who later informed me that he was moved at being reminded about a heritage aspect that he recalled from growing up with his father.

The song's lyrics combine a discussion of the kumera's central role in local farming and subsistence, a list of the types of kumera formerly grown and a discussion of those bird and mammal species that have now disappeared from the island. After listing eleven varieties in verse 2, verse 3 relates that:

Dem fe Berrige, Tongan en Potagee
Se gorn lornga dar bat en dar sunna

Gor-wha bird, black en white sparrow
You nawha gwen see et again

[translation]

The Berrige, Tongan and Potagee[42] kumeras
Are gone, along with Gould's wattled bat, the white headed black-
bird,
The gor-wha (a blackbird of unknown species) and the black and
white sparrow
Which you are never going to see again

The song's chorus emphasises the value of passing on agricultural
heritage (despite its unfashionability in a rapidly modernising environment):

Wi haew larna acklan's yung'un
How fe tull what taytes es wha
By dem leaf en de wines
Cos dar de waye yu larn

[translation]

We have to teach our young people
How to recognise different varieties of kumera
By their leaves and their vine stalks
Since that's the way you learn (to distinguish them)

In one of the few significant deviations from Christian's regular performance style, the album version of this song replaces his usual strummed
guitar accompaniment to the song's descending melodic lines with a warm
swung jazz guitar groove provided by Crowdy's acoustic guitar, bass and
brushed drums.

Released on the DCMS's financially subsidised Coral Music label, the
album achieved considerable international airplay, particularly on public
radio station 'world' and folk music programs in Australia, Germany.
Madeira, New Zealand, the UK and USA. Positive perceptions of its accomplishment and heritage value resulted in Christian's first off-Island performance at the Australian National Folk Festival in Canberra in 2003, where he
appeared, backed by Crowdy and (then) DCMS guitar tutor Erik Damberg,
and gained further exposure by being interviewed on ABC Radio National.
This, in turn, led to his securing a travel grant from the Norfolk Island
assembly to perform concerts in St Johns and Twillingate, in Newfoundland
(Canada) in June 2005[43].

Christian continued writing songs in 2002–2004 and in January 2005
recorded material towards his follow-up album, *White Rose*, with Hackett
and Crowdy, using the DCMS's portable studio facilities. The twelve tracks
written for the CD (slated for release in 2006 through Coral Music) included
five songs in Standard English, five in Norfolk language and two alternating
between the two. In contrast to *Pilli Lornga N.I.*, on which the SE songs
referred to the pre-Pitcairn settlement days and the Norfolk ones to Christian's own life experiences and reflections, the language/topic split is less
marked in his recent material. Ten of the songs are mid-tempo country/folk

197

influenced ballads set to strummed chordal accompaniments and the title track typifies this style. *White Rose* relates Christian's early upbringing, his father's early death and the gift of a cutting of a white rose to his mother (which still grows in the front yard of his family home). The song alternates his narrative account, in SE, with a chorus constructed as a quote from the woman who gifted the cutting:

Fe yus new babe please plunt daye
In wun said ell get dar sun's ray
Fe watch o'er hem es he grow en play
Cos dems twos root yaih fe stop

[translation]

For your new baby – please plant it
Somewhere where it will get the sun's rays
To watch over him as he grows and plays
Because those two are here to stay

Two other SE songs are strongly autobiographical. *Paradise Dancer* is a warmly nostalgic account of a beautiful dancer at the Paradise hotel in the 1970s, with her "waist long brown hair" and "Tahitian complexion", dancing so that the "whole place went wild". Set to a bright, mid-tempo guitar part, the first line of the chorus, "It was the Paradise dancer", rises in pitch above the melody of the preceding verse before falling to the affirmative "She was the Paradise Queen". The lyrics play with the cross-association of 'Paradise' the venue with the recalled island 'paradise' of the singer's youth. *The life of a muso* has a similar topic and setting, in this case, the South Pacific hotel, where the musician in question meets a young woman, falls in love and has a baby with her. The song ends sadly with the mother's choice to end the relationship when the singer decides to resume performing. While the chord progression, tempo and lyrical topic are standard county ballad material, the varied vocal melody and asymmetrical syllable lengths of verse lines give the song a more spontaneous (rather than overtly generic) feel. A third SE song, *The Blue Horizon*, complements the point of closure of *The life of a muso* and reflects on the sadness caused by love lost. Set to a slow shuffle rhythm, the song echoes earlier pop/Blues compositions – such as Frank Ifield's *Lovesick Blues* (1962) – and is based around the visual impression and repeated phrase of "the blue horizon" that surrounds the island and separates it from the rest of the world.

The remaining SE songs comprise *The Norfolk*, a short historical vignette of the construction of the first ship on Norfolk in 1797, during the period of the first penal colony, and *The Lord's Thanksgiving*. The latter is a composition specifically written to commemorate and be used on Thanksgiving Day. This occasion was acquired from whaling captains' wives in the mid-1800s and has become localised as a blend of US-style Thanksgiving celebrations and more conventional Anglican Harvest Festival services. The song represents Christian's most overt statement of his faith to date, ending with the statement:

Birds that whistle in our valleys
Fill the day with melody

The Lord alone could compose it
Thank the Lord in Thanksgiving

In musical terms, the two most distinct songs written for Christian's second CD are the Norfolk language compositions *Surfin' Bombis* and *Boom and Bust*. The former is a nostalgic paean to a popular surf break at Bomboras[44] frequented by Christian in his youth. Sung at a brisk tempo, with a gruffer vocal delivery than featured on *Pilli Lornga N.I.*[45] and set to a typical surf rock modal chord progression – the song's lyrics use period references and experiences of driving down to the break:

Sledgen round a coner out Bombis
Flat out in wun mini moke
Haewa beat wun Holden F.J.
Or chok orn a dust en smok

[translation]

Driving hard round a corner out near Bombis[46]
Flat out in a mini moke[47]
[I] have to beat [go faster than] a Holden F.J[48]
Or choke on its dust and exhaust emissions

and of demonstrating his surfing skills:

Oony Ai gut dar yellow board
Ai'l shoew dem whutta-waye
Fe shoot swal orf Nepean
Oony dem old cats el do et

[translation]

Only I've got the yellow board
I'll show them how to do it
How to shoot the swell off Nepean
Only the older/experienced surfers will/can do that

In addition to its lyrics, the song also celebrates the prowess of veteran local surfer Brian 'Golla' Adams through spoken vocal interjections over the song's concluding dimuendo that proclaim "Go Golla go ... Yu still es king".

The title and refrain of *Boom and Bust* refer to regular local cycles of investment and enthusiasm in new crops and products followed by a collapse in their feasibility, market and/or profitability (exemplified by the 'banana boom' – and subsequent 'bust' – of the 1930s). Reflecting Christian's affection for Jimmy Buffett's work, the song is set to a calypso derived rhythm with a marked ascent and descent of vocal melody on the chorus (which also stresses the "b" sounds of its hook, with the extended, open sound of the "oo" in "boom" suggesting an opening of potential and the abrupt terminal sound "ust" in "bust" suggesting closure). After running through various failed schemes, the song ends by referring to the present boom product, tourism, before ruefully concluding "Wun day es proud rooster/Next day es feather duster".

The four other Norfolk language songs are more typical of Christian's mid tempo ballad style. *Anny, Emelia, Kirar* (named after his three grand-daughters) is a delicate expression of love which identifies the difference in

199

role between parenting and grandparenting and offers the invitation to his granddaughters that " Dar bass said fe be sat/ Es orn poppy's knee" ('The best place to sit/Is on grandad's knee'). Adding to the emotional theme of the lyrics, Christian sings the song with greater use of vibrato than usual in his repertoire. *Gwen Hoem* also has a marked emotional emphasis, conveying the feelings of islanders returning home after a period away, using the image of the island glimpsed from a plane to characterise local experiences and beauty. Set to a jazzy chord progression, the song's feel and theme is akin to both various Jimmy Buffett compositions and songs by Torres Strait Islander Seaman Dan (such as *Sunset Blues* [2000]). *Kam o'er hiah si et* also expresses love of place, this time within the scenario of a tourist experience ('come over here and see it' being an invitation). The song switches between Norfolk language verses that extol the beauty of the island and the pride of its inhabitants and a simple SE chorus that expresses the wish that visitors will make their holiday one they "won't forget" by "sharing in our culture".

Of all the songs written for the *White Rose* album, *Tu-mooti*, a song about returning from a fishing trip, has the strongest, most dense use of Norfolk terms and phrases. Christian's restrained delivery of the lyrics belies their humour. The song revolves around the conviviality that takes place on fishing trips and down at Kingston pier as boats return, fish are filleted, beers are drunk and various locals pass by to check out the catches. The lyrics conclude by relating the frosty welcome the protagonist gets when he returns home inebriated, having given away the fish he has caught. As on his debut album, *White Rose's* songs convey a strong sense (and love) of place and inscribe and commemorate everyday aspects of island life as facets of history and heritage.

Kath King

Following discussions with Don Christian-Reynolds in 2000, I managed to secure some small financial support to enable the island's Multicultural Arts Society to hold a Norfolk language song contest in 2001 (the first since 1984). At my suggestion, the contest was limited to under-30 year olds, in order to stimulate a new generation of songwriters. Due to this, and various other factors, submissions within the contest deadlines were limited but the contest was successful in facilitating the emergence of a new songwriter and performer, Kath King. King's winning entry was an uptempo celebratory song about island life entitled *Ai guud* ('I'm good/happy'). Submitted on tape in an unaccompanied form, Don Christian-Reynolds worked out a fast-mid tempo ukulele accompaniment and the song was performed at the award ceremony at St Barnabus's function room in June 2001.

The verses of *Ai guud* move from detailing various activities (sweeping the verandah and making a woven hat and a pie) leading up to Bounty (Anniversary) Day. The song is expressed in colloquial Norfolk, giving it an everyday speech-like quality, and is humorously inflected, as in its fourth verse:

Den ai gwen hoem f'baeli ap
Ap fas f' dar Bounty Borl

Ai bin et dar swiit en kaa fet mais klorth
En ai nor gwen raun' a horl

[translation]

Then I go home to have a rest
[After] the Bounty Ball
It [the food] was so delicious, I can't fit into my dress
And I'm not going round the hall

which leads to the final celebratory chorus:

Bat ai guud, hieh ai guud
Hell yeh ai fiil guud
Ai bin paati hoel deih
Et dar baelful
So whatawieh ai fiil?

[translation]

But I'm good, hey, I'm good
Hell yeh, I feel good
I've been partying all day
And I've eaten too much
So how do I feel?

and a final answering line: "Ai fiil guud". A version of *Ai guud* sung to Christian-Reynolds's ukulele accompaniment was included on Christian-Reynolds and King's *Kath & Donald @ Norfolk* CD.

Along with *Ai guud*, King also submitted another unaccompanied song to the contest, entitled *Teach me how fer lew*, that the (anonymous) contest judges deemed as ineligible for competition (due, in large part, to perceptions of its strong similarity to the vocal melody of another song which they

Figure 26: Kath King and Don Christian-Reynolds (2002).

couldn't readily identify at the time – Simon and Garfunkel's *Scarborough Fair*). While the opening line and aspects of the melody of King's composition are close to another commonly known western song, the issues underlying this are more complex. Although they have come to be prominently associated with *Scarborough Fair*, Simon and Garfunkel were not its authors, as was stated in the credits of their 1966 album *Parsley, Sage, Rosemary and Thyme*. It was, in fact, a traditional English folk song. More than that, although unacknowledged, the abbreviated version of the song that the duo recorded was based on a version that Simon had learnt from British folk performer Martin Carthy in 1964. The song itself dates back to the medieval period and exists in many lyrical and melodic variants. The lyrics of the original list the tasks assigned to a woman in order to win her suitor's hand, opening with the reference to Scarborough Fair that gives the song its title. Given this context, issues of melodic plagiarism are more complex than they might at first appear.

While King's composition has a similar wistful intensity to the English folk song, a number of factors establish it as an accomplished original composition. The song's lyrics, reproduced and translated below, offer a particular ecological/'Green' reading of island history posited on the vocal protagonist's wish to be able to learn from the turtles that inhabit the waters around the island:

Turtle, turtle daun Blaek Bank
Cum round ya si me
I daun ya waiten me worn
Wall me en dem oefi

Larn bout how bin usa be
When whalen was about
En dem maen bin usa row
Til "There she blows" dem would shout

Fight dem suff
Du mine how big
En maybe turtle ghos
Yu ell teach me how fer lew

Larn bout parrot swarmen theck
Destroyen sullens crop
De Norfolk Ielanders struggle
Fe auwa be orn top

Turtle, turtle daun Blaek Bank
Cum round ya si me
Larn all acklan how
Yu's the guardian of the sea

Fight dem suff
Du mine how big
En maybe lovely turtle
Yu ell teach me how fer lew

[translation]

202

Turtle, turtle down at Black Bank
Come round here and see me
I'm down here waiting on my own
Me and the trevally[49]

Learn about how things used to be
When whaling was practiced
And the men used to row
Until they'd shout "There she blows"

Fight that surf
It doesn't matter how big [it is]
And maybe turtle ghost
You'll teach me how to live

Learn about the parrots swarming thick
Destroying our crops
Norfolk Islanders struggle
For us to stay on top [of things]

Turtle, turtle down at Black Bank
Come round here and see me
Teach us all how
You're the guardian of the sea

Fight that surf
It doesn't matter how big [it is]
And maybe lovely turtle
You'll teach me how to live

The song's melody is in a pentatonic scale, typical of western folk music, and occupies a one octave spread. As vocal educator Leigh Carriage has identified (pc 2004), King's vocals have an "untutored" quality, apparent in her slurring up to notes and occasional flat pitches. These are however stable in their usage and give the delivery an 'authenticity effect' that emphasises the sincerity and mood of the song. King's vocal lines are mainly aspirated and gentle with a switch to a constricted 'reedy' tone on the first two lines of the choruses for dramatic emphasis.

The version of the song submitted to the contest by King was sung unaccompanied and recorded on a small cassette tape recorder. In order to give the sound an echoic quality that would enhance its theme, King recorded herself singing live in the tiled interior of the toilets of a local hotel (a technique also used on occasion in 1950s and 1960s US pop music). Following the contest, Dave Hackett and Kristine Pymont[50] created three ambient/textural backings for the song (named the 'Ocarina', 'Gijan' and 'Gaapen' mixes[51]) and one radically processed techno dance track, entitled *Turtle an naenwe*[52]. Ten copies of the CD were produced, (with a cover design taken from a carving by Pitcairn singer Meralda Warren) and tracks from the EP were subsequently featured on Radio VL2NI in 2001. By virtue of its subtle lyrical themes and its stylistic difference from any prior Norfolk Island material, the recorded song is a notably original contribution to local song culture and one that offers an alternative model to the styles discussed above. The 'Ocarina' and 'Gijan' mixes and *Turtle an naenwe* were sub-sequently included on @ *Norfolk* (where they are referred to as *Tiich me hau fer lew* I, II and IV).

King's third composition on @ *Norfolk* is a lyrically simple, mid-tempo celebration of the rain that sustains Norfolk's rich and varied vegetation, accompanied by Christian-Reynolds's chordal acoustic guitar part. *Rien* declares the singer's "love" for the rain: "Norfolk rain is a thing you can't buy/Norfolk rain falls sweetly from the sky". While less lyrically and thematically complex than *Teach me how fer lew*, the song has a similar sincerity in its affirmation of island life and environment.

2002 Song contest

A further song contest was held in 2002. Open to entries in both Norfolk and English languages and with all-age categories, it attracted a greater number of entrants, from both the Pitcairn-descended community and other residents. Amongst the entrants was Maleah Butterfield, who submitted a short song that she had written in 2000, at the age of eight, entitled *Norfolk Island es talken*. The song, written in mixed SE and Norfolk, is a joyous celebration of life on the island:

> Ai love mais island and it's pretty too
> Got plenty thing here fer acklan du
> We no got Macdonalds or a zoo
> But we gut Emily Bay, wetls and plenty cow too

[*mais*: my; *fer acklan du*: for us to do; *wetls*: food]

Along with its effective simplicity, Butterfield's eager and confident vocal delivery of the song ensured it was well received and won her the junior songwriting prize.

The winner of the adult entrant category in the 2002 contest was a SE song entitled *The ballad of Seth Nash*, with lyrics written by Judy Schmitz to a melody and chord progression closely similar to Gordon Lightfoot's song *The wreck of the Edmund Fitzgerald* (1976), relating the story of a child's death at sea in 1817 while en route to Norfolk Island[53]. Along with debuting songwriters, the competition also received entries from Kath King, George 'Toofie' Christian, Alison Ryves and Alan Maisey. Aside from Christian's *Paradise dancer* (discussed above), the remainder of entries dealt with everyday, contemporary experiences and perceptions of Norfolk Island – Ryves's *Rainbow (on Norfolk Island)* subsequently appearing on her 2003 album *Dancing with the Storm* (discussed in the previous chapter) and King's *Rien* appearing on @ *Norfolk*.

The number of entrants to the 2002 contest illustrated an increased focus on the expression of local identity in song prompted, in no insignificant way, by the cash prizes awarded to the contestants. On Norfolk, as elsewhere, funding is a significant aspect of cultural life and either the personal/family subsidy of recordings (in Ryves's and Pedel's cases) or external assistance (such as the DCMS's support for George 'Toofie' Christian and Kath King) are a necessary element in a music culture that has not, to date, been subject to commercial investment and marketing. Self-funded ('DIY') releases with limited distribution are still the norm and, in the case of CDs such as @*Norfolk* and Ben Boerboom's Caktus albums[54], these have been individually copied on home computer systems. While their packaging may not resemble the standards of commercial releases or heavily subsidised productions, this low cost production option has the benefit of minimising initial financial outlay (once computer equipment has been purchased and/or accessed) and maximising profit from direct sales at performances and/or local shops. As a form of sustainable local production that does not require external assistance this has a number of significant advantages. It is however salient to note that the only Norfolk Island recording to have secured significant international radio airplay to date – and to have assisted in securing the recording artist concerned international performance opportunities – has been *Pilli Lornga N.I.*, with its more industry-standard packaging, sound quality and promotional assistance[55].

As this chapter has discussed, contemporary Norfolk language/Pitcairn heritage songwriting began in the 1980s and has been boosted through the work of new songwriters such as Christian and King. Unlike earlier, orally-transmitted songs and hymns, recent compositions have passed into local culture through radio play and CD purchase and circulation, *in addition to* live performance. While outside influences and agencies have contributed to the latest wave of songwriting, recent compositions have enriched and diversified the heritage that has sustained from the earliest phase of Pitcairn settlement. Through language, theme, music and melody, the songs discussed in this chapter are significant for providing a public expression of a cultural identity that is as located in the present as it is in any myths of origin.

Notes

1. This is not to claim that no individual may have known or sung any such repertoire, rather that there is no evidence of this in documented social music performance, despite there being a considerable amount of literature on island social life between the 1850s-1870s.

2. Along with the distinctive use of the word "girt", the song's lyrical themes are close to verse one of *Advance Australia Fair*:

   Australians all let us rejoice
   For we are young and free
   We've golden soil and wealth for toil
   Our home is girt by sea
   Our land abounds in Nature's gifts
   Of beauty rich and rare
   In history's page, let every stage
   Advance Australia fair!
   In joyful strains then let us sing
   "Advance Australia Fair"

3. When royalty were not in attendance, if they were, the prior anthem had priority as the 'royal anthem'.

4. Other writers suggested included early 20th century headmaster Gustav Quintal and an (un-named) schoolteacher at Anson Bay school.

5. This is Scott and Borg's version, Buffet's has "I wish I'll show a yorlyi" for this line.

6. Borg's version of this verse has a number of differences:

   All auwas examiners es

> *Peter, Tom en Jack*
> *Doo yorlyi worry ef wi nor*
> *Gut any prize des tack.*

7. In its current usage 'wawaha' means pompous or conceited, this earlier 20th Century usage is more suggestive of 'self-importance' and/or 'preachiness'.

8. Buffet's version of these two lines is significantly softer in meaning: "Cos yorlyi know before I larn/De thing I tull es true" – translation: 'Because you know/That what I have told [you] is true'.

9. Not necessarily English nationals, rather English speaking Anglo-Australians.

10. Fookie Young wrote a song while interned in a German concentration camp during World War Two that has been revived by members of the Norfolk Island Girl Guides after having been transcribed from its original written version by Guides leader Colleen Crane. At time of writing (early 2005) I had been unable to obtain a copy but it was scheduled for inclusion in a booklet of island songs collected by Crane and guides due to be published some time in 2005 under the title *Norfolk Songs and Poems*. (Thanks to Coleen Crane for this information.)

11. At time of writing Don Christian-Reynolds was considering the possibility of writing chordal parts and arranging the song for ensemble performance.

12. Archie Bigg recalls that this line was "Where *flying* fishes play" (interview 1999).

13. Eileen Snell.

14. Marina Sellars.

15. Interviewed in 1999, Snell also identified that she had completed lyrics to others that had not been set to music yet.

16. I have been unable to ascertain the specific date.

17. A small local fish.

18. This is a rather clumsy translation that nevertheless indicates the processes referred to.

19. The session also included covers of the Pitcairn *Auwas gubai song* (discussed in Chapter 12) and the *hapa haole* Hawaiian standard *Pearly Shells*.

20. Several prominent Pitcairn descended islanders who championed various aspects of island culture and autonomy have declined to participate in SPD activities due to factors such as their lack of belief in the SPD's central tenet (that the island had been given to the Pitcairners by Queen Victoria and that Australia has no legitimate authority over it) and/or the exclusion of non-Pitcairn descended spouses from SPD activities and policy making.

21. The organisation is also referred to in some 1980s published material as 'The Society of Descendants of the Pitcairn Settlers'.

22. A song about the Pitcairners departing from Pitcairn to Norfolk Island on the *Morayshire* that had been written in English and translated into Norfolk language.

23. Emily Bay, at Kingston, is the island's main recreational swimming spot.

24. Since horse drawn buggies were a common form of transport prior to motor vehicles, this gives the song a nostalgic aspect.

25. Full length and abbreviated versions accompanied by acoustic chordal guitar and a piano accompanied abbreviated version.

26. Thanks to Denis Crowdy for pointing this out to me.

27. A song of unknown authorship that originated in New Zealand's North Island in the early 1910s and was modified into a song popularised by Paraire Tomoana in the latter part of the decade. It is now a New Zealand/Maori folk standard.

28. Schooling on the island cut off at Year 9 level until the mid-1990s, when teaching through to Year 12 was introduced in the island school.

29. In 1959 she also auditioned for employment on the new ABC TV service, which, after a considerable delay, requested her to attend further auditions, unfortunately her

marriage had dissolved in the interim and she had relocated to Norfolk Island (and she did not take up their offer).

30. Also referred to as *Dar said orl acklan kam fram*. ('The place we all come/originate from'). (The Norfolk term 'kam fram' translates as 'come from' but also alludes to ancestry in the compound word form 'kamfram').

31. "Age" being a derivative of 'edge', as in cliff-edge.

32. Engineered by Chris Townend and Murray Cook.

33. The only other track to feature musical extracts is the album closer *Piano man*, which opens with the sound of an unidentified piano rag and ends with communal singing of the standard *Show me the way to go home*.

34. His songs are also known in Melanesia, with a version of his Caribbean-themed song *Volcano* being resignified on the Papua New Guinean Rabaul benefit album *Rabaul: Volcano Town* (1994).

35. It is possible that Snow's hula-influenced tunes were inspired by his key early model, Jimmie Rodgers, who recorded several Hawaiian-influenced tracks in 1927-31, including five tracks on which he was accompanied by Lani McIntyre's Hawaiians in 1930.

36. Its lyrics refer to a pair of lovers separated (one on Bluebird Island, one on a far away shore) only to be reunited when bluebirds fly "over silver seas" to invite the (male) singer to sail his "ship of love" back there.

37. One of the songs on the original demos, *Naenwe*, was omitted since both Christian and the producers were unhappy with its structure.

38. Also see the 'Afterword' to this volume for a discussion of the writing and pre-production of the album.

39. Which, in some accounts, is identified as a different species.

40. The pronunciation here is anglophonic ("love" rhyming with the preceding "above") rather than the common Norfolk pronunciation/variant 'law'.

41. The duo has collaborated on three albums to date, *Follow the Sun* (2000), *Steady Steady* (2001) and *Perfect Pearl* (2003), all of which include hula style tracks.

42. The term 'potagee' appears to derive from the word ' Portuguese ' and was formerly used on the island to refer to something unreliable. (Possibly a retention of a term from whaling days referring to the perceived shortcomings of Portuguese crew members).

43. These concerts were held in conjunction with the "Postcolonial Distances' conference at Memorial University, St Johns, that brought together Canadian and Australian music academics to compare aspects of Australian and Canadian music.

44. The name of a location (and road) on Norfolk Island. The word 'bombora' derives from an Australian Aboriginal language term for a submerged reef. The word's connection with surfing was cemented by US band The Original Surfaris with their 1962 hit single *Bombora*.

45. Closer in style to his rock-orientated live performances of the 1970s and 1980s.

46. 'Bombis': an abbreviation of Bomboras.

47 A small jeep-like vehicle launched in Australia in the mid-1960s.

48. The first Australian manufactured car, which was highly popular in the 1950s,

49. A type of fish.

50. A music graduate from Macquarie University.

51. The 'Ocarina' mix was named after the sampled Ocarina sound that features as an extra melodic line. *Gijan* is a Norfolk word meaning confusion and *Gaapen* means transfixed.

52. The *naenwe* reference suggests the psychedelic effects of eating the fish. This name has not been one subsequently used by King to refer to the track.

53. Appropriately enough, given its musical model, the version of song submitted on

cassette to the contest has an intricate melody and strong folky feel and its victory in the competition was boosted by singer Eileen 'Irish' Sloan's confident and nuanced vocal performance on the demo version and the emotional poignancy of the lyrics:

As the tears slowly rolled down her cheeks
She closed her eyes and began to pray
For her little boy that had passed away
Seth Nash was his name –
And he was eight months old

54. Or one-off singles such as Dave Clayton's 2001 song *Norfolk Island: Jewel in the South Pacific*.

55. *Pilli Lornga* N.I. was publicised through various means, including specialist folk/world music radio DJ e-mail lists.

Chapter Twelve

FROM CULTURAL EMERGENCE TO CRISIS
Pitcairn Island 1945-2005

T he end of World War Two lightened Pitcairn's isolation as ships began
to ply Pacific routes again but the cultural stimulation offered by contact
with the passengers and crews of visiting cruise ships diminished considerably in the late 1940s and 1950s with the growing use of trans-Pacific air
travel by tourists. Information about the island in this period – and
particularly about cultural practices – is limited but there seems little doubt
that hymn singing continued to be prominent[1]. One thing that is known is
that the island's cultural isolation began to be ameliorated from the late
1950s on through the growing possession and use of radio receivers. In the
1950s and early 1960s, the Ecuadorian station Radio Quito became a local
favourite. As part of an affiliation deal with the US CBS network, the station
re-broadcast shows featuring material by early hillbilly/country performers
such as Ernest Tubbs, Hank Williams and Hank Snow. In the 1960s and
1970s country music became even more popular on the island, due in large
part to islanders tuning in to US radio stations such as the Sacramento
(California) based KRAK. In this regard, despite its geographical isolation,
Pitcairn was linked into contemporary musical tastes, since KRAK was one
of the pioneer US stations to switch into country music formatting (a policy
which was promoted by industry figure Joe Allison in the early 1960s). As
a result, artists such as Johnny Cash and Charley Pride became popular on
Pitcairn. The radio station also ran regular listener competitions, including
occasional prizes for the listener tuning in from furthest away. In the late
1960s Steve and Olive Christian heard one such announcement, wrote in
and won a selection of Cash, Pride and Elvis Presley LPs, which were duly
mailed to Pitcairn.

From the late 1970s on, another form of cultural contact and diversion
was provided by visits from the Chilean navy training schooner *Esmeralda*.
The ship regularly included a brass band amongst its crew, which performed
on the island on several occasions. In 1984, a further musical and cultural

stimulus was provided by a different group of visitors, with the arrival of twenty-eight Norfolk Islanders on a (self-styled) 'pilgrimage' to the island of their ancestors. The group flew to Mangareva, via Auckland and Tahiti, then by chartered ship to Pitcairn, arriving on October 25th. Publicised in advance, the Norfolk Islanders were swelled by the addition of a further thirty-five Tahitians and Mangarevans (and a New Zealand television crew, two journalists and a photographer). Following a series of parties and a cricket match, a concert was held on October 30th, with brackets of songs being performed by Norfolk Islander, Tahitian, Mangarevan and Pitcairn performers. This conjunction of styles and repertoires allowed a temporary convergence of those musical traditions that had developed in relative isolation since the initial foundation of the Pitcairn community and their effective bifurcation in the 1850s and 1860s (into the separate communities of Norfolk and Pitcairn islands). One outcome of this contact was that the Norfolk Islanders realised that the hymn known for many years on Norfolk as *The Pitcairn anthem* was not known by Pitcairners (and might therefore be more appropriately named *The Norfolk anthem*). However, as both communities discovered, the hymn *In the sweet by and by* is common to both islands (despite the fact that it was written *after* the re-establishment of the Pitcairn community and could not have been taken by the groups who left Norfolk Island shortly after the founding of that community).

Like Norfolk Island, Pitcairn has no long-established tradition of locally written 'folk' music and the performance of localised versions of hymns has, to some extent, substituted for a vernacular song tradition. However, this situation changed following the opening-up of Pitcairn to new musical styles in the 1950s and 1960s, resulting in what would seem to have been the first attempts at local songwriting since the 1800s. The first example appears to have been the setting of original lyrics written by Australian pastor Lester Webster and Melva Evans (nee Warren) to the tune of Australian Aboriginal gospel singer Jimmy Little's 1963 hit single *Royal telephone*. This song, entitled *We from Pitcairn Island*, was originally written in 1967 but it was not until the mid-1980s that it entered the regular repertoire of Pitcairn singers[2]. It is now regularly performed to welcome and farewell visiting ship's crews and visitors coming ashore.

The song's lyrics comprise:

We from Pitcairn Island
Welcome you today
We're glad you called[3] to see us
But soon you'll sail away

We hope you will remember
The love we've tried to show
The friendship we have made today
Remains though you must go

chorus

We will miss you as you journey on your way
We do wish that you with us could ever stay

But we know that God will keep us in his hands
Perhaps someday we'll meet again on this far distant strand[4]

Our island is so tiny encircled by the sea
Its shoreline is so rugged as you so well can see
Yet we so dearly love it our homes are also there
And if you come our way again our welcome you will[5] *share*

[repeat chorus]

Another song that was premised on the lyrical substitution of a prior song[6] was simply entitled *Pitcairn Island*. Allan Cox, a schoolteacher who worked on the island in the 1980s, wrote this song. In a version performed by Trent Christian in 1999 for the author, the lyrics open with

A long way out in the middle of the sea
A lovely little island just happens to be
Pitcairn island, the place we love the best
The best, the best, the very, very best

and proceed to give a lightning account of the Pitcairn community's history before concluding with the contemporary comment:

Although our numbers dwindle and the ships are less
We still welcome you with a great warmness
To Pitcairn Island ...

Despite Webster's involvement in co-writing *We from Pitcairn Island*, the SDA ministry on the island was uneasy about the increasing availability of radios and record players and the number of islanders listening to popular music on them. Indeed the SDA Church regularly cautioned against them in services and in informal advice to individuals and families. As Meralda Warren has recalled:

When we were teenagers growing up, even to wiggle to the stereo going
was very much frowned upon ... it got to the stage where it really wasn't
on. Most of us who left the island for New Zealand or other places [in
the 1970s] came back with outside influences, we picked up dancing
styles and things ... but it stayed very strict on Pitcairn, it got to a stage
where people stopped going [to church]. (interview 1999)

During the 1970s guitars became more easily available on the island and in 1978 the contracted schoolteacher introduced basic guitar studies into the curriculum. This posed a challenge to the SDA Church, who responded to this drift away from their traditional teachings and prohibitions by attempting to channel the musical diversification into established religious music. To mark this development, the SDA pastor, Wallace Ferguson, penned an article for the island's monthly newsletter, the *Pitcairn Miscellany*, in which he wrote:

Some months ago the schoolteacher introduced guitar training: this has
gone along very well. And the church has taken opportunity by the
forelock. Two divine services have been run almost entirely on special
musical items. On the 3rd of June the programme hinged on music in
the Old Testament, and then again on the 22nd of July the programme
centralised on the life of Christ in a musical presentation – Christ born

211

*into our world – Christ's ministry – Christ's death on the cross – Christ's
resurrection – Christ's return. All these phases of the life of Christ were
presented in vocal items, or instrumental items or a mixture of vocal
and instrumental ... Besides this other items were rendered in other
services and these were much appreciated. (PM July 1978: 2)*

As he went on to emphasise, he judged these musical experiments to be a
success whose "impressions ... will not soon be forgotten" (ibid).

While Ferguson's approach represented a significant liberalisation of
SDA musical policy it was mild in comparison to that affected by Australian
SDA pastor Rick Ferrét, who arrived on Pitcairn in 1988 (and departed in
1991). Ferrét had a markedly different background to his predecessors. Prior
to embracing the SDA faith, and joining the ministry, Ferrét had been a lead
guitarist in a Sydney rock band and soon after his arrival he was enlivening
services by playing guitar. He encouraged young islanders to follow his
example and diversified and updated the repertoire of songs used for
worship. As some indication of the major reversal in SDA policy and practice
at this time, he also performed secular music at social functions and taught
local guitarists such as Trent Christian particular techniques to enhance
their playing. By 1995, the community were musically 'modernised' enough
to accommodate carols accompanied by electric guitars at a pre-Christmas,
candle-lit event (*PM* December 1995: 2).

School music education also developed in the 1980s-90s, albeit somewhat erratically, depending on the individual background and proclivities
of the contracted teacher concerned. One notable development occurred in
1997, when contract schoolteacher John Chan organised a school band
using the school's instruments (five recorders, two triangles, two tambou-
rines and a xylophone) plus the school and church keyboards and his own
flute. Using an Apple Mac computer music program he adapted sheet music
into EZ notation[7] and organised school concerts. This represented an attempt to encourage a broad base of the school students to learn instruments
and perform (and was the first time that computer-based music systems
had been utilised on the island).

The social music performed by islanders from the 1950s to the present
principally comprises well-established 'standards' (such as Jimmie Davis
and Charles Mitchell's 1940 composition *You are my sunshine* and the US
vernacular song *Goodnight Irene*) and country songs (such as Hank
Thompson's 1960 hit *Blackboard of my heart*) together with occasional,
easy-to-play contemporary pop songs added to the social repertoire at the
time of their availability via repeated radio plays and/or access to records
on the island. But as Trent Christian has also emphasised:

*When we get together for a jam session, in the night, usually on a Friday,
people will play the old country classics and the old Pitcairn hymns too.
We'll go straight from a country song to a hymn, all together. Those
songs are all ones everyone likes singing, so they go together. (interview
1999)*

In these jam sessions, the singers are usually accompanied with ukuleles
and/or guitars, the spoons and, on occasion, the piano accordion and/or

'tea chest' basses[8]. Skills on these instruments have been acquired from visiting seamen, such as Captain Frank, of the *Essi Kari*, who visited the island on several occasions during the 1970s, entertaining islanders with his accordion playing.

Since the mid-1970s the island has also been visited every 12-18 months by a French navy ship from Tahiti, whose crewmembers have established a tradition of going ashore and performing lengthy sessions (described by Meralda Warren as "beautiful music: all night!" – interview 1999). The Tahitian members of these crews perform on guitars, ukuleles and impromptu percussion for Pitcairners. During many of these performances Pitcairn islanders have joined in with the singing or dancing, picking up choruses and basic moves, and Trent Christian recalls himself and others strumming along on guitars, vamping parts to complement the material played by the Tahitians[9] (interview 1999). Occasional contact with Polynesians from neighbouring Gambier Isle (Mangareva) has also increased local awareness of (contemporary) Polynesian music. The presence of a Rarotongan temporary worker on the island in the late 1990s was also significant for teaching Pitcairners about Rarotongan dancing[10]. This tentative shift towards embracing cultural Polynesianism has also surfaced in the school curriculum, with contract New Zealand schoolteacher Sheils Carnihan training a group of fourteen year olds to perform Maori dances at the 1989 Christmas concert – including a *haka*, a *poi* dance (involving the whirling of a ball on a stick by dancers) and a *raku* (where sticks are tossed between partners). (The poi, danced to the music of the Patea Maori Club's record *Poi E*, was apparently particularly well-received by the audience and was performed again as an encore [*PM* December 1998: 3]).

One tradition that has firmly established itself on Pitcairn is that noted in Chapter 5, of sending off visitors with farewell songs from those islanders who ferried them to their boat. Innumerable reports indicate that this remains an enduring 'signature' of Pitcairn culture, one that continues to make a significant impression on visitors. Australian adventurer Frank Clune, who visited the island in 1964, commented that:

All hands paddle furiously until we cross the bar, and with Pervis at the helm we row towards our ship, to the strains of "Ship of Fame", sung by the islanders ...

The steamer hoots, the boats cast off, and the Pitcairners sing their hymn of hope, "Shall we gather at the River?" Their song rang in my ears for many a mile as the Athenic *gathered speed and headed west.* (1966: 239)

Bounty mutineer descendant Glyn Christian, who visited Pitcairn in order to research the life of his famous ancestor Fletcher, also identifies the "famous songs of goodbye, ringing with rich, reedy harmonies unique to Polynesia" as particularly heart-wrenching, commenting:

The moment of goodbye, when just we fifteen were left on the deck, was ghastly. We stood mute in harsh floodlight from our mast heads as they sang 'Goodbye' [the Goodbye song] and 'In the Sweet Bye and Bye', and we were grateful we had some preparation for the raw beauty of

213

unaccompanied singing by almost fifty loved people on the open sea. (1999: 407)

While such community singing does not appear to have been recorded in situ, some sense of its musical style is conveyed in a recording made by members of the Christian family at the SDA Voice of Prophecy (VOP) studio in Newbury Park, California in 1991. Tom and Betty Christian's first contact with the recording's producer, Eddie Pullen, and VOP occurred in 1967 when they spent six months in California[11]. They returned in 1990, with their daughters Raelene, Sherri and Darlene, and gave a series of presentations about Pitcairn that ended with them singing a selection of Pitcairn songs and hymns. In January 1991, shortly before their return to Pitcairn, Pullen suggested that they record the material they performed on their tour. For the recording session they were joined by Betty Christian's sister Marie (a US resident) on ukulele and by Pullen on mandolin.

The material was transferred to CD in 2003 and copies were made available for sale from the island on a release entitled *Tom and Betty Christian's Family sing favourite Pitcairn Gospel Songs*. The album features twelve songs, *The Pitcairn welcome song* and *Goodbye song*; locally associated hymns *In the sweet by and by* and *The ship of fame* and eight other hymns. Betty Christian has described the latter as:

old favourites that we sing many times here, at church, Sabbath School and some social events as well. They were also some of our personal favourites and ones that we all agreed on from the list of songs we had to choose from. (pc 2004)

As befits a low-tech live-in-the-studio recording, the album features the Christians singing in their usual spontaneous 'social' manner. Along with Tom Christian's acoustic guitar accompaniment, the ukulele and mandolin parts are significant elements in the arrangements by virtue of reinforcing a pronounced Pacific 'chug' to the rhythms of the *Welcome song* and giving a more country/gospel feel to songs such as *Manger to the Cross* and *Cling to the Bible*. The versions of *The ship of fame* and *In the sweet by and by* included are faster paced than the Norfolk versions discussed in Chapter 9, perhaps reflecting their different status on Pitcairn compared to Norfolk (where they have a more solemn anthemic function). The version of *The goodbye song* performed differs from Young's original composition (discussed in Chapter 5) by following its first verse with the line "Goodbye God bless you one and all" repeated three times, the last with a rising inflection in the final words, before concluding with a melodic dip down to the concluding phrase "Until we meet again".

II. Norfolk Connections

Trent Christian

In 1993 Trent Christian relocated to Norfolk Island and worked for several years as a guide for Pinetree Tours and playing and singing at regular 'Island Dinners' at the South Pacific Hotel, where his repertoire included Meralda Warren's songs *In the blood*, *Bounty burning* and *Away orn Pitcairn*[12] (dis-

*Figure 27: Trent Christian onstage at the 1999
Norfolk Country Music Festival.*

cussed below) together with Pitcairn hymns and international standards, such as the US hillbilly song *She'll be coming round the mountain*.

In 1999 Christian appeared at Norfolk Island's Country Music Festival. During his set he performed a version of Neil Murray's song *My Island home*, popularised in the Pacific by Torres Strait Islander Christine Anu with her 1995 version. As described in his on-stage introduction, the song's lyrics were particularly significant for him, describing his own circumstances (in 1999):

> *Six years I've been in the city*
> *And every night I dream of the sea*
> *They say home is where you find it*
> *Will this place ever satisfy me?*
> *For I come from the saltwater people*
> *We always lived by the sea*

215

Now I'm down here living in the city
And my island home is waiting for me

The identification of Norfolk Island (a community of less than two thousand inhabitants, with a town centre comprising one main street), as the "city" in question provides a telling identification of the scale of the Pitcairn community in which Christian grew up. In the early 2000s Christian performed with his sister Tania in Polynesian culture shows at venues such as the Colonial Hotel, appeared in a duo with Kim Davies (which visited Lord Howe Island in 2003) and made various solo appearances, performing to tourists. While Christian has not (to date) written any original material, he has featured two compositions by Rosie Saint[13] in short sets performed for tourists – *Welcome song* and *Tears for Norfolk*. The *Welcome song* was written by Saint for the 2001 South Pacific Mini-Games and is a cheerful, uptempo composition inviting and welcoming visitors:

Come on over and visit us
Come on over it's a must
Come on over to our sandy shores
And we'll show you more

Saint's second composition is a slower, reflective composition, with lyrics addressing the threat to Norfolk's traditional identity and lifestyle posed by development of the island. As Christian has commented, "Rosie's songs are perfect for the tourists, giving them the welcome and also maybe making them think about what's here and us having to look after it" (interview 2004).

Meralda Warren

Along with Trent Christian's engagement with Norfolk Island culture, a similar acquaintance was also a significant factor in inspiring Pitcairn Islander Meralda Warren to begin writing songs in 1987. Warren first learnt ukulele by ear from her mother Mavis, a social player and singer, when she was five, and then learnt chordal guitar and piano-accordion playing from instruction books and in imitation of visitors to the island. In addition to working as a police and immigration officer and assistant nurse (and, formerly, a ship-to-shore radio operator), she has also taught guitar, intermittently, at the Pitcairn Island school (depending on the willingness of the New Zealand teachers contracted in for fixed two-year periods to let her run such classes).

In 1984 Warren visited Hawai'i on a sponsored study trip and studied hula dancing with George Naope, a traditional dance teacher involved with re-instating Hawai'i's Merrie Monarch Dance Festival. Her studies led her to realise how much of Pitcairn's Polynesian cultural heritage had been lost and to value the forms – such as weaving and cooking – which remained[14]. On her return to Pitcairn she danced at several social occasions and taught dances such as the tamure to adults such as Trent Christian and, for one semester, to children at the island school. She has subsequently confined her (public) dancing to social occasions, such as the visits of French naval vessels, when Polynesian crewmembers would also dance. Warren's introduction to songwriting occurred while on her first visit to Norfolk Island in 1987.

Inspired by the (revived) sense of tradition in Norfolk Island culture at that time, and by her awareness of the imminent bicentenary of Pitcairn settlement, she wrote three compositions based on the shared historical roots of the two island communities: *Away orn Pitcairn*[15], *In the blood* and *The Bounty's gone*, together with a fourth, on everyday life on Pitcairn, entitled *An unsuccessful day*.

The lyrics of *In the blood* emphasise the ancestry of present day Pitcairners, and Warren in particular, opening with the declaration:

I've got the blood of the mutineers:
Christian, Young, McCoy
Quintal, Adams un all hem others

and later stating:

Our mothers come from Otaheite
Toofati, Maimitti
Tiopiti un sweet Maria

Unusually for her (self-accompanied) songs, Warren performs the chordal guitar accompaniment for *In the blood* alternating standard strums with a light rasguedo (flamenco style arpeggio) accent on the second beat, giving the track a rhythmic buoyancy.

The Bounty's gone is typical of her musical oeuvre (and the songs discussed below) by having a rhythmic structure accenting the second and fourth beats in the bar, suggesting a country-meets-hula mixture similar to (but not influenced by[16]) many of George 'Toofie' Christian's songs. Its lyrics centre on the events leading up to the destruction of the *Bounty*

Figure 28: Meralda Warren, Norfolk Island (1999).

217

described in its chorus:

> Higher and higher the flames are burning
> Lower and lower the Bounty sinks
> No more howling in her riggings
> No more wake astern will float

An unsuccessful day is a short humorous song describing one of the everyday realities of island life – a failed fishing trip. While it retains her habitual rhythmic lilt, the song's brisker pace, dense syllabic flow and vocals set slightly higher than her usual median range give a distinctive aspect to the song, matched by its lyrics. Warren's sardonic depiction of the situation – and her colourful language use – provide a particularly vivid vignette of her life on the island, as in verses 2 and 3:

> Sitten orn a rock, waiten for wun fish
> I must catch et, oh how I wish
> Oh how I hate it when always teck my bait
> Har small sleppary bloody pick pick

> I tried it once more but har wave over me poured
> I wish I home wipen in a house
> Nor larna sullun I nor catch anything
> Keep et as quiet as a mouse

[The final line of verse 2 is a statement of exasperation about the fish picking at her bait and the penultimate line of verse 3 states that she hopes no one realises ["nor larna sullun"] that she has been unsuccessful.]

Sung in more standard English, *Away orn Pitcairn's* lyrics summarise the island's lifestyle over a repetitive chordal groove, its chorus painting a broad picture:

> Away orn Pitcairn the sun is shining
> The sea it crashed with a boom on the shore
> The hills are steep up one side down the other
> The plants and flowers are the beauty of the eyes

Warren performed *In the blood* and *The Bounty's gone* on Pitcairn as part of the 1990 Bicentenary celebrations, and later taught them to school students. Subsequently she has also written topical songs for specific occasions, such as a farewell song for Pastor Rick Ferrét and his wife when they departed in 1991 and one for a rat eradication team who visited the island in 1997 and 1998.

I met Warren on Norfolk Island in 1999, during her extended stay there (on a form of long service leave from her duties on Pitcairn) and interviewed her about her work. At our second meeting I offered to record her songs (on the digital minidisk recorder I had with me) and to burn her CD copies for archival and documentary purposes. While initially wary, she accepted the offer and we arranged a recording session in the kitchen of the house she was staying in. On the day of the recording, in mid-April, she revealed that she had written several new songs and we recorded eight of her compositions plus a modified version of Merle Haggard's song *Okie from Muskogee* (similar to the Norfolk *Dreamfish Song* discussed in Chapter 11) entitled *I'm proud to be a Pitcairn Islander*. Like her initial four songs, discussed above, her newer material was written in various combinations of Standard English and Pitcairn language.

The four new songs recorded at the session comprised *The cause*, *Wishing*, *Pitcairn Island* and *Mussa es the same*. *The cause* relates that the cause of the *Bounty's* voyage to Tahiti – and thereby the mutiny and foundation of Pitcairn's community – was the collection of breadfruit to take to the Caribbean. The vocal melody is set to a minor chord accompaniment, with a descending melodic pattern in the chorus lines. Referring to the breadfruit by its Pitcairn name – *uru* – the song's chorus summarises this history and the vitality of Pitcairn culture:

> *The uru grows high on a tree*
> *A fruit that cause the* Bounty *mutiny*
> *Without it our history is just ordinary*
> *Fire still burns strong after the* Bounty

Pitcairn Island also provides a broad history of the community while *Wishing* presents facets of island life and love of place, opening with:

> *The pandanas palm trees*
> *Down by the sea*
> *Orn Pitcairn Island*
> *Are calling me*
>
> *We swim in Bounty Bay*
> *Sometimes fish all day*
> *Make carving un a weavings*
> *Un talk all day*

Mussa es the same ('Most things/aspects are the same/similar') was a song inspired by Warren's sense of the continuing connection and affinity between Norfolk and Pitcairn communities. The song opens with a linguistic celebration of Tahitian origins, rolling the syllables off melodically:

> *From Papanoo Papaeete, Tahiti*
> *Maimiti, Toofati set sail*

before switching to the harder English language:

> *With Fletcher, Edward and William*
> *Across the sea they came*

After mentioning the (then) recent visit of Norfolk Islanders to Pitcairn the chorus asserts that as a result of Tahitian and mutineer interbreeding "a race was born back then" and the final verse declares:

> *We make the same style weckle*
> *Un talk fer sullun jest the same*
> *You had to know the breed we come from*
> *Yes ucklan I hope we nawa change*
>
> [We make the same type of food
> And talk to eachother using similar language
> You have to know (understand) our ancestry
> Yes I hope we all never change]

Complementing the Polynesian syncretic theme of its lyrics, the song's chordal accompaniment has a marked hula swing to it.

After we completed the April 1999 recording session and were packing up Warren discussed her imminent return to Pitcairn and mentioned that she would have loved to have heard her songs performed with a band (but was unlikely to ever do so while she remained on Pitcairn). Upon my return to Macquarie University I designed a Bachelor of Arts (Honours) project for two students, Josh Cameron and Kristine Pymont, which involved them adding instrumentation to the live recordings of Warren's eight original songs (recorded in mono) as a demo for what a more formal studio session might sound like, intended as an encouragement gift for Warren. This project was completed in late 1999, under my supervision and advice as to what instruments and textures might be appropriate. On the arranged tracks Cameron provided piano, ukulele and percussion parts and a guest vocalist, Sydney singer Melanie Horsnel, added high harmony vocals to *The cause*. Pymont recorded and mixed the additional recordings (an awkward activity given the mono nature of the original vocal and guitar recording). The reworked tracks were then sent to Warren with an explanatory note as to why and how the material had been produced. Warren's response exceeded my expectations in that she was pleased enough to want the material manufactured and (self-) released as her debut CD[17]. This appeared in 2000 under the title *Pitcairn Songs* and was sold by Warren to passing cruise ships and via the Internet, providing her with cultural prestige and a financial incentive to continue songwriting and performing.

Inspired by recording her first album, and the potential suggested by the added instrumental accompaniments, Warren wrote four more compositions in 2000, three of which were a conscious attempt to produce "songs about more modern times than *Bounty* times" (pc 2000). *Pitcairn's places* relates the origins of various Pitcairn place names and was written to complement the work of her mother in teaching classes about Pitcairn historical locations at the island school. After detailing particular incidents and locations, the final verse relates:

So young Matt Quintal claimed his set of rocks
Adams the other one too
Maimiti her pool
John catch his cow
Timiti, that crack is just for you
A credit to our kin as the names kept pouring in
Pitcairn's places seen by me and you

Come share with me is a cheerful, mid-tempo song about a visit to Oeno Island, 120 kilometres away, where Pitcairners regularly have annual holidays (usually staying for 10-14 days). The trip involves negotiating shifting sandbars and a jagged coral reef before setting ashore and enjoying its pleasures:

Her lagoon is filled with beautiful fish
The palms with coconuts
Land crabs crawl all over the place

220

Birds put on their strut
Sunsets glow muss every night
Stars are out so bright
Waves lap peacefully on the sand
I'm so glad you're here with me

Warren's third contemporary topic song, entitled *Will we survive?* outlines the difficulties facing the community with the departure of young people, and the potential opportunities offered by a new road, planned airstrip and the development of honey production. Its sense of reflection on the viability of Pitcairn's community, combined with a political comment on the island's status as a colony of the United Kingdom in the chorus:

We are the children of the mutineers
Living an existence in our own way
The British have claimed us as her colony

proved highly prescient in the light of the upheaval that afflicted the island in the early 2000s.

In 1999 a complaint was made to a visiting British policewoman about the alleged sexual abuse of young island girls by older men. This led to an investigation that culminated in charges being laid against seven Pitcairn men residing on the island (and six others now resident in Australia and New Zealand). The five year lead up to the trial of the Pitcairn seven traumatised and polarised the island community. The charges resulted from the extension of British laws (and specifically the legal age of sexual consent) to Pitcairn. Lawyers for the accused men contested the application of British law, claiming that the prosecution had not proved that British law – and, indeed, sovereignty – applied to Pitcairn, a community founded by mutineers who had rejected British law and Tahitian women who had never been subject to it. The matter was eventually heard by the New Zealand High Court in July 2004, which ruled in favour of the British Crown.

As the legal investigations against Pitcairn men progressed, the British government strengthened its administration of the island, sending in social workers and, in the period immediately prior to the trial, ordering the confiscation of islanders' guns[18]. Many on the island perceived an opportunistic agenda behind the British actions in that the imprisonment of the seven men would result in (the already overstretched) community of 47 becoming unsustainable, requiring evacuation of the island and the removal of the British government's responsibility to maintain and service it. (And, indeed, documents disclosed in April 2005 revealed that this was actively considered by the British Government in 2001[19].)

Despite the passage of the 'Pitcairn Trials Act' in 2002 (against the Pitcairners' wishes) – which allowed Pitcairn legal cases to be tried in New Zealand – the accused seven were successful in demanding that their trial should be held on Pitcairn itself. On the eve of the trials in October 2004 a group of Pitcairn women, including Meralda Warren, held a media conference on the island to reinforce the defence's claims that Pitcairn sexual customs and traditions were distinct from Britain, in that it was accepted by the community that there was no arbitrary age that determined when post-pubescent females could consent to have sexual activity. Despite this attempted intervention, the trial found six men guilty, creating deep divisions in the island community.

Warren's feelings about the court case and the motives behind the British Government's actions were expressed in a poem that she published on line on her web site (http://www.maimiti.pn/) in October 2004 and in the *Norfolk Islander* newspaper (6.10.04). Written, perhaps appropriately, in strong vernacular Pitcairn language, aimed at a Pitcairn and Norfolk speaking audience, the poem (which I have deliberately included here without a SE translation[20] and with Warren's original spelling) summarises the views of those Pitcairners opposed to the sexual abuse trials, crystallises perhaps the most polarised moment in Pitcairn history and suggests an uncertain future for the rocky isle:

> *Dem car import a British sullun fer teck us orf ours land*
> *Hem wawaha ones se secummed to Forbes un Fells great crooked hands*
> *Dem make es though dem flyen high but one day gwen land real hard*
> *Cos when hem Brits se pull outa ya, Parn my word ways dem a yah*
>
> *Charisma es one special thing, you gut et ulla nort*
> *Ours Pitcairn sullun gut et all except fer some who thought*
> *You car jes fine et any side un domine how much time dem try*
> *Go wipe un get outa ya, you es oony one pommie spy*
>
> *Short memories youley have of dem, who work dems sweat fer you*
> *Who built yous house dem very men, tubbet you know es true*
> *Fut yourley nor jes move orf ya, un let us sullun be*
> *Or please respect hem very ones who saved yous life you see.*
>
> *Yourley keep on reporten to the world fer clean up ours land*
> *But dem ones I keep on ya'ren et from es barely half a man*
> *Gut more to getten outa shep, with out hem generators orn*
> *Un when you come fer push a bush, Yous tractor nort se born*
>
> *Tourist es the bigger view fer halp ucklan orn ours way*
> *But who gwen come fer see one pom who car say "Wut a way"?*
> *Dem come fer see ucklan carve hem tree, un talk bout history*
> *Dem gwen a come cos dem very ones know ours men nor guilty*

Notes

1. Meralda Warren also recalls that her great uncle Elwyn Christian used to perform hymn tunes on a homemade violin in the 1960s until borers destroyed it. (interview May 1999).
2. Warren also recalls several other compositions being set to borrowed tunes on the island at this time, none of which subsequently entered the local repertoire.
3. "come" in some versions.
4. "land" in some versions.
5. "may" in some versions.
6. I have been unable to ascertain the title of the original song on which this composition was based.
7. Which uses a combined musical symbol and letter notation for rapid student familiarisation.

8. The instrument comprises a resonator, usually a tea chest or similar box, a neck, often a broom handle, and a single string. (The Pitcairn version used a fishing line for the latter function.)
9. Which, Trent Christian recalls, are often played on guitars with open tunings (which Pitcairn Islanders are unfamiliar with).
10. I have been unable to discover his name.
11. When VOP was sited at its previous location in Glendale.
12. During Meralda Warren's visit to Norfolk Island in 1999 he also duetted with Warren on her (just-written) song *The cause*, and *We from Pitcairn Island* at a Bounty Day Celebration concert at the SDA Hall (which also included performances from Don Christian-Reynolds, George 'Toofie' Christian and Susan Pedel).
13. Whose involvement with island Maori music is discussed in Chapter 7.
14. One result of this was that she wrote and published a collection of Pitcairn recipes in 1986, entitled *Taste of Pitcairn*, which has, to date, sold over 2000 copies worldwide.
15. Which she had begun work on in 1984, after her return from Hawai'i.
16. Since Warren recorded her songs prior to Christian writing and recording many of the compositions featured on *Pilli Lornga N.I.* (2001).
17. At this time the DCMS had not initiated its Coral Music label and was unable to assist with manufacturing costs.
18. A number of islanders also alleged British interference with mail and e-mail during this period.
19. See, Harvey (2005: 3) for details of (then) British secretary of state for international development Clare Short's 2001 recommendations in this regard,
20. Readers who have followed the discussions of Norfolk and Pitcairn song lyrics in Chapters 11 and 12 should be to translate the majority of the verses without particular difficulty. One word of particular relevance featured here is "pommie", derived from Australian vernacular, to refer to English/British people and institutions.

Conclusion

UNFOLDING HERITAGE

In the Introduction to this volume I emphasised that the notion of heritage I would be deploying was a fluid, adaptive one that "can develop new objects and put forward new meanings as it reflects living culture", as opposed to one that simply represents "an ossified image of the past" (UNESCO, 2002). In many ways the tension between these two notions (and operations) of heritage typifies much of modern Norfolk and Pitcairn culture. Fundamental to any notion of Pitcairn identity, and to the identity of Norfolk's Pitcairn-descended population, is the historical event of the *Bounty* mutiny and the settlement of Pitcairn by mutineers and Tahitians. While this is a fixed reference point, its interpretation has varied and, as I asserted in Chapter 7, experienced a notable revival in the 1930s-1950s. As a result, the prominence of *Bounty* mythology in present-day public culture on Norfolk Island does not so much evidence an "ossified image of the past" as a refigured one that complements a set of socio-political arguments and feelings that crystallised in the 1980s. It is also possible to discern a similar (although arguably less marked) reassertion of *Bounty* heritage in the work of Pitcairn songwriter Meralda Warren (and her attempts to preserve local lore for successive generations).

Participation in a series of Festivals of Pacific Arts over the last two decades has allowed Norfolk Islanders (and, to a lesser extent, Pitcairners) to present aspects of their culture to a broad Pacific audience. In this context, the material performed and displayed both represents the heritage of its communities and is further 'heritagised' through its inclusion in such prestigious contexts. As with many other forms presented at the Festivals, Norfolk and Pitcairn song, dance and craft are hybridised, syncretic practices derived from (various combinations of) pre-contact indigenous Pacific cultures and post-contact western elements. As in Oceanic cultures in general, this broad characterisation encompasses a spectrum of activities from those that appear close to pre-contact practices and those more obviously contemporary in form, style and/or medium. As befits populations with mixed race origins that have developed at geographical removes from (either of) their cultures of origin, forms of Pitcairn and Norfolk culture tend to occupy the mid to latter band of this spectrum.

In terms of performance culture, the modified Polynesian-style of dancing that has become prominent on Norfolk Island since the mid-1900s is the form that derives most clearly from Pacific traditions. This said, these dance styles are – themselves – modern adaptations of pre-contact cultural traditions; and subsequent western media representations of these have played a significant role in their popularisation with Norfolk Islanders. Heritage here is interdependent with international cultural exchange and mediation.

In terms of music, Pitcairn and Norfolk cultures encompass a range of western traditions (such as Christian hymnody, art music and popular song of various kinds). Aside from historically isolated phenomena (such as the presence of Maori performance troupes in the 1980s and occasional visiting performers), there is no tradition of Polynesian music performance on Norfolk Island and little on Pitcairn (at least, after its re-settlement in 1858). As a result, the melodies, chord progressions and musical structure of the body of Norfolk Island songwriting that emerged from the 1980s on, and Meralda Warren's work on Pitcairn Island, derive from western styles (most notably, country but also 1960s/1970s folk-pop). While there are aspects of rhythmic feel, vocal harmony (and instrumentation) in some of this work that shows Pacific influences, these are, in most – if not all – cases, derived from earlier *hapa haole* Hawaiian and/or 20th Century pan-Pacific styles of popular music.

Lyrically, many Pitcairn and Norfolk Island songs explore local topics and themes. The underlying model for this aspect of the songs largely derives from US country and Euro-American folk music traditions. This is just as much the case with Norfolk and Pitcairn Island language songs as it is with Standard English ones, indicating the manner in which there is a bicultural continuum between them, rather than a separation of topic and approach into linguistically distinct and demarcated genres. One of the only percep-tible differences between Norfolk/Pitcairn language compositions and local Standard English ones is that the former tend to express aspects of the multiple components of local heritage (cultural, agricultural, environmental etc.) in more concentrated forms. Here, specific Norfolk and Pitcairn terms both refer to other aspects of heritage and express and encapsulate them *through* specific words – terms such as *hilli*, *stithy*, *pilli* and *tintoela* representing highly distinctive local qualities and perceptions (rather than being simple translations of SE words). Similarly, the litany of place, flora and fauna names in songs such as Meralda Warren's *Pitcairn's places* and George 'Toofie' Christian's *Sweet taytes* are distillations of heritage within language itself.

In the Introduction to this volume I quoted Doreen Massey, appropri-ating her characterisation of the 'place specificity' of a metropolitan road to apply to isolated island locations, concurring with her that:

> *What gives a place its specificity is not some long internalized history but the fact that it is constructed out of a particular constellation of relations, articulated together at a particular locus ... The uniqueness of a place or a locality ... is constructed out of particular interactions and mutual articulations of social relations, social processes, experi-ences and understandings.* (1993: 68)

In terms of the cultural heritages of Norfolk and Pitcairn islands, the "particular constellation" has involved the twinning of two dots in the firmament of the Pacific in an interactive "constellation" that also links back to Tahiti and Britain, to Australia and New Zealand and out to the USA (through both the history of whaling and modern global media forms). It is this relationship that binds the chapters of this volume together and informs the variously shared, parallel, divergent and intersecting aspects of Pitcairn and Norfolk Island history.

Futures/Heritage Strategies

During my interaction with Norfolk and Pitcairn islanders in 1999-2005 discussion often turned to issues concerning the survival and potential longevity of local culture and language. As a cultural researcher, my views on such matters were often sought and (apparently) taken seriously. My responses can be summarised as follows:

1. The preservation and maintenance of traditional forms, genres and artifacts is a valid and important heritage activity;

2. Local cultural plurality and hybridity are important and are not necessarily antithetical to, nor undermining of, local tradition;

3. The development of new forms and styles of expression are important means of attempting to ensure cultural longevity and relevance.

Point 1 was generally agreed upon. Along with respect for local culture and the education of the young, local traditions were seen as useful tourist attractions. However, points 2 and 3 proved far more contentious and provoked a wide range of responses.

With regard to Point 2, from the mid-1800s on Australian and New Zealand migrants to Norfolk Island have both intertwined with its Pitcairn descended population and, in various ways, maintained and developed aspects of their own identities. The nature of their identity politics and the complexities of interaction (and, particularly, inter-marriage) between residents of Australian, New Zealand (and other) ancestry and Pitcairn descendants merits a dedicated study in its own right. The under-representation and under-theorisation of the histories of non-Pitcairn descendant Norfolk Islanders in this volume reflects the manner in which their experiences and perceptions have not been so obviously expressed through music or dance. Indeed, it is significant that the only aspect of the latter that was identified to me as culturally distinct might, equally as well, be regarded as a sectarian aspect. Here I am referring to the continuance of an Anglican tradition of hymn singing (discussed in Chapter 9) that *some* locals have perceived as distinct from traditional Norfolk-Pitcairn hymnody and have – thereby – regarded as essentially Anglo-Australian in nature[1]. Outside of islanders and visitors of Australian and New Zealand ancestry participating in the mainstream western music and dance culture of the island (discussed in Chapters 6 and 10) there appear to have been no other enduring traditions of distinctly Australian or New Zealand culture on Norfolk Island[2], and no body of songwriting that expresses the perceptions and worldviews of non-Pitcairn descendants. The principal exception to this is the work of Alison Ryves. While her previous residence in North America gives her a distinctly different background to that of the Australian and New Zealand families and individuals who have settled on Norfolk since the 1850s, her songs (as discussed in Chapter 10) include several reflections on issues of local cultural positioning. Through her participation in the Festivals of Pacific Arts[3] and the inclusion of her songs in the Norfolk troupe's repertoire, she – along with other residents of non-Pitcairn descent – has been a pioneer in the presentation of Norfolk culture as a (simultaneously) distinct *and* inclusive form. In contrast to the vocal local lobbying group the Society of Pitcairn Descendants[4], (which only admits islanders of Pitcairn descent to its membership), the performing troupes at the Festivals of Pacific Arts have not been restricted by ancestry and have thereby been representative of a broader contemporary Norfolk community.

The inclusiveness of the Norfolk troupe can be regarded as a positive aspect of a living, thriving culture. Similarly, the inclusion of Ryves's SE songs along with SE and Norfolk language material by songwriters of Pitcairn ancestry might also be viewed as a positive reflection of the culturally plural and (partially) bilingual nature of contemporary Norfolk. In this regard, the bilinguality of Norfolk songwriters such as Don Christian-Reynolds, Susan Pedal and George 'Toofie' Christian represents Norfolk as both a place of particular community and origins and a location that has had a strong and continuing cultural and political implication with Australia and New Zealand.

It should be emphasised at this point that there is no *requirement* for heritage to be representative of all the members of the localities that sustain it. As discussed in the Introduction, culture is fluid and notions of heritage are contentious and often disputed. In this sense, some of those seeking to defend a specific Pitcairn descendant identity might well regard the inclusivity of the Norfolk troupe and its song repertoire as problematic (and, indeed, such a view was expressed to me by several islanders). Equally, as another other local cultural activist expressed to me, referring to the number of individuals on Norfolk not of Pitcairn descent, "you can't pretend it hasn't happened, things aren't like what they were before, you have to make the best of it ... for everybody ... we all live together here" (pc 2002).

The issue here concerns local engagements with history and identity. Historically we can view the establishment of the first Pitcairn community as an 'accidental' result of the initial phase of European proto-colonial incursion in the Pacific; the move to Norfolk in 1856 as an internal relocation within an imperial zone; and the settlement of Australians and New Zealanders on Norfolk as a process of transmigration in the British Empire's south western Pacific fringe. Within this, the Pitcairners are part of an imperial cast involved in a global narrative and their co-existence on Norfolk Island (first with the Melanesian Mission and more latterly with a substantial population of Australian and New Zealand origin) is just a fact (and facet) of a larger transnational history. In this 'big picture' Pitcairn and Pitcairn-descendent Norfolk cultural identity and language are an incidental outcome of particular processes of infra-imperial settlement and relocation. Culture, like any other element in an historical narrative, 'moves on', changes and adapts to circumstance.

In opposition to such a scenario, Pitcairn and Pitcairn-descendant Norfolk activists have, particularly in recent years, proffered an alternative history that regards the original Pitcairn community as having been (somewhat indistinctly) outside the British Empire, of the relocation to Norfolk having been to a place granted exclusively to the Pitcairners, of Australia having no legitimate claim to Norfolk; and, most recently, of British law not applying to Pitcairn. From this viewpoint, Pitcairn cultural identity and language can be seen as having been subject to imperial oppression and dilution through uninvited and unwelcome settlement that continues to require active resistance and counter-measures.

The polarity of the two positions creates the tension and stage upon which (particularly) Norfolk and (also) Pitcairn culture is enacted. While Pitcairn culture largely remained an internal oral/folkloric form in the late 19th and early 20th Centuries (under the loose ambit of the British Empire and the hegemony of Seventh Day Adventism) Meralda Warren's songwriting, and especially her verse responses to the 2004 crisis in Pitcairn (posted on the Internet), represent a new cultural phase. Warren's work communicates internally, drawing on cultural heritage, *and* signals itself to outsiders as an expression of cultural distinction. In this, Pitcairn culture, especially as mobilised at a time of stress and turmoil, shows itself as active and strong.

Warren's work is a practical illustration of my third argument about cultural survival and longevity, namely that "the development of new forms, styles and manners of cultural expression are important means of attempting to ensure cultural longevity and relevance". My belief in this area of unfolding heritage had broader ramifications for my research on Norfolk and with Pitcairn Islanders, and its extension into cultural production. These are more fully discussed in the following Afterword, which represents a more personal perspective on matters of Norfolk and Pitcairn cultural heritage and development than the chapters that constitute the bulk of this volume.

Notes

1. I should also emphasise that this view was refuted and, indeed deemed offensive, by several Anglican Norfolk Islanders I discussed it with.
2. There were however the short-lived phenomena of the local Maori performance troupe (discussed in Chapter 7) and the Australian bush band The Norfolk Whalers (discussed in Chapter 10) both of which operated in the 1980s, in a period when TEP (Temporary Entry Permit) workers were prominent on the island.
3. As both a singer and an exhibiting potter.
4. See discussion in Chapter 11.

Afterword

ENGAGING IN FLUX:
The politics and practice of collaboration

T his chapter provides a discussion of two linked aspects that have run through the book. The first concerns a number of ways in which heritage can be understood as a continuing process of cultural identification and modification. The second reflects upon my role as a player in that process through my work with musicians and my subsequent analyses of their views and material. While these concerns obviously go beyond the thematic and chronological studies offered elsewhere in this volume, I hope to establish that the processes that I examine are useful to understanding the development of heritage as a central form of cultural identity. Neither heritage nor cultural identity are solid 'totems' or 'anchors' for a community – immutable points of reference amidst the storms of modernity and social change. They are projections constructed from combinations of empirically verifiable history, the 'imagined' history of folklore, vaguer assumption and supposition, wishful or fearful thinking, conjecture, fabrication, invention and various curdlings or blossomings of the above.

In the sections that follow I draw on my experiences of communicating with Norfolk and Pitcairn islanders. For reasons that will become apparent, I do not identify each of my informants and discussants by name; the phrases and opinions that are quoted are, nevertheless, those of specific individuals.

I. Engagement
During my first few weeks on Norfolk Island in Autumn 1999 I was repeatedly asked the same question – "Are you related to the Thomas Hayward who sailed on the *Bounty*?" This question initially took me by surprise but I soon came to realise that Norfolk and Pitcairn are the centre of a global network of individuals fixated with the events of the *Bounty* mutiny and the subsequent histories of the Pitcairn and Norfolk communities. Over the years, several descendants of the *Bounty* crew have travelled

to Norfolk Island and, by dint of shared family histories, hold some interest for locals. From Day 1 on Norfolk I smiled good-humouredly, stated that the surname was coincidental, emphasised my status as an academic and tried to identify why my research and presence on the island was substantially different to that of the *Bounty* aficionados who regularly visit.

This position was more than a little undermined about three weeks into my stay as a result of a phone conversation with my mother in England. Informing her about local queries about whether I was related to the *Bounty's* Thomas Hayward (and my polite dismissal of these) I was considerably disconcerted when she told me that the Hayward side of my family originated from a similar area of South East England to that of Thomas Hayward (and, therefore, that *some* form of family kinship was a distinct possibility). As any reader familiar with the *Bounty* story will be aware, such a connection is far from an advantage in a location such as Norfolk Island, where Thomas Hayward is regarded as second only to Bligh as a villain in the *Bounty* history, on account of his not joining the mutineers and later returning to the South Seas on the HMS *Pandora* to help track them down. Due to my desire that such an association should not become my dominant 'identity marker' (especially in advance of any degree of close family connection being substantiated), I have largely kept this historical spectre a private one. The shadowy figure of Thomas Hayward has nevertheless lingered at the fringes of my consciousness and I should acknowledge that a slight unease about the connection to my namesake strengthened my resolve to provide an accurate and informative account of Norfolk and Pitcairn Island cultural history for members of the two communities.

This tangential personal link to the *Bounty* mutiny and the personality clashes that led to the founding of the Pitcairn (and, subsequently, Norfolk) Island community was compounded in early 2001. Whilst preparing a paper on my Norfolk research for an international colloquium at Macquarie University, I was interrupted by a knock at the door. A delivery driver presented me with a large wooden box mailed from Pitcairn Island. Opening it I found a detailed, hand-carved model of the *Bounty*, complete with rigging and sails. An accompanying note from Pitcairn Island singer-songwriter Meralda Warren informed me that she had made it as a 'thank you' for my having produced her *Pitcairn Songs* CD. Both the nature of the gift and its representation of the physicality of the *Bounty*, at a moment when I had been engaged in intense consideration of the mutineers' legacy, dizzied and unnerved me. I stopped writing and spent some time gazing at the model, almost hearing the creak of timbers and feeling the spray of the water as the model gave me a mental image of the genesis of the societies I discuss in this volume.

Breaking from the norms of presenting research to academics in a studiedly objective form, I decided to discuss my response to Meralda's gift of the *Bounty* model and my mild sense of implication and (however irrationally) guilt-by-association with Thomas Hayward as part of my paper. This aspect of my presentation produced a strong sense of discomfort, and even embarrassment, amongst several of my colleagues from Australia and the USA. After the session in which I gave my paper I received a number of variously caustic, sarcastic and dismissive remarks about the 'indulgence' and inappropriateness of my confession of such subjective and/or irrational feelings in an academic forum. More than a little bruised by these, I retreated to the cafeteria to refresh myself. I was joined there by veteran Australian Aboriginal singer and gumleaf player, Herb Patten and an Aboriginal PhD student, Peter Mckenzie. As individuals with heightened awarenesses of the complexities of personal identification, responsibility and reconciliation in post-colonial, early 21st Century Australia, their responses were very different, and far more considerate and reflective, than those of other colleagues. Patten told me that people from his community in Victoria were familiar with the troubling traces of figures from the past and informed me about a traditional remedy. When someone from Patten's community wished to quiet a preoccupation with an ancestral figure they would hold a smoking ceremony, using specific leaves. He suggested that I should try something similar to quiet my ghosts.

My responses to this remark were complex. One image that came instantly to mind was that of the *Bounty* in flames – its smoke the result of its burning at anchor off Pitcairn in 1790 in a process that obliterated the material evidence of the mutiny and hid the whereabouts of the mutineers from pursuers. Yet this was a smoking that had only briefly quieted the mutiny's 'ghosts', the Pitcairn community *had* been discovered and the mutiny continues as a powerful foundation myth in Pitcairn and Norfolk culture. Engaging with Herb's suggestion, I commented that smoking rituals were foreign to my Anglo-Australian culture and I conjectured whether giving conference papers and inscribing the leaves of books with facts and analyses were my western equivalent of such a ritual. On reflection – and in my specific case, at least – aspects of the parallel ring true. Postcolonial guilt-by-association with the Australian authorities' various repressions and underminings of Norfolk-Pitcairn culture has been a motivating factor in my work. The desire to achieve reconciliation, has, in turn, influenced the research methodology of this book and my wider engagement with the Norfolk and Pitcairn communities.

As a result of my collaboration with Norfolk and Pitcairn musicians and cultural activists in 1999-2005, the awkward figure of Thomas Hayward has dimmed in significance as other identifications have intensified. As I complete this manuscript, with Meralda's *Bounty* model positioned on a shelf to the side of my desk, my 'spirit' – my 'affective alliance', in more academic terms – is with those whose bloodlines continue on in the Pacific communities I have had the privilege of working with. While subjective, 'fanciful' engagements with research topics and communities remain so problematic to academics as to necessitate their quarantining in an Afterword such as this, the writing of this book has been substantially informed by the issues I raise here and any account that did not acknowledge them would not be as true to my Norfolk and Pitcairn friends, colleagues and acquaintances as I wish to be.

II. Culturally Engaged Research and Facilitation
In between 1999 and 2004 I worked with my Macquarie University col-

league Denis Crowdy and various postgraduate students to develop an approach we came to term Culturally Engaged Research and Facilitation (CERF)[1]. We deployed this in our interaction with the Norfolk Island community (and in similar engagements with communities on Lord Howe Island, in the Whitsunday islands and on East New Britain and Mioko) during the years in question. Like the UNESCO YCH documents discussed in the Introduction to this volume, there was nothing particularly novel about individual elements of our approach. What to us was distinctive was the identification of CERF as a specific agenda and our advocacy of it.

From its outset, CERF was consciously conceived as an activist project. It is one of the paradoxes of much anthropological and ethnomusicological work that it tries to explore and document the inner-workings of societies and cultures in an essentially passive manner. 'Deep contact' is seen as exemplary whereas active involvement and development are always wrapped as problematic. Even with the tendency in ethnomusicology to learn music through traditional methods of training and/or participation in community music making, the emphasis has been on learning a set of established musical (and knowledge) 'grooves'.

One of the more welcome developments in anthropology, ethnomusicology (and linguistics) over the last two decades has been the combination of traditional forms of scholarly research with subsequent community-orientated and/or community-beneficial outcomes. The practical-political result of such research is made manifest as a complement to its gathering and analysis.

CERF locates itself within an essentially similar frame of reference but borrows its political inflection from a different context. One foundational point is the application of a Green politics to culture. CERF is premised on the assertion that just as it is important to maintain biodiversity in (and *through*) diverse local habitats, so it is important to maintain cultural diversity and distinct local heritages. This is not simply a restatement of 1970s' pre-occupations with media-imperialism nor more recent concerns with the impact of globalism (although it is congruent with these); it is also a more local-regional reading that recognises micro-differences as important.

Having established a Green paradigm as a basic referent, it should be made clear that CERF acknowledges that forms of culture are far more fluid and volatile than biological species and that heritage is far less fixed and able to be 'restored' than local biological habitats. Here CERF takes a cue from the founding principles of the quadrennial Festivals of Pacific Arts (discussed in various chapters of this volume). The inaugural FPA was held in Suva in 1972 with the express aim of *preserving* traditional forms of culture; *protecting* traditional culture against swamping by outside cultures; and of *developing* local culture. In ecological terms, the first two aims are also those of environmentalists, the latter – and its conjunction with the former – are a point of difference. The FPAs were established to preserve and promote traditional cultures simultaneously with their development. The emphasis here is not so much on a purist 'freezing' and protection of traditional cultures as a maintenance of the old along with the new.

232

With particular regard to Pacific cultures, I have regularly recalled the principles and components of the FPA agenda while familiarising myself with other recent research in Pacific communities. Each time I read some scholar's (learned and conscientious) account of some (supposedly) doomed and disappearing practice, I have recoiled at the passivity involved. Time and again I have also recalled a different text that has become something of a shadow referent for many of the strategies I have pursued. The text is a novel by British writer Clive Barker, best known for his metaphysical horror stories and films. Entitled *Sacrament* (1996), the book follows the parallel and intersecting paths of two linked characters, a supernatural being in human form named Jacob Steep and a photographer named Will Rabjohns. Each is preoccupied with the extinction of species of animals. Steep roams the Earth with his consort, Rosa McGee, finding and killing the last surviving members of a species, while Rabjohns records the last moments of endangered animals and their environments. The similarities between the academic documenting final cultural moments in parallel with global and local enterprises' destruction of unique local habitats is a troubling one. In my case, it proved so troubling as to galvanise my resolve to pursue a different path.

CERF retains a major element of traditional academic inquiry in that scholarly documentation, analysis and historical research is regarded as a primary and essential part of its project. In common with more progressive developments of other disciplines it also advocates a shift to thinking of members of local cultures as *collaborators* rather than research *subjects*. As other researchers have found, this approach has major benefits all round. Collaborative research is a reciprocal, engaged and interactive form that can prove far more productive than passive observation. Yet it also raises an immediate issue. It is clearly not enough for the researcher to ask someone to collaborate with them in undertaking *their* research. The collaborative aspect requires consideration of what the collaborator wants.

My research on Norfolk and Pitcairn culture in this book has been enabled by (and is reflective of) the needs, desires (and sometimes unintended stimuli) provided by collaborators. The needs and desires of collaborators are not simply those that exist fully formed and ready to be asked of the CERF worker, they are also ones that can be stimulated and formed through discussion of what the CERF worker can realistically offer. In the case of my research on Norfolk and Pitcairn, this book project formed a component of a series of collaborative activities. With the research of this volume as *one* of my identified areas of interest, I undertook and/or facilitated the following reciprocal activities with colleagues in the DCMS[2]:

1. Transfers of old vinyl records, reel to reel and cassette tapes to CD for individuals.

2. Location recordings (using a digital minidisk recorder) that were subsequently transferred and mastered to CD format for musicians, either for individual reference or (in the case of recordings of Eric Craig and Don Christian-Reynolds) as the content of a self-released CD (entitled *Unplugged*).

3. Location recordings, using a digital minidisk recorder, that were subsequently modified, enhanced and mastered to CD and duplicated, either as a small private run (Kath King's *Teach me how fer lew* EP) or for manufacture and retail as a self-released CD (Meralda Warren's *Pitcairn Songs*).

4. The studio recording, mastering and packaging of an album of material for commercial release (George 'Toofie' Christian's *Pilli Lornga N.I.* CD).

5. The recording of a CD album on location on Norfolk Island for commercial release using portable studio equipment (George 'Toofie' Christian's forthcoming *White Rose* CD).

6. Funding, design input and facilities assistance for Norfolk Island song contests (in 2001 and 2002).

7. Funding and institutional assistance for performers to visit island events (Denis Crowdy, Erik Damberg and Ruth Wilson to the 2002 Norfolk Island Multicultural Festival).

8. Assistance in arranging performances of artists at international events (George 'Toofie' Christian's appearance at the Australian National Folk Festival in Canberra in 2003 and at the Canadian-Australian music conference in St Johns, Newfoundland in June 2005).

9. Promotion of Norfolk Island and Pitcairn artists through media interviews, mail-outs (etc.).

10. Provision of professional advice about music, education and funding opportunities; writing letters-of-support (etc.).[3]

While we are not claiming any originality in contributing the above (as researchers from various fields have provided similar 'extended services' to other communities) it is pertinent to note that the activities go beyond those usually expected of a researcher and are more akin to those expected of and provided by a community arts worker. The professional function of the latter is to enable communities to collaborate in artistic enterprises that stimulate bonds and interactions and produce work that is expressive of those communities. While discussion of the history of community arts activity is beyond the scope of this Afterword[4], it is most salient to note that the principal critiques of this activity have been in terms of the (implicit) assumption that communities *require* intervention; the nature of the interventions supplied; and the relation of their organisation and outcomes to pre-existing community networks and expressive traditions. The similarity of aspects of CERF work to community arts facilitation necessitates consideration of these critiques.

Western community arts work largely originated in the 1960s and was derived from models of local experience in communities that were perceived to have suffered from socio-economic disadvantage and various kinds of social disruption, decay and/or demoralisation. Community arts work was seen (by its advocates and practitioners, at least) as a corrective and empowering project that allowed communities to create focal activities and channels of expression. Its agendas and, often, chosen activities and media were however largely imported into the communities that workers dealt with. As such, it was open to criticism that it did not so much encourage and facilitate distinct, autonomous cultural expression as replicate a series of cultural practices (community murals; inner-city garden projects; video polemics etc.) in different localities.

One fundamental difference between established western community arts practice and CERF work is that CERF is fundamentally committed to (the FPA model of) preserving, protecting and developing *distinct* local practices. This necessitates a more responsive, reactive perception of local cultural character and its potential. It is important to acknowledge that any individual or enterprise comes laden with ideology – in the form of values, preferred models and perceptions that have been inculcated through institutional training and broader cultural osmosis. Far from claiming or attempting to transcend an ideological position (and thereby bias) CERF operates within the specific ideological position asserted earlier in this Afterword. This said, it attempts to minimise its presumption of required intervention and privileged practices in favour of flexible, locally-appropriate activities. The question remains however, as to what (if any) extent is it legitimate to 'interfere' in local culture – that is, to encourage and/or facilitate developments that may not have occurred without external intervention?

With regard to the Norfolk and Pitcairn cultures discussed in this volume, my colleagues and I have clearly intervened through our support and facilitation of local songwriters' recordings. Even if it were simply the 'benign' intervention of helping record, release and promote songs that already existed, it might be considered interference. The fact that we have (deliberately) sought to stimulate the production of new songs and, in Kath King's case, the emergence of a new songwriter, represents more than facilitation. In the case of George 'Toofie' Christian's work, as discussed in Chapter 11, the recordings and discussion of material and its packaging constitute a collaboration between local and overseas performers. In this regard, the purist might want to identify our actions as a *pollution* of pre-existent Norfolk music culture. But while it is possible to make such a case, the purist would also have to consider the string of cultural outsiders who have exercised a powerful influence on the music and general culture of Norfolk and Pitcairn since their communities' foundations. Settlers, whalers, whalers' wives, missionaries, educators, visiting artists and others – not to mention various external media forms – have all played an important role in developing local music and dance culture. In this regard, as my colleague Steven Feld suggested to me[5], individuals such as CERF workers are just the latest in a long line of foreigners who have connected with local communities in order to follow and deploy their own agendas. From this perspective, communities such as Norfolk and Pitcairn are not so much isolated, pristine environments as localities within a global matrix that experience and accommodate aspects of cultural change as part of their dynamic.

Aside from Christianity and the imposition of colonial power, late 20th and early 21st Century globalism (and its regional fractals) have provided the most significant impact on local Pacific cultures experienced over the last three hundred years. It can be seen to have unrolled in a dual form, as both specific media imperialism (through conscious attempts to destabilise and penetrate local markets) and through the indiscriminate 'collateral' impact of internationalisation in general (GATT, the general agreement on trades and tariffs being a prime example). The volume of external input increasingly challenges the limits and elasticity of local cultural identity. Compared to these massive forces, CERF workers are minor players. Their influence is dependent on various factors, chief amongst which is the degree to which they establish trust with communities and find collaborators. Assessment of the CERF worker's success and/or the appropriateness of their actions and outcomes is – of course – highly complex. Whereas there is no requirement for globalism to be *anything but* indiscriminate in its impact, the CERF worker is accountable on several levels. Most importantly, they are responsible and answerable to the community. This characterisation only gets us so far though, since communities are inevitably diverse, with various factions, and various concepts of cultural purity and integrity (and micro-personal perceptions of these).

Ultimately then, CERF is far more risky and problematic than conventional research, whose professed distance and non-disruption of its object of study gives it a distinct (if often dubious) rhetorical armour. There are no hard and fast guidelines for CERF but rather, a broad set of protocols that serve to orientate its workers and their projects. As identified and formulated in the projects described above, these comprise:

(a) *Methodological, contextual and precedential study* – This is the familiar territory of academic training, the literature study and consideration of methodologies. By the study of precedents, I refer to research into similar cultures and cultural situations and into research conducted in them.

(b) *Possession of relevant skills/ access to relevant resources and expertise* – Intellectual training is not on its own sufficient to ensure the effectiveness of CERF activities, other skills and access to equipment and facilities are also essential. The nature of these varies with specific fields of activity (some of the relevant ones for music-related research being sketched above).

(c) *Project design* – As discussed above (with regard to my particular work with Norfolk and Pitcairn Island communities), this involves being able to formulate and modify project design with regard to the perceptions and suggestions of the communities involved (rather than the simple retention of a provisional design or the imposition of one that doesn't complement local perceptions). It also depends on:

(d) *The ability to acquit project design and/or to sustain continuing project development* – These require the CERF worker to ensure (to the best of their abilities and facilitation) that they can acquit the project they design and agree to undertake. If they cannot, they should either only agree to undertake a suitable part of this or else obtain assistance with the broader project.

(e) *Returning produced materials/ensuring circulation of materials* – It is increasingly recognised that any materials produced by a researcher should be returned (in appropriate forms) to the individuals and communities involved. There are various levels to this. At its most basic, this involves the provision of scholarly publications to individuals and community resource centres (such as libraries) but more importantly, it involves the provision of what might be considered 'byproduct' by the researcher – word processed copies of various accounts or transcribed cultural texts, audio or audio-visual recordings etc. to various members of communities.

(f) *Producing locally accessible and useful materials* – In addition to written and/or audio-visual material aimed at a scholarly audience, the CERF worker should also aim to present their research to communities in various appropriate formats, through talks, accessibly written papers, locally-orientated publications etc. presented in appropriate style(s) (and/or language[s]).

(g) *Assistance with the publication/presentation of cultural work by local producers* – In parallel with f), the CERF worker should assist the public presentation and circulation of cultural work in a manner that is advantageous for the cultural producers concerned.

(h) *Access to funding/funding knowledge networks capable of acquitting the above* – Aspects d-g (above) all require funding and resource assistance and it is a prerequisite of any CERF activity that the worker should have access to either (and ideally both) designated funding or schemes for provision of funding for CERF activities. Such provision should be a pre-requisite for any CERF project (not something that a CERF worker should be expected to conjure as a test of ingenuity and/or undertake as part of a research rite-of-passage).

(i) *Commitment and ability to impart skills and facilitate autonomous production and development* – The essential corollary of the CERF worker's involvement as an external agent is that they communicate and convey as many of their skills and knowledges to the local community as possible to ensure that local, self-initiated projects can develop along with those the CERF worker has been involved in.

CERF work is essentially interventionary in that it involves itself in stimulating and facilitating cultural activity (within the ambit of local heritage). A further level of intervention is contributed when the CERF worker is an outsider to the community concerned (a common though by no means necessary or universal situation[6]). Whatever the status of the individual worker, one of CERF's aims is to empower the community to develop autonomously (rather than slip into a relation of dependence on the worker). At the same time, it must be acknowledge that CERF is not simply a package that can be delivered, it is one that requires servicing (in both senses of the word); periodic upgrades (of technology, knowledge and training); and also benefits from being linked into and informed by the experiences of communities and initiatives in other regions.

In these regards, (geographically isolated) small island cultures are no differently placed than any geographically located community on a 'mainland' (or elsewhere). Specialised centres and facilities cannot be replicated in each and every community. The ideal is a mixture of as many locally accessible and autonomously used facilities as possible with as much access to external facilities and equipment as is necessary (the balance changing at different times and in different circumstances). This recognises that not only does technology change at a rate that small communities (let alone arts and academic institutions) find hard to keep up with but that information agendas, processes and bureaucracies are also constantly modifying. Technologies also 'leap', new hardware and software offering new potentials while previous technologies are still being sought and applied. Rather than dependency, we need to imagine a global grid of resources and communications that communities can access, share and dialogue within.

For many more politically progressive researchers, much of the above will be an increasingly assumed 'common sense' ethical framework for practical research. It has been one of the more reassuring aspects of late 20th and early 21st Century academia that there is a declining cohort of vampiric researchers (in the field of culture, at least). Few researchers would be prepared to admit to simply latching on to informants and communities in order to extract knowledge 'blood' and then flying on to use its nutrition to further academic careers; far fewer still would seek to publicly defend such a position (even within terms of an inflated academic rhetoric of the virtues of knowledge gathering and theorisation as worthwhile things-in-themselves).

What is still prevalent however, is an assumption that the CERF components identified above should eventuate as a 'gift' – a form of beneficence – from the committed researcher working with a deserving (ie 'compliant' and [ideally] grateful) community. The model here is of the religious missionary or altruist doing 'good works'. As should be immediately apparent, such a model is so untenable as to be offensive. Conventional researchers and CERF workers alike are involved in remunerated and/or or grant assisted professional activities that require the input and assistance of the communities they target. If beneficence still has any currency as something that communities and external groups acknowledge, it simply shows that traditional researchers and the research enterprise have tapped into a persuasive paradigm that continues to cover itself with rhetorical smoke and mirrors. Perhaps, in this regard, a further category needs to be added to the above list:

(j) *The ability to communicate the nature of CERF activity in such a manner as to demystify and enable it.*

In terms of *all* of the above, my colleagues and I would argue that it is a fundamental ethical responsibility of universities and research and arts funding organisations to affirm and support CERF's model of engaging with cultural communities. As should be apparent, this is a radical, idealistic call in the current intellectual, educational and cultural climate of the West. In the early 21st Century 'economically rationalist' notions developed in the 1980s have come to dominate research policy and funding to the extent that any alternative approaches are openly denigrated and disadvantaged by national, regional and institutional bureaucracies – choked as 'deviant', dismissed as 'naïve' and disparaged at every turn. With a few exceptions, CERF activities continue to be largely dependent on its workers' successful exploitation of niches within institutional and research bureaucracies and an extension of their work into collaborative projects at one remove from their principal professional activities. Commendable as this might be, it must also be fundamental to CERF's broader project for it to seek and obtain a firmer and more facilitated institutional base.

III. Networking
As discussed, my colleagues and I developed the notion of CERF in 1999–2005 through reflection on activities conducted with members of the Norfolk and Pitcairn Island communities and similar projects on other islands. We were also informed by dialogue with colleagues engaged in parallel work and reflections, such as Steven Feld and Jonas Baes (who both contributed to the 'Trajectories' research colloquium we hosted at Macquarie in 2001). Feld's perceptions and experiences are referred to elsewhere in this volume but we should also acknowledge the importance of Baes's reflections on the nature of ethnomusicological fieldwork in the Philippines (2002) as an influence and as a forceful reminder of the need to consider factors such as human rights, land rights and security as fundamentally intertwined with culture, its maintenance and development.

While the DCMS's focus has been primarily on musical activity in a specific area of the west and central Pacific, we have been aware that the CERF approach was one that had wider application and ramifications. Contact with a group of interdisciplinary researchers concerned with the Ogasawara islands (to the far south east of Japan's territorial waters)[7] who were also committed to community facilitation and development proved insightful in expanding our agenda. The work of linguist Danny Long (from Tokyo Metropolitan University) and ethnomusicologist Junko Konishi (from Shizuoka National University) was particularly convergent with ours and an exchange of expertise and engagement took place, with my accompanying Konishi and Long on a research visit to Ogasawara in mid-2003 and Long accompanying me to Norfolk Island in early 2004. By far the most productive aspects of these visits were our mutual opportunities to meet local cultural activists and to familiarise ourselves with locally originated projects and their perceptions, needs and ambitions. What became apparent was that there were many factors in common between the communities (and other similar ones that we had been involved with)[8].

One outcome of this sharing of knowledge and contacts was our resolve to initiate an international network of small island cultural activists and researchers. This was established in mid-2004 as the Small Island Cultures Research Initiative (SICRI). Its designation as an *initiative* (rather than a society or association) reflected the manner in which we designed it as a coalition of researchers and island activists and communities involved in collaboration, networking and development. While the specific CERF designation and agenda was one developed by the DCMS at Macquarie University, our shared vision for SICRI was one in which CERF's principles were fundamental (and which inform the organisation's "Background and Mission' statement at www.sicri.org/[9]).

One key aspect of SICRI is its intended function as a communication network. While we were fully aware that the Internet is far from the universal, transglobal service it is often hyped as, we envisaged an online resource function as a key aspect of SICRI's operation. In addition to the development of SICRI's main site, my colleague Eve Klein designed an online bibliographic database and project register entitled 'SICREF' (www.sicref.org) that was launched in February 2005 at the inaugural international meeting of SICRI, held at Kagoshima University (Kyushu, Japan) at the Research Center for the Pacific Islands[10].

Fittingly enough, for such a culturally vibrant community and one that has been involved in collaborative interactions with CERF workers over the last eight years, the 2nd international SICRI event has been scheduled for February 2006 on Norfolk, hosted by Norfolk Island Museum with the assistance of the Community Arts Association. The meeting has been planned to present various aspects of Norfolk Island culture, cultural policies and initiatives to international delegates; to encourage discussion of these; and to allow international delegates to facilitate further discussion of small island cultures internationally. As such, both the organisation and the conference are projects that have been envisaged as interactive and collaborative, positioning island cultures as developing entities in 21st Century contexts (rather than as peripheral relics of cultural diversity that flicker on the edge of disappearance in an increasingly 'grayed-out' international cultural order). As this book attests, Norfolk Island is a singularly apposite venue for such a consideration of the cultural heritage and development of small island communities.

Notes

1. I would also like to acknowledge David Hackett's role as a central technical facilitator and contributor to this project.
2. As the reader will note, the list refers exclusively to music related activities. While I was asked to work on various tasks for dancers, these were all music-orientated.
3. In addition to other activities on the island to assist research collaborators (driving, moving equipment, childcare, erecting a watertank, running other errands etc.).
4. Adams and Goldbard (1982, 1996) provide a useful interpretation and advocacy of community arts work (based on North American experience) in terms of culturally democratic *animation*.
5. In the course of a wide-ranging discussion with the author conducted in Sydney in Spring 2001.
6. On Norfolk Island, for instance, I have worked with local museum curator Eve Semple, who has an active approach to developing the museum's project and community links informed by her training in Australian universities. The Vanuatu Kaljoral Senta's (Cultural Centre's) community fieldworker scheme is another notable regional example.
7. Which have a history of occupancy by a mixed European/North American and Pacific

Islander community and Japanese migrants, several linguistic hybrids and syncretic music and dance practices.

8.   This is not to argue that the CERF model is (necessarily) universally applicable, it is at an early stage of design and testing in different locations and with researchers from different research cultures and academic 'heritages'.

9.   Which states:

• SICRI was established in 2004 to facilitate communication and collaboration between researchers and cultural practitioners working with small island communities.

• SICRI's principal aim is to research and assist the maintenance and development of the language, music, dance, folkloric and media cultures of small island communities. It aims to identify potential research partners and appropriate strategies and funding sources to benefit small island cultures and those researching them.

• Key to SICRI's activities is the principle that external researchers should develop their projects in consultation with island communities and should reciprocate such co-operation with appropriate assistance and facilitation of local cultural initiatives.

• SICRI operates with reference to broader concepts of cultural heritage [see UNESCO, 2003: What is Cultural Heritage and Types of Cultural Heritage]; consideration of island communities as (simultaneously) isolated and connected; and is concerned to address the impacts and potentials offered by tourism.

10. With the endorsement of The Pacific Society (Taiheiyo Gakkai), The Japan Society of Island Studies (Nihon Tousho Gakkai), The Non-profit Organization for the Advancement of Pan-Pacific Higher Education; The Japanese Society for Oceanic Studies; The Council for the Promotion of Kagoshima Prefectural Islands; and The Japan Consortium for Area Studies.

Bibliography

Adams, D and Goldbard, A (1982/1996) 'Animation – whats in a name?' fs24 http://www.wwed.org/animation.html accessed 3.3.05

Anderson, B (1983) *Imagined Communities – Reflections on the origin and spread of Nationalism*, London: Verso

Armstrong, E (1900) *The Melanesian Mission*, London: Isbister and Company

Baes, J (2002) "That's Ethnomusicology! or Could my study of songs help indigenous Philippine peoples in disputes over ancestral domain?", *Perfect Beat* v5n4, January 2002

Ball, I (1973) *Pitcairn: Children of Mutiny*, Boston: Little, Brown and Company

Bambrick, N and Miller, J (1994) 'Exotic Hula – 'Hawaiian' Dance Entertainment in post-war Australia', *Perfect Beat* v2 n1, July

Barker, C (1996) *Sacrament*, London: Harper Collins

Beaglehole, J (ed) (1962) *The Endeavour Journal of Joseph Banks 1768-1771 (Volume One)*, Sydney: Angus and Robertson

––––– (ed) (1967) *The Journal of Captain James Cook – The Voyage of the Resolution and Discovery 1776-1780 (Volume Two)*, Cambridge University Press (for the Hakluyt Society)

Beechey, Captain F (1831) *Narrative of a Voyage to the Pacific and Beering's Strait* Volume 1, London: Colburn and Bentley

Belcher, L (1871) *The mutineers of the Bounty and their descendants in Pitcairn and Norfolk Islands*, London: J. Murray

Bligh, W (1792) *A Voyage to the South Sea*, London: George Nicol

Bligh, W (1794) *An answer to certain assertions contained in the appendix to a pamphlet entitled Minutes of the proceedings on the court-martial held at Portsmouth, August 12th, 1792, on ten persons charged with mutiny on board His Majesty's ship the Bounty* , London: George Nicol

Briand, P (1966) *In Search of Paradise*, New York: Duell, Sloan & Pearce

Buffett, A (1999) *Speak Norfolk Today: an encyclopedia of the Norfolk Island Language*, Norfolk Island: Himii Publishing

––––– (2004) *Coconuts to Computers: a concise illustrated history of Norfolk Island and its people*, Norfolk Island: Himii Publishing

Carr III, J.R (2004) 'In the wake of "John Kanaka": Musical interactions between American whalers and Polynesians, 1800-1875', paper presented to the 25th Annual Sea Music Symposium, Mystic Seaport Museum (USA)

Carriage, L and Hayward, P (2003) 'Heartlands: Kasey Chambers, Australian country music and Americana', in Hayward, P (ed) *Outback and Urban: Australian Country Music Volume 1*, Gympie (Queensland): Australian Institute of Country Music Press

Chauvel, C (1933) *In the Wake of "The Bounty": To Tahiti and Pitcairn Island*, Sydney: Endeavour Press

Chauvel Carlsson, S (1989) *Charles and Elsa Chauvel – Movie Pioneers*, Brisbane: University of Queensland Press

Christian, G (1999 [rev of 1982 ed.]) *Fragile Paradise: the Discovery of Fletcher Christian, Bounty Mutineer*, Sydney: Doubleday

Christian-Reynolds, C (2004) '9th Festival of Pacific Arts – Palau', (unpublished) Head of delegation's report, Norfolk Island: Community Arts

Clarke, P (1986) *The Norfolk – Bounty – Pitcairn Saga – Hell and Paradise*, Sydney: Viking

Clifford, J (1997) *Routes: Travel and Translation in the Late Twentieth Century*, Cambridge (USA): Harvard University Press

Clune, F (1966) *Journey to Pitcairn*, Sydney: Angus and Robertson

Comins, R (1879) in (unattributed ed) *Melanesian Mission: The Island Voyage 1897*, Ludlow (UK): Melanesian Mission

Coombe, F (1909) *School-days in Norfolk Island*, London: Society for Promoting Christian Knowledge

Coyle, J and Coyle, R (1995) 'Aloha Australia: Hawaiian Music In Australia 1920-55', *Perfect Beat* v2 n2, January

Coyle, R (2000) *Radio VL2NI on Norfolk Island: Finding the "community" in " community radio"*, report to Norfolk Island Administration

Davies, K and Davies, K.A (eds) (nd) *Old Norfolk Town: the past in pictures*, Norfolk Island: self-published

Dening, G (1992) *Mr Bligh's Bad Language: Passion, Power and Theatre on The Bounty*, Cambridge (UK): Cambridge University Press

Druett, J (1991) *Petticoat Whalers: Whaling Wives at Sea 1820-1920*, Auckland: Collins

Elcum, C (1885) 'Visit of the Rev. C.C. Elcum', chapter appended to Murray (1885)

Ellis, W (1832) *Polynesian Researches* (revised second edition), London: Fisher, Son and Jackson

'Elise' (1883) 'A Visit to Norfolk Island' – reprinted in *New Zealand Mail*, 30/11

Feld, S (1991, 2nd expanded edition) *Sound and Sentiment – Birds, Weeping, Poetics, and Song in Kaluli Expression*, Philadelphia: University of Pennsylvania Press

Firth, R (1970) *Rank and religion in Tikopia*, Boston: Beacon Press

Firth, R and McLean, M (1999) *Tikopia Songs: Poetic and musical art of a Polynesian people of the Solomon Islands*, Cambridge: Cambridge University Press

Fullerton, R (1923) *The Romance of Pitcairn Island*, London: Carey

General Conference of the Seventh Day Adventist Church Committee on Music (2003), 'Philosophy of Music' – archived at fs24 http://www.adventist.org/beliefs/other_documents/other_doc9.html accessed 18.7.04

Harvey, C (2005) 'British in bid to quit Pitcairn', *The Australian* 28/4

Hayward, P (2001) *Tide Lines: Music, Tourism and Cultural Transition in the Whitsunday Islands (and adjacent coast)*, Lismore (Australia): Music Archive for the Pacific Press

———— (2002) *Hearing the Call: Music and Social History on Lord Howe Island*, Lord Howe Island (Australia): Lord Howe Island Arts Council

Hilliard, D (1978) *God's Gentlemen: A History of the Melanesian Mission*, Brisbane: University of Queensland Press

Hitch, G (1992) *The Pacific War 1941-45 and Norfolk Island*, Norfolk Island: self-published

Hoare, M (1978) *Norfolk Island – An Outline of Its History 1774-1977* (second edition) Brisbane: University of Queensland Press

———— (1996) *Norfolk Island in the 1930s: Administrator Pinney's Term*, Brisbane: Boolarong Press

Hobsbawm, E and Ranger, T (eds) (1983) *The Invention of Tradition*, Cambridge: Cambridge University Press

Hood, T (1863) *Notes of a Cruise in H.M.S. "Fawn" in the Western Pacific in the year 1862*, Edinburgh: Edmonston and Douglas

Howard, F (1856) unpublished letter to Emily Howard (his sister), Mitchell Library Collection

Hugill, S (1961) *Shanties from the Seven Seas*, London: Routledge and Keegan Paul

Hunt, A (1914) *Memorandum By Secretary, Department of External Affairs relating to Norfolk Island*, Melbourne: Parliament of the Commonwealth of Australia

Kennedy, G (1989) *Captain Bligh, the man and his mutinies*, London: Duckworth

Laycock, D (1989) 'The status of Pitcairn-Norfolk: Creole, dialect or cant?' in Ammon, U (ed) *Status and Function of Languages and Language Varieties*, Berlin: Mouton de Gruyter

Lomax III, J (2001) *Red Desert Sky: the amazing adventures of the Chambers family*, Sydney: Allen & Unwin

Maidment, J (1981) *Gazetteer of New South Wales Pipe Organs – and those of Australian Capital Territory and Norfolk Island*, Melbourne: Society of Organists (Victoria) Incorporated

Massey, D (1993) 'Power, geometry and a progressive sense of place', in Bird, J et al (eds) *Mapping the Futures: Local Cultures, Global Change*, London: Routledge

McKay, I (1994) *The Quest of the Folk: Antimodernism and Cultural Selection in Twentieth Century Nova Scotia*, Montreal: McGill-Queens University Press

McKee, A (1989) *HMS Bounty: A True Account of the Notorious Mutiny*, London: Souvenir Press

Meade, H (1871) *A ride through the disturbed districts of New Zealand; together with some account of the South Sea Islands*, London: John Murray

Mercer, M (1987) *An Island Education: A History of the Norfolk Island Public School (1856-1987)*, Norfolk Island: Norfolk Island P & C Association

Montgomery, H (1908) *The Light of Melanesia: a Record of Thirty-Five years of Missionary work in the South Seas*, London: Society for Promoting Christian Knowledge

Moran, L (1942) 'Origins of Polynesian Club' [letter to the editor], *Pacific Islands Monthly*, November

Moran, M (1998) *Point Venus*, Sydney: Brandl and Schlesinger

Morrison, J (1792) *Diary* (transcribed Mayes, A [1917]), unpublished manuscript copy [held it Mitchell Library, Sydney]

Moulin Freeman, J (1998) 'East Polynesia: the Society Islands: Dance', in Kaeppler, A and Love, J (eds) *The Garland Encyclopedia of World Music Volume 9 – Australia and the Pacific Islands*, New York: Garland Publishing

Murray, S (1992) *Pitcairn Island: The first 200 years*, La Canada (USA): Bounty Sagas

Murray, T (1860) *Pitcairn: the Island, the People and the Pastor*, London: Society for the Promotion of Christian Knowledge

———— (1885) *Pitcairn: the Island, the People and the Pastor* (revised and expanded edition of 1860 original) London: Society for the Promotion of Christian Knowledge

Murrell, B [(ed) Quintal, S] (2001) *Norfolk Island: 1914-1916*, Norfolk Island: Quintal, S

Nicolson, R (1997) *The Pitcairners*, Auckland: Pasifika Press (reprint of 1965 edition published in Sydney by Angus and Robertson)

Nobbs, R (1984) *George Hunn Nobbs 1799-1884: Chaplain on Pitcairn and Norfolk Island*, Norfolk Island: Pitcairn Descendants Society

———— (1990) *St Barnabas and the Melanesian Mission*, Norfolk Island, Norfolk Island: Friends of Saint Barnabus

Nordhoff, C and Hall, J.N (1921) *Faery Lands of the South Seas*, Garden City (US): Garde City Publishing

———— (1932) *The Mutiny on the Bounty*, Boston: Little, Brown and Co.

———— (1933) *Men against the Sea*, Boston: Little, Brown and Co.

———— (1934) *Pitcairn's Island*, Boston: Little, Brown and Co.

Oliver, D (1974) *Ancient Tahitian Society* (three volumes), Honolulu: University of Hawai'i

Oliver, D (1988) *Return to Tahiti: Bligh's Second Breadfruit Voyage*, Melbourne: Melbourne University Press

Palmer, B Nobbs (1986) *A Dictionary of Norfolk Words and Usages*, Norfolk Island: self-published

Pike, A and Cooper, R (1980) *Australian Film 1900-1977: A Guide to Feature Film Production*, Melbourne: Oxford University Press in association with the Australian Film Institute

Ramsay, D (1821) extract from journal – unpaginated typed manuscript formerly in personal historical archive of deceased Norfolk Island historian Merval Hoare (accessed 1999)

Rutter, O (ed) (1931) *The Court-Martial of the Bounty Mutineers*, Sydney and Melbourne: Butterworth and Co.

Selwyn, Bishop (1872) *Notes of a Visit to Norfolk Island, the headquarters of the Melanesian Mission* (private circulation monograph) Auckland: William Atkin

Shapiro, H.L (1935) *The Heritage of the Bounty: The story of Pitcairn through six generations*, New York: Simon and Schuster

Silverman, D (1967) *Pitcairn Island*, Cleveland and New York: The World Publishing Company

Smith, G (2004) 'Celtic Australia: Bush Bands, Irish music and the nation', *Perfect Beat* v5n2, January

Society of Pitcairn Descendants (1996) *A political history of the Pitcairn people in Norfolk Island from 1856 to 1996*, Norfolk Island: Society of Pitcairn Descendants

Sprusom, J (1884) *Norfolk Island: an outline of its history from 1788 to 1884*, Sydney: Thomas Richards

Swift, A (1983) 'Let The Island Praise Him: A collection of Biblical Songs and Pslams set to Original Music', Norfolk Island: self-published

———— (1984) 'The Story of Creation in Song', Norfolk Island: self-published

———— (1985) 'Father Abraham: A Musical Play', Norfolk Island: self-published

Tiakihana, T [aka Jackson, T] (1966) *Norfolk Island*, Rotorua (New Zealand): United Publishing

Tudor, J (1943) 'We take kava: an evening with the Polynesian Club in Sydney', *Pacific Islands Monthly* June

Unattributed (1880) 'Consecration of the Patteson Memorial Church, Norfolk Island, by one of the visitors" in (unattributed [ed]) *Melanesian Mission: The Island Voyage, 1880*, Ludlow (UK): Melanesian Mission

Unattributed (1940) *Famous Maori Songs*, Auckland: Charles Begg & Co.

Unattributed (1942) 'Eric Ramsden Farewelled: Founder of the Pacific Islands Society', *Pacific Islands Monthly*, September

Unattributed (ed) (1952) *Blue Mist – Musical Settings of Colourful Australian and New Zealand Place Names*, Auckland, Sydney and Melbourne: Southern Music Publishing Co.

Unattributed (ed) (1971) *Hymns of Norfolk Island*, Norfolk Island: Greenways Press

Unattributed (ed) (1976) *Hymns of Norfolk and Pitcairn Islands*, Norfolk Island: Seventh Day Adventist Church

Unattributed (ed) (1984) *Hymns of Norfolk Island*, Norfolk Island: Uniting Church

Unattributed (ed) (198?) *Pitcairn Hymns and Norfolk Favourites*, Norfolk Island: Church of England

UNESCO (2002) 'Year of Cultural Heritage' documents http//:portal.unesco.org accessed 11.5 03

W.M.E. (1944) 'Army picnic: NZ Garrison on Norfolk Is.', *Pacific Island Monthly*, March

Walker, P (1999) 'Preserving culture: history as dance', *Pacific Islands Monthly*, January

Ward, P (nd) 'Music In The Early Adventist Church' http://www.tagnet.org/advent-ist.fm/articles/music.htm accessed 18.7.04

White, B and King, E (eds) (1860) *The Sacred Harp*, Philadelphia: S. Collins

White, E (1890) *Patriarchs and Prophets*, Mountain View (California): Pacific Press

Whiteoak, J (1999) *Playing Ad Lib – Improvisatory Music in Australia 1986-1970*, Sydney: Currency

———— (2003) 'Two frontiers: early cowboy music and Australian popular culture', in Hayward, p (ed) *Outback and Urban: Australian Country Music Volume 1*, Gympie (Queensland): Australian Institute of Country Music Press

Young, R (1882-1891) 'Some Letters from Pitcairn Island to a Sailing Ship Captain' (typed manuscript held in Phillips Library, Peabody Essex Museum, Salem, Massachusetts [USA])

———— (1894) *Mutiny of The Bounty and Story of Pitcairn Island 1790-1894*, Oakland (California): Pacific Press

Index